PRELUDE TO STRUGGLE

African American Clergy and Community Organizing for Economic Development in the 1990's

Katie Day

University Press of America,® Inc.
Lanham · New York · Oxford

University Press of America,® Inc.
4720 Boston Way
Lanham, Maryland 20706
UPA Acquisitions Department (301) 459-3366

12 Hid's Copse Rd.
Cumnor Hill, Oxford OX2 9JJ

Printed in the United States of America
British Library Cataloging in Publication Information Available

Library of Congress Cataloging-in-Publication Data

Day, Katie, 1951-
Prelude to struggle : African American clergy and community organizing for economic development in the 1990's / Katie Day.
p. cm
Includes bibliographical references and index.
1. African American churches. 2. African American clergy. 3. Economics—Religious aspects. 4. Church and social problems—United States. 5. Church work with the poor. 6. African Americans—Economic conditions. I. Title.

BR563.N4 D39 2002
361.7'5'08996073074811—dc21 2002018861 CIP

ISBN 0-7618-2154-6 (cloth : alk. ppr.)
ISBN: 978-0-7618-2154-0

♾™ The paper used in this publication meets the minimum requirements of American National Standard for Information Sciences—Permanence of Paper for Printed Library Materials, ANSI Z39.48—1984

This book is dedicated
to the Pastors of North Philadelphia
who continue to work with energy, intelligence,
imagination and love
to make their corner of the city
a better place.

And to
Molly and Julian,
who exude ample amounts of the same qualities
and make our home a better place.

Contents

Preface		vii
Chapter 1	Introduction	1
Chapter 2	Research Methodology	25
Chapter 3	Results from the Congregational Questionnaire	41
Chapter 4	Leading the Flock: The Role of the Pastors in Social Change	91
Chapter 5	"The Extension of our Dreams"	115
Chapter 6	"A Place to Let my Light Shine"	149
Chapter 7	Conclusion	187
Appendix	Survey	207
References		211
Index		217

Preface

As the new millenium unfolds, policy makers have rediscovered faith-based organizations as partners in the delivery of social services. Overcoming political commitments to keep "church and state" separate, long-held biases have been trumped by a fresh appreciation for the effectiveness of religious organizations to care for the most vulnerable in society. Data gathered by the Bush Administration supports the argument that many programs springing out of faith commitments and communities are, in fact, more effective than government initiatives in working with urban gang members, rehabilitating the addicted, feeding the hungry, sheltering the homeless, and enabling welfare moms to move successfully into the workforce.

But as any reader of the Bible can tell you, there is nothing new under the sun. Religious congregations have been involved in improving the quality of life in their communities in this country since the Mayflower. The degree of service and nature of "outreach ministries" varies by religious tradition, congregation and leadership. However, humanitarian efforts by religious folk have long addressed the needs of the poor both with and without government resources. Before President George W. Bush established the office of Faith-based Initiatives, the Clinton Administration had written in the "charitable choice" proviso in the Welfare Reform Act of 1996. This also made public funding available to local ministries with the poor. There was an office within HUD (Housing and Urban Development) during the Clinton years which was charged with linking religiously-based development projects with government funding. This echoed Lyndon Johnson's War on Poverty policies in the 1960's. Committed to encouraging "maximum feasible participation" of local communities in federal anti-poverty programs, the federal government co-opted and empowered many religious groups to deliver a wide range of services aimed at lifting poor people out of inferior housing, schools and job markets. In intervening years when the rhetoric around church and state separation seemed most strident, religious entrepreneurs found ways to access federal funds for their programs. While not proselytizing directly in service delivery, religious groups could organize separate corporations to receive funding, particularly for economic development projects. On a smaller scale, housing Headstart programs in their buildings kept many struggling urban churches financially afloat even as they recruited the families into their membership.

Not all faith communities have felt theologically or politically comfortable accepting government funding. The perceived new wrinkle promoted by the Bush Administration is that a religious provider may weave their message into the service delivery as long as there is a non-sectarian alternative available. (This is the same proviso written into Clinton's Welfare Reform Act of 1996). This has particularly made religious liberals nervous. Who is to define what is faith-based and what is not? Who will monitor the availability of alternatives? Will religious groups lose their prophetic edge, reticent to "bite the hand that feeds them?" Conservatives, too, dampened their enthusiasm when they realized that now public funds could be used to support, for example, the Nation of Islam to carry out their ministries with addicts in the name of Allah.

Since the War on Poverty one religious community has felt consistently comfortable at the table with the feds--African American churches. While maintaining a critical voice when the government cuts back its funding for poverty programs, or tries to shift the responsibility to other players, Black churches by and large have also been savvy in leveraging public monies to develop much-needed community programs. This comes from sheer pragmatism rather than political ideology.

African American churches have had a long tradition of entrepreneurship, born out of necessity. As the first and most prominent independent institution in the Black community, the church emerged as the base for leadership development, community organizing, social change and economic development. When no burial services were available to African Americans in cities, churches organized funeralizing businesses. When access to job skills training was severely limited in their communities, Black churches organized catering and other businesses that would literally capitalize on the talents at hand. Later in the 1960's, the Rev. Leon Sullivan of Philadelphia organized national programs to prepare African Americans for participation in the mainstream workforce. Through sophisticated strategies such as economic boycotts, he and other leaders pressured corporations to make sure the jobs were waiting when the newly trained workers applied.

While other religious traditions focused on the spiritual needs of their members, provided soup lunches once a month for the homeless and debated whether in fact they were mandated to take on a larger role in the public welfare, African American churches could not afford such luxury. "If the Black church doesn't do it, who will?" has continued to be a mantra and more deeply, a core motivation. There is impressive diversity within the African American religious communities, which the legacy of community economic development reflects. Significant development projects have been organized by all kinds of Black churches: small and large, urban and rural, those within the historic denominations as well as independent churches, and those representing all socioeconomic classes. Diverse, too, are the types of projects taken on: developing high-rise housing for the elderly, organizing banks and credit unions, developing commercial malls within urban neighborhoods, sponsoring job skills programs. These are not insignificant undertakings, since many are in areas long redlined by private investors. African American churches have generated all kinds of capital which make such uphill development possible--financial, social and cultural. The mantra rings true. If the Black church hadn't done it, no one would have.

During the 1990's there was a resurgence of interest in, and support for, community economic development based in the African American churches. New training, technical assistance resources and funding supported the renaissance, which was building on a solid track record. At the same time, faith-based community organizing was making a comeback from years of seeming hibernation in the 1970's and early 1980's. Ecumenical coalitions were springing up all over the country, and were taking on citywide and regional issues. A diversity of issues are identified for action by member congregations. For example, the community organizing agenda can focus on quality of life issues such as public safety, as well as economic development concerns such as housing.

While sharing many of the same goals, the two approaches to improving the quality of life in a city or region differ greatly in their methods, commitments and tactics. This book is an examination of faith-based organizing and economic development efforts among African American churches in North Philadelphia during the 1990's. Both approaches were strongly defined, yet pursued their similar goals through very different means. The tension between the two was evident as churches made decisions about the approach that made sense for them. History, congregational culture, understandings of power, political expediency and leadership, even personal biography all interacted as a course of action was developed.

For the study a diverse sample of ten churches was selected in North Philadelphia--the poorest and most solidly African American section of the city. The congregations were small and large, liberal and conservative, and coming from a variety of traditions: independent, historic Black and mainline Protestant denominations. All were demonstrably invested in improving the quality of life for the community, as they defined it. Strong, articulate male pastors led all ten churches. As I spent time in each congregation surveying the members and interviewing the clergy, I developed a deep respect for the commitment and integrity I encountered. I am indebted to these congregations and especially their ministers for the graciousness with which they opened their doors and their lives to this outsider. All of the identities have been changed to preserve their privacy, except in one case. The Church of the Advocate (Episcopal) and its former rector, the Rev. Paul Washington, have an identity that is impossible to conceal. With their permission, real names have been used in telling their story.

There were four churches in which I spent significantly more time conducting ethnographic research during 1992-94. The degree of trust extended to me was truly a gift. I talked to members at church, on the job or in their home, often with a tape recorder. Church records and project documents were provided. I was allowed to be a "fly on the wall" at closed-door meetings of the churches' economic development projects and community organizations. The pastors patiently talked with me about their beliefs and questions, their programs and their dreams, their own journeys and their visions for the future. Perhaps the greatest privilege for this researcher was participating in weekly worship with the congregations. Here the deeper meanings of community action were articulated and celebrated through word, song and prayer.

I therefore dedicate this book to those whose lives and faith are represented in its pages. I can only hope that my respect for the members and pastors of the ten churches is apparent throughout. They certainly deepened my understanding of faith-based initiatives, and I further hope that through my work their experience will make a larger contribution to our knowledge of community transformation springing from religious communities.

There are so many others who have helped this book take shape. I am indebted to the critical feedback of Howard Winant, Carolyn Adams, Dave Barteldt, Kevin Dulaney, Lawrence Mamiya, Hart Nelsen, and David Roozen. When I hit the limits of my technological abilities, the talents of Sal Saparito and Ellen Harper McGarr were invaluable. Grants from the Fund for Theological Education and Aid Association for Lutherans made my field research possible.

This book will forever be identified in my mind with my two children, Julian and Molly, who made their entrance into the world during the project. They provided entrees into many conversations during field work and even though they distracted me during my writing, they will always be my favorite distraction.

Katie Day
Philadelphia, PA
September, 2001

Chapter 1

Introduction

Background

Currently there are two social movements seeking to address the political and economic well-being of disenfranchised communities. During the 1980's, community organizing experienced a renaissance, particularly as it came to be based in religious congregations. The increased popularity of **church-based community organizing** (CBCO) in the U.S. was aided by the re-orientation of the Industrial Areas Foundation (I.A.F.) toward congregations as a primary vehicle for organizing. Other community organizing networks, not nearly as large, but also based on the work of Saul Alinsky, followed suit.

A more recent, and less documented trend has been the increased interest in African American churches to become involved in **community economic development** (CED). In the past several years, conferences have been held to equip African American church leaders to do CED. "The Black Church" has become a sub-specialty within the organizations and networks devoted to promoting CED, from the National Congress on Community Economic Development to the conservative Heritage Foundation. While development activities have always been a part of the ministry of African American churches, there is a decidedly fresh commitment to a more focused and sophisticated approach to creating housing, developing commercial ventures, capital formation and other activities related to directly bringing economic resources to the communities in which the churches carry out their ministry.

This study examines the relationship between these two trends as observed among ten African American congregations in North Philadelphia. All have been strongly involved with CED, yet they have pursued strikingly different strategies and serve to highlight the differences between the two paradigms.

The recent growth of CBCO as indicated by the growth of community organizing networks has been stunning. For example, the I.A.F. developed twelve new organizations around the country in as many years, between 1973 and 1985. In the next five years they doubled that number. Currently, there are over forty local chapters in the U.S., U.K., and South Africa, all training members of their affiliated churches in leadership skills and organizing them to bring about change in their communities.

The executive director of I.A.F. since Alinsky's death in 1972 is Edward T. Chambers, who defined their approach this way:

> Our culture is very simple. We start with family, a congregation. We start with the teachings of the Bible. We start with basic values that are given us. Then we try to practice a genuine democracy -- not the artificial democracy of the sound bite (Greider, 1992, p. 225).

The I.A.F. considers relationships the basic unit of organizing. Their strategy begins with one-on-one conversations, then house meetings which enable issues of concern to be named. These are fed into a larger body of congregational representatives who decide on an agenda and a course of action. (Most of those in the higher leadership circles have attended I.A.F.'s intensive Ten Day Training, and have been taught skills in everything from listening skills to issue analysis to decision making.) The bonds of the diverse religious groups newly in coalition are preserved by a strict non-partisanism and a commitment to working only on those issues of common concern. Politicians are "held accountable" to the organization's agenda, which sometimes leads to confrontational tactics in their public actions.

By "organizing people and organizing money," I.A.F.'s fundamental approach to developing power, local chapters have cultivated enough clout to have an impressive record of changes in policies and services to show for it -- housing constructed, schools reorganized, jobs created, banks reoriented to community investment and community policing instituted. The ultimate goals of the organization are broad and include the restructuring of work and redistribution of income in this country. For many, the CBCO facilitated by the I.A.F. and similar groups represents the only viable hope for social change. One observer articulating that position is political journalist William Greider: "..American political history suggests that this kind of politics, difficult as it is, is the only kind that leads to genuine change" (Greider, 1992, p. 235).

Yet for many within the African American community, it is the congregations, not the community organizing coalitions, which hold the key to more economically viable, self-determining communities. "If the Black church doesn't do it, who will?" is often heard in conversations about community development.

This sentiment is more fully explored by Harold A. McDougall in his book, Black Baltimore. He credits much of the development in the neighborhoods of that city to the efforts of the African American churches. He has a high level of respect for BUILD (Baltimoreans United In Leadership Development, an affiliate of I.A.F.), yet shares a Weberian pessimism that large organizations eventually become bureaucratized, hierarchical and indeed coopted by the very powers they initially seek to confront and change. Instead, he puts more faith in smaller units of development which are "more indigenous, more flexible, and more intimate" (McDougall, 1992, p. 110). Local congregations (not the "megachurches," he specifies) as well as smaller ministry groups, such as Habitat for Humanity, are better equipped to generate microenterprise development, rooted in what he calls the "vernacular culture" of the African American community which values smaller social groupings.

Fueling the CED trend among African American churches has been the dramatic decline of federal funds for cities. As a result, individual churches become more crucial to development in urban communities. Through necessity created by policy changes and a tradition of leadership in CED, African American churches are poised to be able to put together funding packages from local sources -- religious, philanthropic, municipal, and private -- for development projects in their own neighborhoods. Whether out of the cultural self-understanding or the critique of larger coalitions espoused by McDougall, a sense of moral imperative or political pragmatism, African American churches are experiencing a revival in their commitment to CED, even as CBCO is also accelerating.

While the two trends may represent compatible sets of goals, they do not necessarily intersect in reality. The goals of CBCO are broader and more diverse than that of CED. The community organizing coalitions engage a plethora of issues of concern to a community, only one of which is economic development. In addition, the approaches taken by African American churches to CED usually do not utilize the tactics of community organizing. Yet both CED and CBCO are seeking, finally, the self-determination of their communities, as they define them. Although each approach can evolve into the other over time, among African American churches, CED and CBCO represent very different strategies in the 1990's.

The Philadelphia Context

Philadelphia has a rich history of church involvement in CED in the African American community. W.E.B. DuBois documented a wide variety of economic activity in congregations here during the late 19th century, ranging from employment services to cooperatives (DuBois, 1903). North Philadelphia has served as the home base for Rev. Leon Sullivan (now retired) who, through his impressive development work in the community and through the establishment of the Opportunities Industrial Centers (OIC), has left a strong legacy which continues to be a model for church-based CED. He has been described as "perhaps the most prominent example of the modern black minister involved in the complexities of economic development issues" (Lincoln and Mamiya, 1990, p. 264).

Sullivan's philosophy was that African Americans needed more educational and employment opportunities in order to function as full participants in the economic system. During his tenure as the pastor of Zion Baptist Church on North Broad Street (1950-1988), the OIC developed Progress Plaza, the first and largest shopping plaza developed by and for the African American community. Beyond North Philadelphia, the OIC created training programs in 160 cities; by 1980 almost 700,000 people had received job training and employment placement. His influence extended beyond the U.S. He is widely known as the author of the Sullivan Principles in the late 1970's (incorporated by the Reagan administration in its foreign policy), which were voluntary ethical guidelines for multi-national corporations in South Africa. Rev. Sullivan did not attack apartheid directly or call for economic divestment until the end of the Reagan era. Until then he had hoped to preserve the corporate presence and employment opportunities for South African Blacks, while urging their fair treatment.

Sullivan's operational philosophy of stressing self-help while maximizing opportunity, whether at an individual or collective level, has set a standard for local pastors interested in becoming involved in economic development. This approach (which I call the **traditional strategy**) relies on lone entrepreneurial pastors who access the system in order to get resources for development projects in their immediate neighborhoods. It has been, and continues to be, the dominant model for CED among African American clergy.

In a study commissioned by the Black Clergy Association of Philadelphia and Vicinity in 1989, forty credit unions were identified based in local African American congregations, and having assets which totaled $15 million. The Association was interested in consolidating and reinvesting these funds in the Black community. However, they confronted resistance as entrepreneurial pastors preferred to control their own funds and develop their own projects. In North Philadelphia alone, there are two other shopping plazas developed by individual congregations and one in progress. Further, there are numerous elder housing projects, low and moderate housing developments, job training programs, and commercial ventures peppered throughout this section of the city, all generated by individual churches and their pastors operating in the traditional paradigm which is definitive of so much CED activity in African American churches.

Church-based community organizing is also strongly represented in Philadelphia. In the winter of 1992, a new citywide, ecumenical community organization was officially unveiled after four years of groundwork -- Philadelphia Interfaith Action (P.I.A.), affiliated with the I.A.F. In the first three years of its life, P.I.A. has worked on a number of issues but most prominently, housing. They have just completed construction of the first phase of Nehemiah Housing -- 170 single family units for low and moderate income buyers -- and are moving into successive phases which will result in a total of 1000 units. In its short history, P.I.A. has distinguished itself through its aggressive grassroots organizing, boisterous public assemblies and willingness to employ confrontational tactics when holding public officials accountable to their promises and P.I.A.'s agenda.

While many of the 44 charter groups were in fact African American congregations, what was especially interesting was who was not among the P.I.A. membership. Some of the African American clergy who had initiated the process of organizing the P.I.A. (and even a few who had attended the ten-day training) had opted not to join. Other congregations noted for their commitment to community development also eschewed the coalition which is the CBCO effort with the highest profile in Philadelphia. Why would some African American clergy and their congregations within the same urban context, confronted by the same issues and opportunities, choose to affiliate with P.I.A. while others decide against this approach in favor of the more traditional one?

It is true that the I.A.F. has been the target of suspicion and criticism from the African American community since the early days with Alinsky, when the objectives of some community activism in Chicago became identified with thinly-veiled racism. Currently, however, the local leadership of I.A.F. organizations is racially diverse. In Baltimore, for example, the citywide coalition (BUILD) is largely African American in leadership and membership; in Texas, Chicanos represent the majority. The Lead Organizer in Philadelphia is African American, as are many of the clergy and member congregations which are most active in the coalition. Major assemblies ("actions") certainly reflect these demographics, and are marked by some of the music and enthusiasm of a church revival.

The I.A.F. continues to have its critics of its relationship to the African American community, however. James Jennings, for example, contends that Alinsky groups have ignored race as a particular dynamic in community empowerment. Instead, they tend to focus primarily on economic, political or institutional issues and, *de facto*, have considered race only as a secondary, or complicating dynamic. While this criticism focuses on what is perhaps a weakness in the social analysis of Alinsky groups, there is a more insidious dynamic at work, Jennings suspects:

> For the continuing presence and weight of America's racial hierarchy implies that the Black struggle for equality, and its leadership, do hold a vanguard position in the movement for change. This situation undermines the priestly and missionary function of white activists who, sometimes unknowingly, seek to define for the Black community the parameters and style of social change in American society (Kling and Posner, 1990, p. 118).

This study will focus on how and why African American congregations construct their strategies for CED the way they do. Whether or not non-members perceive P.I.A. diluting the political agenda of the African American community remains to be seen. What is clear is that the two models of pursuing CED goals in North Philadelphia churches -- the traditional and CBCO approach as represented by P.I.A. -- have evolved into very different approaches.

Action Frames

As the strategies for community development have evolved, they have distinguished themselves around four polar dynamics which I identify as **action frames**. Since this concept was first introduced by Erving Goffman (1974), it has primarily been used in reference to consciousness -- much like Kuhn's concept of paradigm. However, in current literature on social movement theory, the definition of action frames is being expanded beyond "ways of thinking about political issues," (Morris and Mueller, 1992, p. 71) to include modes of activism (p. 138). As an analytical tool, therefore, it is helpful in understanding collective consciousness and action, and recognizes that the two cannot be considered separately.

For the purposes of this study, an action frame functions for clergy and congregations by organizing their social action in a way which is related to their world views and larger narratives of theology, congregational history and culture. It is expressive of their ideology and political consciousness; it can also shape how an issue is interpreted. Theology, history, ideology, and political consciousness are embedded and reinforced by an action frame, but are not synonymous with it. Action frames organize not only how congregations perceive their social reality, but also the strategies for mobilization they will pursue.

Clerical versus Shared Leadership

The leadership for CED projects in the traditional model has predominantly come from charismatic, entrepreneurial pastors. Often these clergy have spearheaded enormously complex development projects single-handedly, not collaborating with other clergy or laypeople but occasionally working with a consultant. This is consistent with the tradition of the strong patriarchal preacher in most African American churches who is highly revered and whose authority is unchallenged.

This action frame is in contrast to that used by P.I.A. which stresses shared leadership. Like all I.A.F. chapters, the local group is led by a leadership team (the Strategy Team), the membership of which rotates frequently to bring in "new blood." The Strategy Team reflects an intentional diversity, comprised of both clergy and laypeople, women and men, African Americans, Latinos, and Anglos, as well as Catholic and all stripes of Protestant. P.I.A. even has a synagogue which is one of the strongest member congregations. This diversity is reflected in the careful choice of the 6-10 leaders who will be on the podium during public actions. Their commitment to shared, diverse leadership does not necessarily reflect how the individual congregations always operate, however.

Parochial versus Coalitional

While there has been some collaboration among African American churches in traditional development projects, it has tended to be exceptional. When there is collaboration, it is with other African American churches, usually just among clergy. Within the parochial action frame, these lone clergy have focused their CED activities within their immediate neighborhood -- so houses might be developed across the street, a 202 project might be built in the parking lot, or a commercial strip redeveloped down the street from the church.

Usually working alone and locally, congregations have relied heavily on resources which they generated, then could leverage for public and private funding.

On the other hand, P.I.A. is a coalition built mostly of congregations representing denominational and racial diversity. Member congregations find themselves working with others they might never encounter in any other context. Further, member congregations come from all over the city and a few suburbs. This means that while actions might be focused in local neighborhoods, the issues being addressed are citywide. Members believe that it is in their interest to work for policy change at the level of city government or to close a crack house, build housing or get community policing in other neighborhoods in the city.

Resources are also generated from within and used to leverage larger moneys. I.A.F. chapters are dependent on member dues, equitably requiring a *per capita* tax of $10 for each member congregation. While congregations utilizing the traditional model might rely on their own offerings to initiate their CED projects out of necessity, P.I.A. has a different reason for internal fundraising. They believe that by not seeking outside funding for their own operating budget they can maintain their independence, as well as demonstrate their strength when approaching sources for CED projects.

Power Access versus Empowerment

Two different understandings of power constitute distinct action frames operating in the construction of CED strategies -- accessing the power structure as opposed to empowering the disenfranchised in order to bring about change (Jennings in Kling and Posner, 1990). Those who ultimately seek integration into the dominant culture are more likely to build alliances with those within the public and private power structure in order to influence them to direct resources into their interests. In Philadelphia, many of the CED projects pursued by clergy utilizing the traditional model have depended on gaining such access. Partnerships with leaders in City Hall, the banking and real estate communities have been nurtured, often quite effectively. Deals have been negotiated and commitments made out of such relationships, far from public scrutiny or congregational participation. Congregants have been mystified by their pastors' connections and influence.

This again stands in contrast to the understanding of power and the political strategy pursued by P.I.A. Their goal is the empowerment of their broader constituency, the "grassroots" population which is often politically disenfranchised. While P.I.A. seeks to engage political figures and business leaders, they will not form permanent alliances, but want to maintain their independence and a posture of critical distance. Often their demands, which have been culled through a participatory process which aims at being consensual, are presented to officials in a public forum. Small delegations will meet behind closed doors, but usually report their process to a larger group soon afterward.

There is a clear sense in the I.A.F. philosophy that the process of empowerment (through training, process structure, and discipline) is as important as any final outcomes of social change. As explained in the booklet, "Everything you wanted to know about P.I.A.":

> P.I.A. is a multi-issue organization. It is not organized for the purpose of just one issue, but to enable its leaders to raise and address many issues. Several issues will always be in process at P.I.A. and those issues will change over time. These issues are addressed not only to win, but are also occasions for the training and development of a growing body of leaders in P.I.A. able to act collectively and powerfully.

Accommodation versus Change

The action frames described above, representing approaches to leadership, organization and power, result in different outcomes in relation to the existing political and economic structures. In the traditional model, public and private systems are accessed by clergy who do not critique them, much less seek fundamental change. This is not to say that they might not be privately critical, but that whether for philosophical or practical reasons, they do not attempt to bite the hand they hope will feed them.

A recent newspaper article described a classic traditional model CED project being launched by one of the congregations in this study. The pastor is pictured in front of a dilapidated grocery store two blocks from his church. Within a month demolition will begin and a new shopping center will be developed. Of the $4.2 million needed for the project, $400,000 came from the offering plates (and the balance from a combination of public grants and private financing). While the idea for the project came to the pastor as a result of poor service and rude treatment at the last super market chain to occupy the property, he in no way wants to challenge the economic system but to enable his constituents to more fully participate in it:

> It just makes good sense for our community...Black people need to have that kind of economic empowerment..if we are going to survive in a capitalist society ("Faith and capitalism," Philadelphia Inquirer, 7/21/95).

On the other hand, in response to the question "What does P.I.A. want to do?" posed in the informational booklet, the answer:

> CHANGE THE CITY! We are tired of the old ways of doing things. There is too much corruption and too much non-production. The old power-brokers control too much and do too little, leaving our city weak, impoverished and without direction. P.I.A. members are people of faith -- we believe it can be different.

The language is that of reform rather than revolution. In reality, the coalition identifies a number of issues affecting the quality of life in the neighborhoods of the city.

At the present time the priorities include housing, safety, education and public finances. They develop their own goals and policies, some of which are more easily implemented through the system as it is currently operating. For example, targeting abandoned houses to be cleaned and sealed was a "winnable" goal when they approached the Department of Licenses and Inspection for the city. However, in advocating an aggressive policy on crack houses, it became apparent to the organization that the policy-making process itself needed to be challenged. This led them into a head-on confrontation with the powerful District Attorney, Lynne Abraham. In other cities, I.A.F. chapters have moved from modest reform goals to more significant changes in the private and public structures of distributing opportunities and resources when the coalitions grew in numbers and political power. While systemic change is secondary to the goal of the empowerment and democratic participation of citizens, I.A.F. groups will engage in such change efforts if they feel the systems are not serving the interests of citizens.

Theoretical Approaches

Clearly, there are two distinct approaches being employed by African American congregations in North Philadelphia who are engaged in community economic development. Four areas have been identified in which different action frames are utilized in the construction of the overall strategy -- leadership, collaboration, power and change.

The choice of strategy is not always historically neat. For example, a church which at one time employed community organizing might now have adopted a more traditional approach. In the same way, some involved in P.I.A. had previous experience in CED using the traditional approach. A few churches are pursuing both strategies with different projects, working at once on citywide and local development projects. However, in such cases, one strategy is more clearly the dominant model.

Because of the coexistence of strategies within a congregation's history or even current engagement with CED, it is important in analyzing collective behavior to consider the action frames to be dynamic, rather than static categories. The polar tension between clerical and shared leadership, for example, represents a spectrum rather than pure categories. Congregations and clergy live and move within the spectrum; change and tension are to be expected.

Further, the action frames are related to each other, but must be assumed to function separately. Certainly the relationship between clerical leadership, accessing power and accommodation to the *status quo* is understandable, but it is not inevitable. Clerical, rather than shared leadership can also be employed in the pursuit of systemic change.

In brief, action frames must be used as analytical tools which can describe collective behavior in its complexity, rather than reifying it. Certainly a central purpose of this study is the descriptive task -- how do preachers and their people develop their own CED strategy?

But the deeper question is why. Why would churches in the same geographical context construct such different strategies?

Besides their context, these churches also share a historical moment of shifting political opportunities. During the 1980's there was a strong relationship between African American clergy in Philadelphia and the governmental power structure. The Black Clergy Association had one of its own in Congress -- Rev. William Gray, the pastor of Bright Hope Baptist Church in North Philadelphia, who had risen to the powerful Chairmanship of the House Budget Committee. Wilson Goode, a Baptist Deacon, was elected as Philadelphia's first African American mayor, and served two terms from 1984-1992. He relied heavily on the support of Black churches in both his campaigns. This political alliance between the Black Clergy Association, the Mayor's office and Gray enabled some resources and services to flow into Philadelphia's African American neighborhoods even during the Reagan-Bush administrations. This was a heady time for the Black Clergy Association, under the leadership of Rev. William B. Moore (who also headed Gray's local office). Candidates sought their endorsements, and recognized the importance of the churches in gaining access to the Black voting bloc.

Then the political landscape changed dramatically. Wilson Goode was leaving office and William Gray unexpectedly resigned from Congress in the spring of 1991. The MOVE tragedy had cost Goode some support among B.C.A., which divided over whom to endorse in the Mayoral election. Support for Goode's candidate was weak; West Philadelphia clergy gravitated to another candidate. The infighting was exposed in the media. The result was that Black Clergy Association (B.C.A.) was left weakened and divided; their public image was tarnished and they did not have a natural alliance with the popular new mayor, Ed Rendell.

The Black power structure had supported traditional approaches to CED; the connections between church-city hall-Congress had resulted in some significant development projects. The political vacuum did provide a window of opportunity for P.I.A., which was launched soon after Rendell came into office. Some clergy, disenchanted with B.C.A., were attracted to the new coalition. However, the political shift led other pastors away from coalitions altogether; they redoubled their efforts in the spiritual care of their congregations and parochial ministry within their neighborhoods. While the changing political opportunities affected individual clergy, it was catalytic in leading them both into and away from CBCO as a vehicle for pursuing their interests in community development.

African American clergy in North Philadelphia at this time responded differently to the change in political opportunity which affected them all. There are a number of explanatory theories which might be employed to analyze the dynamics at work. Most approaches would focus on variables related to either the **congregation** or the **clergy** themselves as determining the outcome.

Focus on the Clergy

Much of the historical and sociological study of African American religion has revolved around the tension between **resistance** or **protest** and **accommodation** (Marx, 1967; Marable, 1983; Wilmore, 1973; Baer, 1992). This is particularly evident in studies of clergy.

Quantitative studies on clergy activism have generally shown that those African American pastors actively involved in seeking social change are in the minority; most concentrate their energy on maintaining the *status quo* in church and society or only pursuing modest, reformist goals -- accommodationism (Baer, 1992; Broom, 1966; Johnstone, 1971; Shaw, 1973; Turner, 1973). Those variables associated with liberal to radical activism (or protest) are education (Turner, 1973; Lincoln and Mamiya, 1990) and size of congregation (Johnstone, 1971; Lincoln and Mamiya, 1990). Pastors with higher levels of education serving larger churches are more likely to be political activists.

Other studies have also found a correlation between clergy activism and denominational affiliation. In the Black churches as well as their predominantly-Anglo counterparts, activism is more evident among the denominational families which allow for more congregational autonomy. The more "connectional" the denomination, the less activism is seen among the clergy (Pope, 1942; Baer, 1992). A caveat to this is that African American clergy affiliated with the Euro-centric mainline Protestant groups (Methodist, Episcopal, Presbyterian, Congregational) are more likely to be activists (Marx, 1967).

The data suggest that institutional growth and bureaucratization have a deradicalizing effect on clergy (Wilmore, 1983); those in larger, more independent congregations (and affiliation with a mainline denomination could create independence) have more freedom to mobilize their congregations. Again, activism is more likely where clergy have higher levels of education.

While these data describe social trends, they must be tested in microanalysis. At the outset it is evident that there are churches which challenge the data and their ability to be predictive in the context of CED in North Philadelphia in the 1990's: How can we explain the mainline Protestant clergy in North Philadelphia who have chosen not to participate in the more change-oriented P.I.A. coalition, but prefer the more traditional approach to CED? How would the aforementioned studies account for those in large congregations who have eschewed the more progressive strategy or the clergy with lower levels of education from smaller churches who have embraced the CBCO strategy? The weight of the data on African American clergy would indeed lead us to expect little activism among North Philadelphia religious leaders. Those who might be predicted to respond to P.I.A. have not necessarily done so. Other theoretical approaches must be tested.

Focus on the Congregation

Congregations are comprised, of course, of individuals who come into a religious community with their own class interests and political perspectives as well as their religious beliefs. Like any social grouping, coherence is related to a degree of homogeneity. If CED strategies represent the mobilization of interests, then empirical data on the congregations themselves should identify factors which could be driving the approach taken by congregations.

In Lincoln and Mamiya's study of over 2000 African American churches, it was evident that class stratification exists in Black religion along denominational lines (1990). As with the predominantly Anglo churches, the more bureaucratized, connectional denominations (such as the African Methodist Episcopal Church) generally have memberships with higher levels of education and income. The Baptist and Pentecostal groups, characterized by more congregational autonomy, attract greater proportions of their membership from lower socio-economic strata. If such class stratification persists at the congregational level, could not class interests be driving the strategy construction?

The relationship between class, theology and political consciousness has been the subject of much research. Recent research confirms the observation that African American congregations hold more conservative theological beliefs, than their counterparts of European descent (Kosmin, Keysar and Lerer, 1991).

It had been a long-standing tenet in the field of the sociology of religion that conservative theology was linked with conservative positions on political and economic issues and that the opposite was the case among those espousing liberal theology (Stark and Glock, 1968; Marty, 1970; Rokeach, 1969). However, more recent research shows that religious conservatives can hold a variety of political positions (Wuthnow, 1973; Petersen and Takayama, 1984; Johnson, Tamney, Halebsky, 1986; Tamney, Burton, and Johnson, 1988; Demerath and Williams, 1989). The variable of class status seems to be more determinative of political and economic views than does theology. For example, research data show that while upper middle class religious groups might be liberal in their theology, they are more likely than the lower class religious conservatives to hold conservative political and economic views.

African Americans church-goers, despite their more conservative religious beliefs, are more likely than Anglo Christians to hold more liberal political views. In one recent study comparing samples from the two groups, the African American church members were more likely to support increased government social spending and intervention to equalize income differences and raise the standard of living for the poor (Pyle, 1991).

The dominance of class in identifying political beliefs which best represent class interest is consistent with a Weberian framework, although Weber himself would also explain religious belief as related to class interest. Because conservative religious beliefs cannot be a predictor of conservative political views does not mean that they are unrelated. The poor, or disprivileged, classes seek "a sense of honor," "just compensation," and "a release from suffering" (Weber, 1964). Salvation-oriented religion (such as fundamentalist or conservative Christianity) offers them such rewards, as could political activism;

acquiescence is not inevitable. Religion does not necessarily only serve to legitimate the *status quo*, especially for the poor.

That being the case, how does class function in the African American churches as they develop their strategies for CED? If political behavior is consistent with political beliefs, then a Weberian approach might be employed. In such an approach, we would expect to find a relationship between the socio-economic class status of congregations, their political beliefs and choice of strategy. Therefore, it could be predicted that the action frames developed in the traditional approach would more represent the interests of middle class and upper middle class congregants. That is, those churches with more members from higher socio-economic strata would be expected not to affiliate with P.I.A. Conversely, those churches with more poor people would be attracted to the coalition.

Those from the middle and upper classes have benefited from the system; it would be in their interest to access it, but not seek to change it. Further, as those who are more likely to function within bureaucratized institutions with articulated specialization, they would also expect their pastor to function in a specialized role; they would be comfortable with clerical leadership in CED project development. In addition, a parochial orientation could also be in the interest of those members from higher socio-economic status (s.e.s.). Development projects around the church improve the neighborhood, making it a safer destination for commuters and contributing to the future viability of the church.

On the other hand, a Weberian approach would also predict that the congregations with greater representation from the urban poor would be drawn to P.I.A. affiliation. The coalition's orientation toward change and confrontational tactics would better represent the interests of those who seek "just compensation" and alleviation of their suffering. Without strong connections to the system, they are freer to challenge it yet will have to expand their political base in order to have an influential voice. Shared leadership within the coalition is especially attractive to the poor who have otherwise been denied "a sense of honor."

The commitments of CBCO best serve the interests of the poor not only in a Weberian interpretation: certainly this is intentional on the part of the I.A.F. and groups like it. True to their history and central to their philosophy, the organization founded by Alinsky seeks to empower the disenfranchised, to incorporate the alienated into the democratic process which will result in changing the system which has not responded to their needs or served their interests.

A theory of class interest in the construction of strategy will be tested in this study for its explanatory value. Establishing what the class interest of a congregation is represents methodological challenges, to be sure. How can class interest be operationalized? Is it a matter of a simple majority of class representatives, or cannot a minority rule (as is seen in so many social contexts) and have their interest predominate? First it will be important to survey the class status and political consciousness at an individual level before collective behavior can be analyzed.

The methodological challenges lead us to consideration of how complex the dynamics are within African American churches. Black churches exist because of, in spite of, and always in the context of a racist society. Those who are socially and economically upwardly mobile do not have an unambiguous class identification. Despite the fact that they have benefited from the system, African Americans in the middle and upper social strata remain all too aware of racism (Cose, 1993). Racial consciousness increases with education and African Americans do not easily abandon their communities of origin. Therefore, many journey in from the suburbs every Sunday morning to worship in urban churches which draw members from a diversity of social strata, and which are deeply committed to improving the quality of life for the urban poor.

This suggests that an explanatory framework for looking at such churches will need to be comprehensive -- that is, looking not only at the clergy and the class interests of the congregants as the driving factors in the construction of CED strategies. The action frames and the strategies themselves utilized by the congregations are forged within the congregational subculture itself as well as within the broader political and social context. Some of the recent theoretical developments within social movement theory offer theoretical frameworks which are more comprehensive, considering the relationship of dynamics both at the macro (political) and micro (congregational) levels.

Social Movement Theory

The literature on collective action is diverse and growing, focusing on a number of factors which lead to the creation and demise, internal structures and contextual pressures of social movements. As the body of theories have developed, they have moved away from functionalist and reductionist interpretations to a more comprehensive approach which incorporates attention to culture (within and outside of social movements) and social psychology.

An important critic of earlier work on social movements, Doug McAdam expands the field of factors which must be examined out of his own study of the political movements among African Americans between 1930 and 1970. McAdam's definition of social movements would include much of CBCO, and in particular, the goals and activities of I.A.F. and P.I.A.

> ..those organized efforts on the part of excluded groups to promote or resist change in the structure of society that involve recourse to non-institutional forms of political participation (McAdam, 1982, p. 25).

His approach, as well as more recent contributions of others writing in the field, provides a helpful lens for analyzing the dynamics at work which are leading some African American churches beyond their localized ministry into participation in more broad-based organizations working for social change.

His analysis begins with an examination of the external context, particularly the political realities. More specific than attention to the **political culture** (Tarrow, in Morris and Mueller, 1992), McAdam is looking for shifts in **political opportunities** -- that is, those reversals of political fortunes, changes in policy makers, the sudden propulsion of a public issue, or social changes over time -- any factors which alter the political landscape making it possible, although not inevitable, for new voices to emerge. The deterioration of the alliance of African American clergy and politicians described earlier is the political ground tremor felt by African American clergy throughout Philadelphia, creating both a loss of power for some, but opportunity for others. It was in the aftermath of these events, in this political context, that P.I.A. entered the public forum in this city.

Political changes only become opportunities when there is some pre-existing organizational strength which becomes a vehicle for mobilization. Congregations bring a number of critical elements to a social movement -- members, leadership, communication networks and capital (including buildings, funds and the capacity to raise money). The institutional stability and resources they offer expedite movement-building when compared to the prospects of recruiting individuals. I.A.F. certainly realized this when their leadership decided to reorient their recruitment efforts to congregations.

McAdam argues that political opportunities and organizational strength are but preconditions to mobilization for social change. There also has to be a **transformation of consciousness**. Organizers within CBCO recognize that religious communities also bring resources into a movement which can facilitate such a transformation: their frames of meaning. Congregations come with their own collective identities -- which have evolved out of their history and context, and find expression in their symbols language, and ritual. The shared meanings which exist in congregations can, of course, serve to inhibit change. However, they can also promote change as they interpret grievances as injustice, and provide an ideological framework for understanding social suffering as morally intolerable.

The key to incorporating congregations into movements is therefore in finding congruence or resonance between the frames of the movement organization and church members. That is, there needs to be enough consistency between the frames of meaning so that participation in the movement does not challenge the identity of the congregation but in fact expands it. Participation in the movement is therefore interpreted as an extension of participation in the community of faith. (Gamson; Tarrow; Friedman and McAdam in Morris and Mueller, 1992) This can dilute the strength of a coalition, if it incorporates a number of congregational identities rather than recruiting only those congregations with which there is a natural resonance. However, this dynamic, referred to by some theorists as **frame extension** (Snow et al., 1986) can actually serve to fortify a social movement. Tarrow argues that by making use of existing "ideational materials," it will be harder for opponents to delegitimate a movement than if meanings are constructed. (Tarrow in Morris and

Mueller, 1992) It is harder for a politician to publicly criticize a coalition of churches than it is for her/him to denounce a group comprised of individual activists.

The I.A.F. has developed frame extension to a high art in their organization-building. The action frames (shared leadership, collaboration with other churches, empowerment and social change) are not antithetical to the Judeo-Christian tradition, but are embedded in it. The tactics of relationality, small cell discussion, mass meetings and even challenging "the principalities and powers" are familiar to many, if not most, church-goers. Interpreting unnecessary suffering as injustice is part of the moral discourse of religious communities. While the response to social suffering can vary (from patronizing concern to outrage to solidarity within individual congregations), each of these elements could find resonance with the interpretive schemes -- frames of meaning -- in community organizations seeking change.

Of course, not all congregations find that particular social change movements are congruent with their own way of interpreting reality and acting in response to that interpretation. In the Philadelphia context, the role of congregational identity and culture needs to be brought into the analysis of how and why African American congregations choose to pursue their goals of impacting the quality of life for the poor in the city. If in fact the congregations which have affiliated with P.I.A. perceive a resonance between their frames of meaning and action and that of the coalition, is the converse true -- that those who have opted out of P.I.A. experience an ideational incongruence? Are they alienated by this organization? Do they perceive it as pursuing the same goals but through different means, or does the construction of the traditional strategy reflect a very different cultural context which is exclusive of the frames of meaning in congregations which do resonate with the CBCO coalition?

Perhaps the critical issue affecting the capacity for cultural resonance or frame extension is the parameters of the cultural identity itself. That is, does a congregation identify itself primarily with "our church," "the Black community," or "the Christian tradition"? The boundaries of their self-identification -- the relative weight which they place on the greater or little traditions -- will certainly inform the degree of resonance which they might perceive with a social change organization such as P.I.A.

McAdam introduces a fourth component of social change movements which he considers the most critical. Even when grievance has been framed as injustice through the **transformation of consciousness**, even when there is a sense of **intolerance and imperative** (i.e., "This cannot continue! We must do something!") collective action is not inevitable. The potential actors must also be convinced that effectiveness is possible. Participation in a movement must be seen as a **viable** means for bringing change.

The I.A.F. intentionally cultivates such a sense of viability in its outreach to potential participants and training of leaders. Scouts from one community are usually introduced to the organization through exposure to Nehemiah Housing developments in cities where they have been operating longer -- dramatic monuments to the effectiveness of local organizing efforts. Ten-day training sessions take place in cities where major actions are planned, so new leaders from other locales can be exposed to "success stories."

Still, some of the African American clergy from Philadelphia who saw Nehemiah Housing in East Brooklyn and participated later in ten-day training returned to the traditional model of CED. Were they not convinced of the viability of CBCO, or did the traditional approach seem more viable? How much does viability factor into the decision -- does pragmatism outweigh cultural resonance and consciousness as McAdam contends?

The questions raised out of social movement theory necessitate ethnographic research, out of which comes the "thick description" of the determinative dynamics within a limited universe. However, they beg methodological questions: is it possible, for example, to measure a degree of identity resonance and compare it to a level of viability? Perhaps not. But the comprehensive theoretical approaches coming out of analyses of social movements reflects the complexity of the subjects being studied.

The African American church is an enormously complex set of traditions and institutions. The tensions which exist internally, in relation to the African American community and to the dominant culture are not easily understood in historical or sociological analyses.

African American churches are perhaps best understood in paradoxal terms, having seemingly contradictory realities which exist in "dialectical tension" (Lincoln and Mamiya, 1990) or "ambiguity" (Marable, 1983).

Detailed research of African American churches is surprisingly limited, although their relationship to social movements has received much attention by scholars. Most studies have focused on the activism of clergy, although even such a narrow focus betrays the complexity of the dynamics at work. The ethnographic study of four activist clergy by John Brown Childs demonstrated the embodiment of the paradox, with clergy speaking "two languages" of piety and social change (Childs, 1980). Even the quantitative studies of clergy activism remain inconclusive, supporting conflicting interpretations of Black churches as accommodationist or protest organizations.

Other sociological studies have analyzed activism along denominational lines or in relation to discreet variables related to the congregation -- such as its size (Lincoln and Mamiya, 1990) or the expectations of the laity of clergy activism (Harris, 1987). More attention has been focused on differences in political perspectives by age, gender and education, but not as much on how socio-economic status affects congregational activism.

This study is looking at competing paradigms among urban African American congregations as they engage in CED activities -- different strategies, representing different styles, tactics and commitments. A major task of the study is descriptive: How do the different approaches operate? How do they differ? How have they been constructed?

But finally this is also a test of the explanatory power of theoretical approaches. I will argue that the complexity of both the African American church and social change movements demand a comprehensive scheme which resists reductionism. An understanding of the congregation as a collection of individual interests is inadequate, as the collective whole becomes greater than the sum of the parts. Further, the preacher is certainly critical to the construction of strategy, but cannot be isolated for analysis. Even charismatic leaders do not exist in isolation but in the social context of their congregation and community.

All of this argues for an analytical framework which is inclusive of clergy and congregation as they engage one another, acting out of a dynamic subculture and in relationship to both their community and a CBCO.

The larger question under consideration is not **if** African American churches can utilize broad-based community organizing in economic development efforts, but under what conditions will they do so? The issue of if they should move from the traditional approach to one which is seeking social change as well as community development must finally be made by the churches themselves.

Chapter 2

Research Methodology

Introduction

The research design utilized both quantitative and qualitative methods. In order to determine whether ideological or socio-economic variables correlated with the general approach taken by a congregation to community economic development, a questionnaire was developed and congregants in ten churches were surveyed. However, since religious congregations are complex social organizations and the process for determining social behavior is not easily reduced to the simple confluence of particular variables, ethnographic methods were also used. In building on the quantitative data, ethnographies within congregations contributed to developing a "thick description" of how and why particular approaches to community development were constructed.

Sample

Ten African American congregations participated in the study, all of which are now, or have been, involved in community economic development (CED) activities. For purposes of this research, CED is defined as **those activities which seek to attract capital to a neighborhood in order to improve the economic well-being and quality of life for those who are economically disadvantaged.** Churches in the study have been involved in a wide array of economic development projects including building housing for low-income people, organizing credit unions and even a bank, creating jobs programs, and redeveloping a commercial enterprise (shopping mall).

The congregations pursued different strategies in successfully developing their projects. Each approach was evaluated, through interviews with the pastors, as to where they fell on the four continua: parochial/coalitional, clerical/shared leadership, access-to-power/ empowerment, accommodation/change. Half of the churches in the sample represented the more traditional approach to CED and half were utilizing the community organizing model, although there were certainly variations within each grouping. The five congregations using the community organizing approach had chosen to join P.I.A., while the other five had decided not to work with the coalition in pursuing their CED goals. This enabled a comparison between the two approaches among African American churches.

All ten churches in the sample are located in North/Northwest Philadelphia. While African American churches in other parts of the city are certainly involved in CED, there is a concentration of activity in this region. North Philadelphia is the site of Zion Baptist Church; the legacy of Dr. Leon Sullivan is still strong and highly visible in this area of the city. Further, this area is disproportionately represented in the membership of P.I.A.

Despite their geographic proximity, the congregations in the sample represent a diversity of denominational affiliations, worship styles, and membership size, all key factors in the definition of congregational identity. Half are identified with predominantly white Protestant groups, and the others are from African American faith traditions (Table 2.1).

In selecting congregations for the study, relevant individuals and organizations were consulted to facilitate identification of those within the geographic area designated which had experience in CED, as defined above.[1] Articles about the study appeared in The Philadelphia Tribune and Connections (a newsletter of the Metropolitan Christian Council of Philadelphia), inviting participation.

Four congregations which fit the criteria and are in fact well-known for their CED, activities were not included in the sample for different reasons: 1) One congregation is so large (11,000 members) that it would have skewed the results of the survey and would have presented atypical social dynamics in the ethnographic aspect of the project. 2) Another congregation which has had a strong track record in CED, has been under investigation by the I.R.S. and was withdrawing from this activity and from discussing it. 3) A third church is also unusual in its

TABLE 2.1 Sample Congregations

P.I.A. Churches	Denomination	Membership/Attendance[2]
Advocate	Episcopal	150/60+
Sanctuary	Baptist*	1200/600
Northwest	Church of God in Christ*	1000/800
Third	Presbyterian	138/90
Corinthian	Baptist*	800/400
Non P.I.A. Churches		
Grace	Baptist*	1100/800
Knox	Presbyterian	695/325
Victory	Baptist*	2200/1100
Taylor	Methodist	300/100
St. John's	American Baptist	500+/25

* identified with African American Protestant groups

pastoral leadership and social dynamics. The minister is somewhat of a celebrity, having held a high level political office. Because their CED, project (202 housing) was almost exclusively a result of his efforts and connections, it did not represent congregational commitment or involvement. 4) Zion Baptist itself was not included in the study because it was in the process of leadership transition at the time of the research.

Pastors of appropriate churches were initially contacted by phone and the purposes of the study were outlined. In most cases, a follow-up meeting was scheduled. Letters were also sent describing the process of administering the questionnaire and conducting a structured interview with the pastor. For the four congregations to be involved in the ethnographic research, attention was given to describing the process. (In two cases this involved a separate meeting.)

While most seemed genuinely enthusiastic about participating, there was an added incentive: the results of the questionnaire would be shared with the pastor. Information about the beliefs and demographics of the congregation were of particular interest to them. The pastors' verbal responses to the survey results, and the interpretations which they gave to the data were also revealing from the researcher's point of view.

Finally, eleven churches in North Philadelphia were approached, with only one declining to participate. The sample is strongly representative of the CED activities of African American churches in North Philadelphia in the 1990's. One church is located outside of North Philadelphia, in the neighboring Northwest section of the city. (As can be seen later, the demographic profile of this zip code area does not differ greatly from the areas in which the other participating churches are located, although it is somewhat more integrated and has higher income levels.) The inclusion of this church in the sample has been important in that it represents a Pentecostal tradition and is also involved in P.I.A.

While membership in P.I.A. is a definitive indicator of the community organizing approach to CED, it was not always a simple task to assign churches to the P.I.A. or Non-P.I.A. groups. Two of the congregations paid dues yet participated at a minimal level. One of these did not contribute full dues, nor did their members participate during the research period, so it was assigned to the Non-P.I.A. group. The other was kept in the P.I.A. group, as their participation (by paying dues and sending representatives to meetings) has been more consistent even though they are among the least active in the organization. This sorting was also confirmed by the lead organizer who keeps close tabs on the membership.

There has also been some fluidity since the research ended: two of the Non-P.I.A. congregations have been attending meetings and one church has since joined. Nevertheless, during the research period, participation and non-participation in P.I.A. was clear and deliberate for eight of the churches. The other two, while more ambivalent, defined their relationship to the community organization primarily through the payment or non-payment of dues, and to a lesser extent through representation. They do represent a certain constituency: namely, congregations which, for whatever reasons, are not at the core of activity, but remain on the fringes of the organization.

Research Instruments/Tools

Questionnaire

Rationale

There are a number of variables which could affect the outcome of a strategy for community economic development. The **size** and **denomination** of a congregation are institutional factors have been correlated in previous studies to the construction of its social outreach (Lincoln and Mamiya, 1990; Paris, 1985; Pope, 1942). Generally it has been concluded that larger congregations affiliated with less centralized traditions (thereby granting them more autonomy) are more likely to become involved in community issues.

Personal characteristics have also been linked to political orientation and social activism. **Theological conservatism** and **socio-economic class** indices have been the focus of a substantial amount of research, respectively. There had been a long-standing tenet in the field of the sociology of religion that a conservative personal theology is correlated with conservative approaches on political and economic issues, and that the opposite is the case with those espousing liberal theological views. (Stark and Glock, 1968; Marty, 1970; Rokeach, 1969) Some more recent research has shown that no such identification can be easily made -- those of more conservative perspectives on theology instead demonstrate a diversity of political and economic views. (Wuthnow, 1973; Peterson and Takyama, 1984; Johnson, Tamney, Halebsky, 1986; Tamney, Burton, Johnson, 1988; Demerath and Williams, 1989). Since most of this research has been done among white Protestants, and given that African Americans hold more conservative theological views (Kosmin, Keysar and Lerer, 1991), it would be important to investigate the function of conservative theology among African American congregations in shaping a strategy of CED. With its commitment to empowerment and challenging public institutions, sometimes through confrontational tactics, does community organizing primarily attract those of more liberal theological leanings? Or, as more recent research might suggest, is personal theology not a predictor of public witness among African American congregants as well?

The **political consciousness and attitudes** of individual church members should also be considered a variable which might impact the approach to CED the congregation would take. Since the publication of Protest and Prejudice in 1967, Gary Marx launched a lively debate among sociologists on the effect of religion on political consciousness and activism among African Americans. He contends that participation in faith communities has a de-radicalizing effect; that is, religious beliefs, behaviors and affiliations erode an individual's capacity for social critique and confrontation. His thesis has been critiqued by some scholars (Nelsen and Nelsen, 1975; Lincoln and Mamiya, 1990) and echoed by others (Reed, 1986).

For the purposes of this study, it was important to know something about the political and economic views of the congregants, and how these views relate not only to their theological perspectives, but to the strategies for change which they adopt. Obviously, none of the participating churches are sectarian (that is, separatist and other-worldly) and all have already demonstrated a degree of activism in creating positive change in their neighborhoods. They are groups which have clearly not been de-activated by participation in their faith community -- but have some been de-radicalized? The divergent approaches which have been taken by congregations suggest differences in consciousness about society and politics. Would members with more individualistic perspectives be drawn to different strategies of implementing community change than those with more communitarian views? Would higher levels of dissatisfaction with the present economic system provide fertile ground for a more confrontational approach to social change? Does it effect the outcome of the congregation's ministry if larger numbers of members have a higher sense of empowerment for social change?

As well as theological conservatism and political consciousness, another set of variables to consider in understanding the construction of congregational strategies for CED relate to the social location of individual church members. There is a vast and varied body of research on the effects of socio-economic class status on patterns of religious belief and behavior. However, there has been little work done on how social class functions within African American congregations. Because African Americans are more likely to worship in racially segregated congregations, there is a higher degree of socio-economic diversity within these congregations than is found in white churches. (Kosmin, Keysar and Lerer, 1991) Still, sociologists C. Eric Lincoln and Lawrence Mamiya note the increasing class stratification of African Americans and wonder if congregations will follow the same pattern, eventually identifying exclusively with the middle classes and abandoning the poor (1990, pp. 383-385). Certainly this is an appropriate concern for the churches in the study: located in poor communities, they also have large proportions of their congregations who commute to church from more affluent areas both within and outside of Philadelphia. The sample congregations maintain a concern for the neighborhoods in which they are located, as evidenced in part by their involvement in CED activities. However, the degree to which the class status and interests of the congregation contrasts with that of those living in the neighborhood could impact how the congregation articulates its strategy for economic development. In a Weberian framework, class interests would dominate the process. Therefore it might be expected that middle class members would prefer the more traditional approach to CED. Such strategies do not essentially challenge the *status quo* of political and economic systems within which they have had a measure of success. Those of lower education and occupational levels might favor strategies which challenge the current political and economic systems -- there is less to lose and more to gain.

Certainly social location is a factor which permeates belief and behavior patterns in many dimensions: theological, political, social. A questionnaire cannot explain the structures of meanings and interactions which exist -- but it can provide important descriptive data which give clues as to where more investigation is needed in understanding the complex dynamics of faith, consciousness, class interests and social action.

Structure of the questionnaire

A questionnaire was developed which solicited responses in each of these areas. Fourteen multiple choice questions were asked, in addition to two questions related to residence. The questionnaire was printed on four half-pages of a folded 8 1/2 X 11" sheet, so that they could easily be inserted into a Sunday worship bulletin (program) (Appendix: Survey).

The first three questions addressed issues of personal belief, intended to help identify the respondents theologically. The first two questions dealt with views on the Bible and salvation -- two generally recognized doctrinal points which most clearly distinguish orientations to Christian belief. The third question is a rather standard inquiry into theological self-identification, the options ranging from fundamentalist to liberal.

Questions D and E addressed attitudes toward poverty -- whom respondents held responsible for causing and ending it. Here the intention was to expose individualistic or structural approaches to understanding how people become poor and what needs to change.

The next two questions (F and G) were drawn from research done by the National Opinion Research Center (NORC) so that comparisons with the general population could be drawn. These, too, focused on political opinion: the role of government in redistribution of income (F) and the need for "major changes in our economic system."

Questions H, I, and J elicited perspectives on social change: how it might best happen, the role of the Church, and the appropriateness of a pastor's involvement in effecting social change. The first question in this section ("The best way to change society is:") was intended to expose various components of worldview: individualistic/communal, spiritual/secular, empowered/disempowered. For example, a more individualistic-spiritual approach to social change would be reflected in completing the sentence "through spiritual conversion." A more secular, yet also individualistic, perspective would be "for individuals to speak up." Those with faith in government, and perhaps some sense of empowerment through electoral politics, would choose "through electing better officials." Also reflecting empowerment, but through non-electoral processes, is the response, "to join with others and organize protests." A disempowered, passive worldview would be indicated by the response, "to leave it to the experts;" a more religious construction on passivity would be "to wait for God to act."

While understanding the socio-economic status of the congregations was critical to this study, it was decided not to directly ask the individual respondents questions about income. Church members are understandably very guarded about their financial situation; such questions could discourage participation in the study. However, questions were asked about educational attainment (K) and occupational category (L). There was also a question whether one worked full or part-time (M).

Of particular interest is the proximity of residence to the church. What proportion of members walk to church from within the neighborhoods? What proportion drive in, particularly from more affluent areas either within or outside the city? Public transportation was also given as an option. Again, information elicited by Question N sheds light on the self interest of members: would congregations with higher proportions of members residing in the area be more open to the more aggressive tactics of community organizing in working for economic betterment?

Information about the social location of respondents was derived more indirectly. By providing their zip code (O) and closest intersection (P), census data could be accessed and a demographic profile for the whole congregation could be drawn. The major problem with this process was that not all respondents provided usable responses. (Many would simply indicate their street of residence or two major streets close by which might not intersect.) Still for those who provided usable data this was helpful, especially in conjunction with the data on education and occupation.

Respondents were not asked to indicate their gender, marital status or age. An attempt was made to limit the number of questions and to minimize the possibility that the research might be perceived as too invasive or personal. Further, an analysis of differences by gender, generation or life situation, while important, are beyond the scope of this research. Women, however, did comprise a strong majority in all of the churches in the sample.

There were a number of ways in which the data were analyzed. Cross-tabulations were done comparing responses by P.I.A. affiliation, but also by church, denominational grouping, theological conservatism and socio-economic class (educational levels and occupational categories). Statistical analyses were done (both individual respondents and by congregation) to determine the relationships between variables and the factors which correlate with P.I.A. affiliation.

A number of hypotheses were tested. Most importantly, would those of the professional-managerial class be less likely to adopt the more social-change oriented strategy of P.I.A.? Again, in a Weberian framework, it would be expected that those who have had some success in the system would not be as willing to challenge it. They could be expected to be more individualistic in their theology and political orientation.

On the other hand, exposure to education can have the effect of liberalizing perspectives and creating a sense of empowerment and indeed entitlement for change. If this held true, we would expect to find that higher education and occupation levels would be correlated with an attraction to strategies seeking social change. Lincoln and Mamiya found that, among Black clergy, education (as well as age and denomination) was strongly related to a knowledge of, and commitment to, liberation theology (1990, pp. 169, 179-180).

The questionnaire was also designed to test McAdam's contention that social change occurs when conditions are perceived as intolerable and therefore change is imperative, and that it is possible. It could therefore be expected that those opting for community organizing strategies would express dissatisfaction by attributing poverty to structural causes (D), and more strongly agreeing that major changes are needed in the system (G). Further, they would also be more empowered, and more likely to feel that social change is best accomplished through active means -- electoral politics, protest, and to a lesser degree, individual leadership (H). As church members they would more strongly agree that the church has an important role to play in social change.

The questionnaire was not intended to provide exhaustive descriptive data; rather, it was used as a backdrop for the ethnographies. The data served as an important source of clues, suggesting where relationships might exist in the complex system of congregational dynamics.

Procedures for administration

The questionnaire was field tested in a Baptist church in North Philadelphia. An additional question solicited feedback on the instrument itself, and asked what questions might have been confusing or difficult to answer.

Once the instrument was "fine tuned," arrangements were made with the ten churches in the sample to distribute the questionnaire. An appropriate number of copies were taken to the church the week before it was scheduled to be administered during the worship service. They were inserted into the programs to be distributed to church-goers.

In seven of the congregations, the questionnaire was administered by the author (a female of European descent). An African American male doctoral student (who is also a pastor) distributed it in three congregations. Despite our dissimilarity, procedures were standardized and there did not seem to be a difference in response because of the researcher.

The pastor's endorsement and encouragement was, of course, critical. Therefore, during the service, the pastor introduced the researcher and promoted participation in the survey. The researcher then spoke to the congregation and invited all members over the age of 12 to participate. A statement was made generally describing the purpose of the research. Some instructions were emphasized: to only choose one response and to include two intersecting streets closest to one's home. Anonymity was assured. Ushers then made pencils available and usually there was a musical interlude to provide time for completion. Ushers then collected the surveys either upon completion or at the end of the service.

The number of valid cases ranged from a low of 40 to a congregation in which 590 completed questionnaires were usable. There were 657 respondents from P.I.A.-affiliated congregations, and 929 from the non-P.I.A. churches, with the total sample size of 1586.

Structured Interviews

Within two weeks of the congregational survey, an interview was scheduled with the pastor. The interviews were semi-structured and lasted between one and three hours. The interviewer kept detailed notes, but did not tape record the interviews. While a tape recorder gives a more accurate documentation of the discourse, symbolically it can become a barrier to trust and communication if it represents for the subject a possible breach of confidence or implies condescension. An attempt was made, despite differences in gender and race with the interviewer, to close the social distance between interviewer and subject and to identify with their concerns and circumstances. (All the pastors were aware that I am Christian, ordained and teach in a seminary.)

Results of the survey were shared with the pastors; all were interested in the findings and offered their own interpretations. There were few surprises -- for the most part the results confirmed the observations of the pastors. It should be noted that this type of data collection was not part of the typical experience of any of the churches, so that the pastors often expressed genuine appreciation for inclusion in the study.

During the interview, the pastors were asked to describe their route to ministry at their current position. The narrative included information on age, tenure, education, marital status, theological/faith formation, political activism and worldview. The pastors were also asked about the congregation's program and particularly their involvement in CED. They were encouraged to "tell the story" of why and how they had developed their projects. They were also asked to give their perspectives of P.I.A. In the analysis of the interviews, their comments were organized according to the following categories: self-interest, leadership style, degree of dissatisfaction, sense of empowerment, and leadership style according to the four operational poles (clerical/shared, parochial/coalitional, access to power/empowerment, commitment to the *status quo*/seeking social change).

These ten interviews added dimension to the quantitative portion of the study by providing a context for the congregational data. African American congregations often enjoy an organic relationship with their pastor. Sampling congregations without interviewing the pastors would provide a very limited picture. The interviews with the pastors also served as prolegomena for the ethnographic research in the four churches. It sharpened the questions which needed to be addressed and raised other hypotheses to be tested.

Ethnographic Research

For approximately two years prior to the formal research, background research was conducted. Key informants who were knowledgeable about community organizing and economic development involving the African American churches were interviewed. These conversations provided a broad depiction of the "lay of the land" -- the history, current issues, and significant players in this area.

For further background, I did participant-observation in the developmental stages of the organization which became P.I.A. This included attending monthly meetings of the Sponsoring Committee and the clergy group, as well as participating in a two-day retreat. I also attended an "action" (large rally) of an I.A.F. organization in another city, as well as actions in Philadelphia as they were organized, beginning in February of 1992. Through the course of these events, contacts were made, relationships established and many informal conversations took place. All of this background research needs to be acknowledged as it was an invaluable source not only of information and contacts, but also an immersion into the complex dynamics of building a broad-based coalition out of independent congregations, all of which come with their own traditions, agendas, leadership and to some degree, culture. Indeed, the background research crystallized some of the questions as anomalies became apparent.

In exploring the dynamics at work within congregations as they construct their own commitment to and strategies for CED, ethnographic research was conducted in four churches. All had a history of involvement with community development projects, having pursued similar goals but through different strategies. Two of the churches were leading congregations within P.I.A., and the other two had chosen not to participate in the city-wide coalition. In each group there was a larger Baptist church and a smaller congregation affiliated with a mainline Protestant group (Presbyterian and Episcopal). The P.I.A.-affiliated churches were Church of the Advocate (Episcopal) and Sanctuary Baptist Church; the non-P.I.A. field sites were Grace Baptist Church and Knox Presbyterian Church.

Research was more extensive at Advocate and Grace. Approximately three months was spent at each site. During this time I attended Sunday worship each week, which is the centerpiece of activity. I also attended meetings, participated in a soup kitchen, toured the buildings, reviewed written histories and church documents, participated in a church retreat, and "hung out" at the church. All of this was considered text -- one could interpret the commitments of the congregations not only through stated business, but through such sources as who came through their doors during the week, what was hanging on the walls, the condition of the building, announcements in the bulletin, and the allocation of funds. Field notes were kept on each event.

Semi-structured interviews were conducted with 10-15 laypeople in each congregation, as well as with the staff members (both lay and clergy). Most of these took place in the church building during the week or on Sunday; other venues included restaurants and the homes and workplaces of the informants. As with the clergy interviews described above, these ranged from 1-3 hours and focused on the laypersons' involvements and perception of the church, pastoral leadership and CED activities. Careful notes were taken and the interviews were analyzed in a similar manner immediately afterwards.

More limited ethnographic research was conducted at the P.I.A.-affiliated church Sanctuary Baptist and at Knox Presbyterian Church, which is not a member of the coalition. I participated in worship for at least a month at each site and conducted 8-10 interviews which paralleled those at Grace and Advocate.

Of particular interest in the congregational research were organizational matters: What is the level of organization of the church? What are their resources--capital, cultural and human? What is the self-identification of the church and their corporate consciousness about problems in the world and the possibility for change? How do they view their pastor, and themselves in relation to him? As conversation focused on their CED activities, there was much information shared about how the church became involved, who provided leadership, how decisions were made, and their perceptions of the relative effectiveness of the effort.

The research period began in February, 1993 and lasted until February of 1994. This included the collection of both the quantitative and ethnographic data.

Limitations of the Research Methodology

Because of the complexity of the subject, a comprehensive research design using a highly defined sample was used. By focusing on a limited geographical area and a specified set of activities, the actual universe of study is quite small: i.e., African American Christian congregations in North Philadelphia involved in community economic development. Most of the possible cases are in fact in the sample. Therefore, the results can be generalized to this universe, but no farther. This study can only suggest interpretive schemes for other churches in other cities (or in other parts of Philadelphia, for that matter). Still, what is sacrificed by having such a limited universe is offset by the depth afforded by more comprehensive research (using quantitative as well as qualitative methods within a selective sample).

Within the quantitative portion of the project, there were some unavoidable limitations. In constructing the questionnaire, it became apparent that there were no pre-existing instruments which solicited the particular combination of data needed -- religious beliefs, views on poverty, the government, social change, and the church, as well as demographic information. When possible, questions were used from other sources and are helpful for comparative analysis. Still, it is always preferable to utilize a pre-existing instrument which has already been tested for validity and reliability.

Secondly, a questionnaire by definition eliminates the possibility of response by those people who are functionally illiterate. There was no reliable way of knowing what proportion of worshipping members might have been excluded from participating. However, in inner-city congregations which represent a diversity of socio-economic classes, this is an important concern. While it is hoped that the interviews did not exclude those who might have been prevented from responding to a questionnaire, it is not known whether those who were illiterate were represented in the study (or even the church).

A final problem with the questionnaire is that those who do respond represent the most active members (i.e., those attending worship), who also have higher levels of motivation and comfort with survey forms. This could have biased the sample toward higher social classes.

However, both the demographic data and interviews with clergy support the notion that the membership has income and education levels that are disproportionately high when compared to the neighborhood populations where the churches are located.

It is more difficult to ascertain the problems inherent in the ethnographic components of the project. There is some evidence suggesting a Hawthorne effect: when asking pastors their perceptions of community organizing and particularly P.I.A., several seemed to suspect that I was representing the organization and asked questions which betrayed this assumption. Later, as mentioned previously, two of the unaffiliated congregations began to "check out" the organization; one has since joined. It is impossible to decipher what role, if any, participating in this research project had in that decision.

A more obvious question to be raised in the context of this research is the same one asked by Carol B. Stack in the introduction to her study of African American family life, All Our Kin: “Is it possible for an outsider who symbolizes the dominant culture to enter a black community, win the community's participation and approval, acquire reliable data, and judge its reliability?” (1974, p. ix) Two sets of dynamics affect data collection and interpretation in such a situation -- the perception of the researcher by the informants, and her own biases.

It was clear from the outset that I could not easily “blend into” the landscape of congregational life in North Philadelphia. In almost every situation I was the only person of European descent. Physically remaining on the fringes was often not an option. At one ethnographic site it was the practice of the pastor to have “special guests” ushered to the front pew at the beginning of the worship service and publicly introduced. (This continued throughout my entire stay at the church, until I was finally “trained” to seat myself in the front!)

Certainly there was curiosity, and sometimes suspicion, about the motives of my presence. Many times I was directly asked about my purpose; at other times a polite reserve communicated a wait-and-see attitude. More often in public and in individual conversations the informants were interested in the project, enthusiastic about participating and communicated that they were “honored” to be part of the study. The fact that I was clearly identified as a Christian and a church person by my affiliations generated assumptions about shared values and theology, creating a bridge in many situations. At both of the major ethnographic sites (Grace and Advocate), I was asked to participate in worship leadership on my last Sunday at each church. This indicated, if not assimilation, at least a level of trust extended to this outsider. The dynamics of identification and inclusion, as well as those of maintaining distance, also have the capacity to bias the data. It can create a motivation to "tell the researcher what she wants to hear," on the part of the informants. The researcher can identify with the informants to the point of wanting to "protect" them by filtering out unflattering information.

To summarize: I have no doubt that the responsiveness of the clergy and laypeople in the study was influenced by their perceptions of the researcher -- an Anglo female, who is a teacher and clergywoman. It would be naive to believe that I was free of bias as I negotiated my way in a culture which was at once familiar and foreign. In what ways and to what degree this subjectivity was the case is less clear.

It was apparent during the research that in the process of collecting data, assumptions and biases which I had about African American church life were exposed and challenged. This was often expressed in journaling at the end of each installment of field notes. Here I tried to identify my own experience during the course of an interaction: what had been confusing, uncomfortable or resonant in what was being received. There is no doubt that as listener, observer, and indeed student, I was not unchanged by the research process.

---

[1] Thanks to Joe Kalacky of Delaware Valley Community Reinvestment Fund, John Mosley and Bill Moore of Black Clergy Association, Inc., Michael Gecin of Industrial Areas Foundation and Martin Trimble of the National Association of Community Development Funds.

[2] Membership and attendance figures were reported by the pastors, most of whom said that they were "guesstimates." Exact records were not kept, or were not available.

Chapter 3

Results from the Congregational Questionnaire

Introduction

The purpose of this chapter is to report and discuss the results of the questionnaires which were administered in the ten sample congregations between March 1993 and January 1994. Data were collected on socio-economic status (s.e.s.), religious beliefs, and opinions about poverty, social change, and the church. After a description of the whole sample, beliefs and opinions will be presented in relation to class and faith indices, and finally P.I.A. affiliation.

The total number of valid responses was 1586, with congregational totals ranging from 40 to 589 with a mean of 159. It is not possible to calculate the response rate because the total number of bulletins containing the questionnaire taken by individual church members was not counted. What was known was the number of available questionnaires, as suggested by the pastor. However, non-members and under-aged members took bulletins; some couples and families only took one.

Of the total sample, 657 responses came from the P.I.A.-affiliated churches and 929 were from congregations which had chosen not to join P.I.A. The respondents represented all occupational categories indicated, with the largest number identifying themselves as professionals (27%) (Table 3.1). The rest are distributed throughout semi-skilled occupational categories. It should be noted that when compared to the 1990 census data for the city of Philadelphia, the sample had a higher proportion in professional-managerial positions (31.3% versus 24.8%) and a lower unemployment rate (5.3% versus 9.7%).

Table 3.1 Frequencies of Occupational Categories

Categories	Respondents	Percent
Professional	401	27.0
Clerical/office worker	222	14.9
Salesperson	34	2.3
Manager	64	4.3
Merchant/proprietor	12	.8
Service worker	155	10.4
Tradesperson	47	3.2
Factory worker	78	5.3
Retired worker	225	15.2
Student	102	6.9
Unemployed	78	5.3
Volunteer/non-paid worker	53	3.6
Other	14	.9

Those sampled represented higher levels of education than the city-wide norm. In Philadelphia, the proportion of those who have graduated high school is 65.9%; among respondents at least 81.8% had high school diplomas.[1] About one third indicated that high school was their highest completed level of education (33.2%); but a substantial proportion had also had some college instruction (26.7%), had graduated college (9.9), attended graduate school (4.9), or received a graduate degree (7.1%). In addition, 8.4% had received some sort of vocational training

Despite the higher levels of education, the proportionately weighted census data indicated that the median income level for congregational members (based on the tracts from which their members are drawn) was slightly below the citywide level: $24,617 compared to $25,287.

Five of the churches had median income profiles above that, with the highest being $29, 287. The lowest congregational median income profile was $17,509 (Chart 3.1). Seven of the congregations had members residing in tracts with poverty rates above that for Philadelphia (20.3) (Chart 3.2). Further, the composite socio-economic profile shows that members reside in tracts with substantially higher percentages of female-headed households (Chart 3.3).

Residential patterns reflected the homogeneity of worship patterns. All of the congregations drew members from census tracts with much higher proportions of African Americans than the city-wide rate (Chart 3.4). All but one congregation had members coming from tracts with lower proportions of Latinos than found throughout the city (Chart 3.5).

Variation from the city-wide norms should come as no surprise when considering the commuting patterns. Despite the fact that these churches are located in densely populated neighborhoods along the Broad St. corridor, they all have large proportions of their membership which commute to church from other parts of the city, as well as from outside Philadelphia. Only 15.5% (n=230) of respondents indicated that they walk to church. Nearly 3/4 drive to their home congregation (71.7%). Although these churches would be easily accessible by public transportation, only 12% utilize public services on Sunday mornings. The questionnaires which could be matched with census data[2] show that the sample congregations only drew 22% from within their zip code areas, even though 29.7% indicated that they "drive from within the neighborhood." (The discrepancy could be attributed to the imprecise definition of boundary.) Still, the locally drawn membership (less than a quarter of the whole congregation living within the church's zip) comes to church by walking, taking public transportation, and driving. That leaves a substantial portion which comes from outside the neighborhood in which the church is involved in social ministries of community economic development. Whether these commuters are bound by family history or are more recently attracted to the church from outside the neighborhood, will influence the degree and nature of their loyalty to the pastor, the church, and the neighborhood. This will be explored in the ethnographic research.

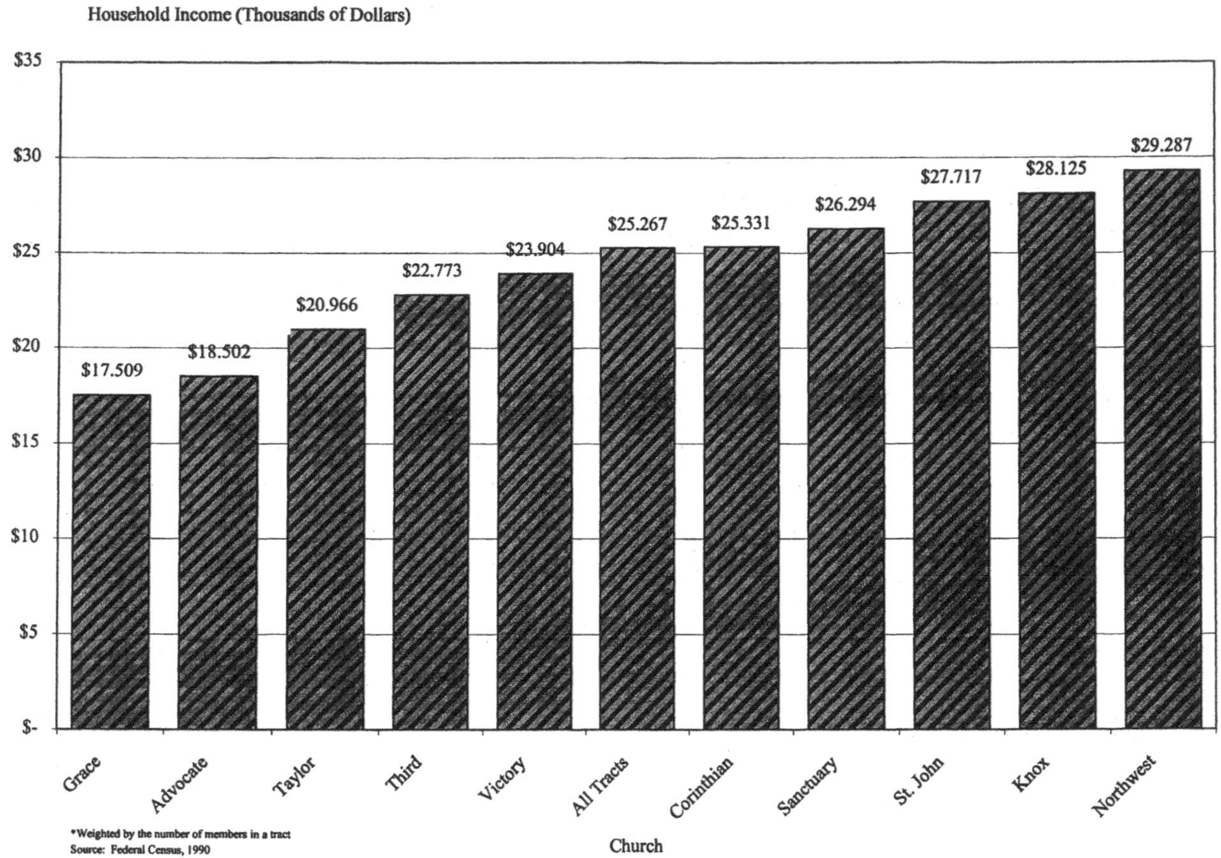

*Weighted by the number of members in a tract
Source: Federal Census, 1990

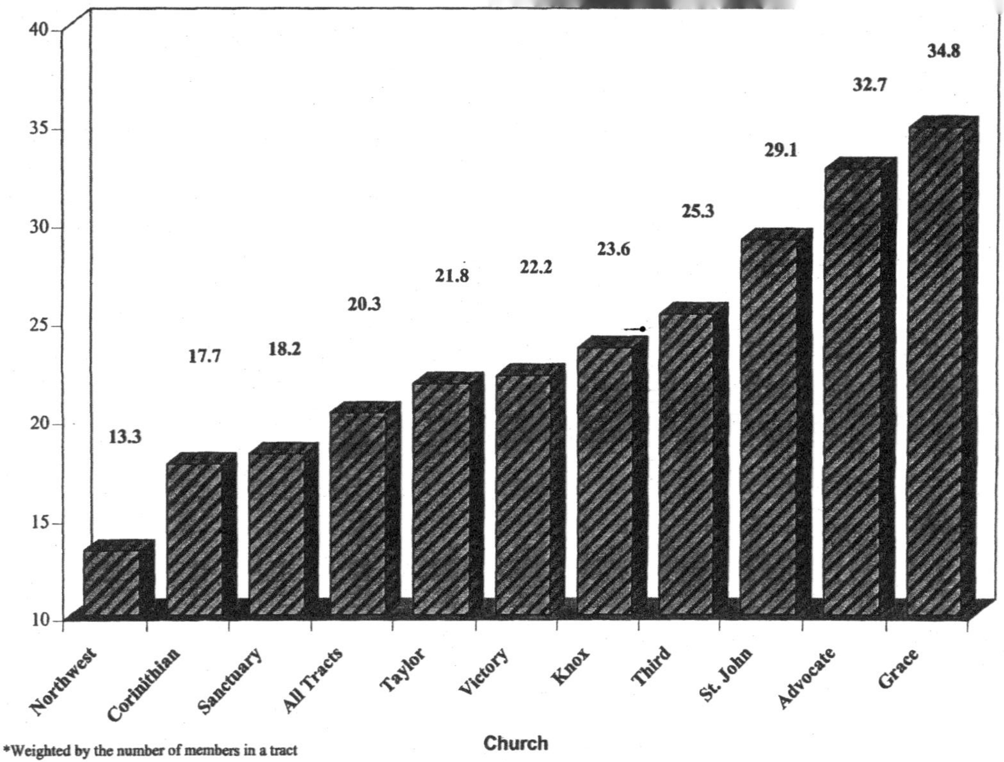

*Weighted by the number of members in a tract
Source: Federal Census, 1990

Chart 3.2 Poverty Rate of Tracts from which Churches Draw Their Congregation*

Pct. Female Headed Households

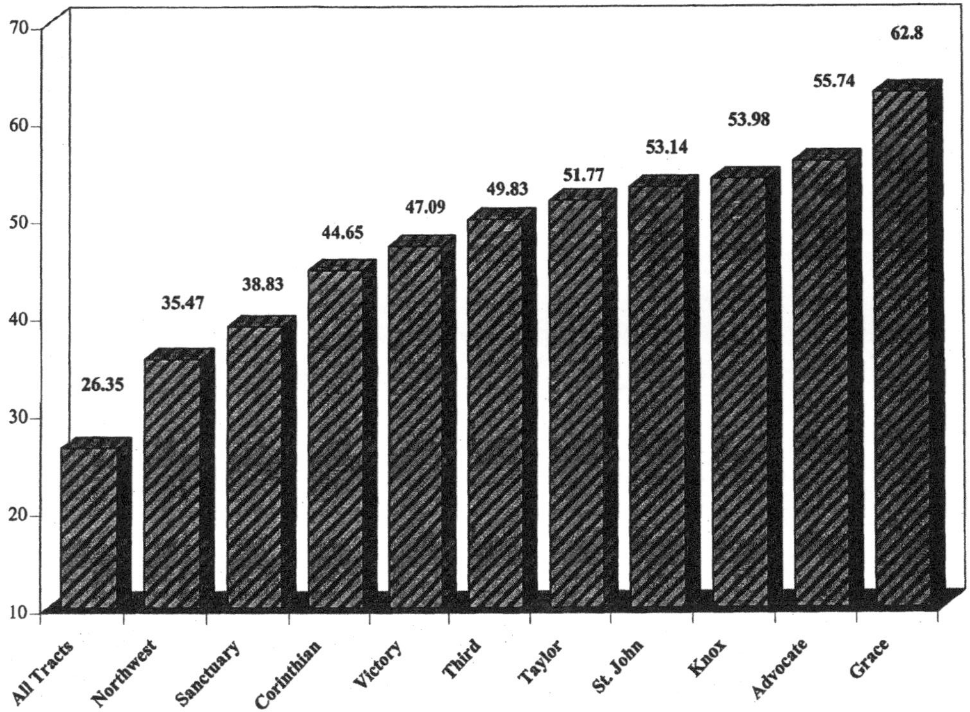

*Weighted by the number of members in a tract
Source: Federal Census, 1990

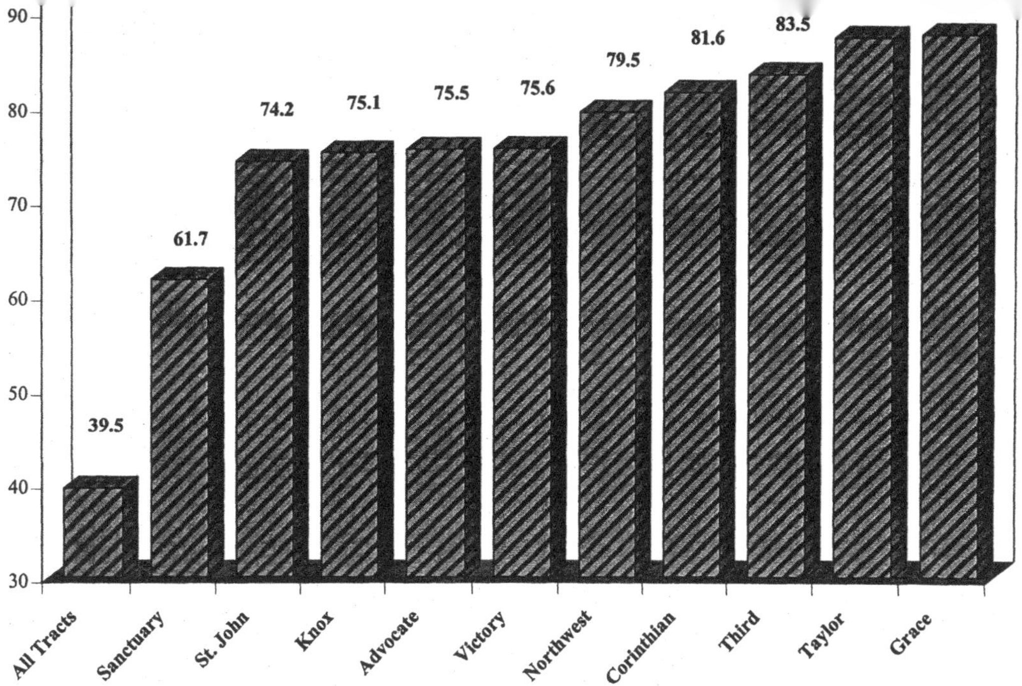

*Weighted by the number of members in a tract
Source: Federal Census, 1990

Chart 3.4 Racial Composition of Tracts from which Churches Draw Their Congregation*: Percent Black

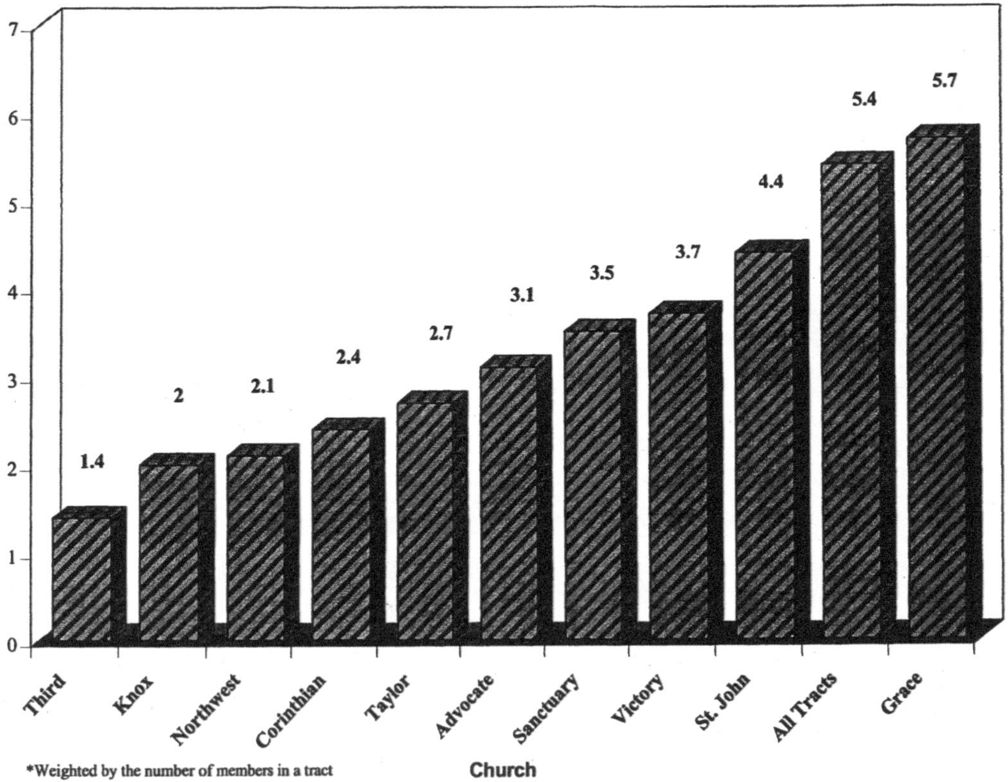

*Weighted by the number of members in a tract
Source: Federal Census, 1990

What is clear at the outset is a difference in the socio-economic status of those who walk to church when compared to those who drive or take public transportation (Table 3.4). While 51.5% of the commuters have some education beyond high school, only 35.2% of the walkers do. Further, they are less likely to be in professional occupation categories (15.7% versus 29.1%). Their unemployment rate approaches that of the city: 8.3% compared to 4.7% for the commuters. The discrepancy is even more apparent when looking at income data: although 59.3% of those who walk to church come from tracts with incomes below that of the city, only 26.9% of the commuters represent low income residential areas. How residential context is related to patterns of belief and opinion will be examined later.

On the theological spectrum, those sampled hold conservative views about the Bible and salvation. There was a high level of consensus (72.1%) that "the Bible is the actual word of God and should be taken literally." Similarly, more than half (53.5%) held the view that "Only those who have been born again will be saved by God." The formulation of personal faith commitments is complex and resists being distilled into a few multiple choice questions. Still, the majority responded with views most often representative of fundamentalist/evangelical orientations to the Christian religion.

To summarize, the sample population can be described as African American evangelicals, largely representing the working and middle classes (as indicated by occupation and census data on income) with higher levels of education than the urban population at large. The congregations maintain more diversity along socio-economic status lines than they do according to racial/ethnic representation. Members are largely drawn to these racially homogeneic congregations from outside the zip area, and most reside in other neighborhoods which are highly segregated by race. Still, those who walk to church clearly represent lower socio-economic strata than do the commuters.

In analyzing the survey data, six independent variables will be considered to determine their relationship with political opinions and P.I.A. affiliation. While it is assumed, in the construction of the research formula, that political consciousness is related to the choice of strategy for CED, the relationship between the two dependent variables will also be considered. The independent variables have been recoded into consolidated categories to facilitate analysis: conservative/moderate conservative/non conservative (belief)[3], professional-managerial/non-professional (occupation)[4], high school and post high school (education)[5], high and low (income),[6] walkers/commuters (proximity)[7] and traditional African American and mainline Protestant (denomination)[8]. Interactions among the independent variables will highlight which are producing the strongest effects.

It is hypothesized that socio-economic status (education + occupation + income), theological beliefs, denominational affiliation, and residential proximity to the church will all be related to political consciousness which in turn will influence the preference of strategy for CED (Figure 3.1). It is incumbent upon the data to disprove the null hypothesis that these factors are unrelated to the choice for or against affiliation with P.I.A.

[belief] + [occupation] + [education] + [income of tract] + [proximity] + [denomination] ➔ political opinion➔ P.I.A.

Figure 3.1 **Hypothesized Relationship of Variables**

In the following section, the results of the questionnaire related to each of the variables, independent and dependent, will be reviewed. The data will be presented at both individual and congregational levels. This is done so that the relationships of the variables can be seen more clearly as they are descriptive of both individuals and the religious congregations with which they affiliate. It is also possible that we might be able to tease out how variables which are correlated at an individual level but not so within congregations.

Religious Beliefs

Views on the Bible

Despite the high level of consensus on the Bible, some variations can be seen among those holding conservative views. Congregations differed widely, with an independent Baptist church having 85.4% of its members affirming that the Bible should be taken literally. In contrast, only 26.3% of the Episcopal church maintained the same belief. Denominational affiliation made the biggest difference here, with members of the traditional African American churches holding more conservative views than their counterparts in the mainline Protestant churches (Table 3.2).

The effect of socio-economic status was ambivalent. While occupation and income did not make a difference in beliefs about the Bible, there was a significant difference between those with higher and lower education levels on this question. Those with more education did not hold literalist views to such a proportion. Further, those who lived within walking distance of the churches were not as conservative on the question as their commuting sisters and brothers.

It is clear that there is no real difference between those affiliated with P.I.A. and their counterparts. The members of churches which have chosen to pursue the course of community organizing in bringing about change are just as likely to hold literalist views on the Bible. Looking at the congregational data further confirms this finding (Chart 3.6). A comparison of the mean scores of P.I.A. and non-P.I.A. congregations failed to disprove the null hypothesis: beliefs about the Bible did not differ significantly.

Views on Salvation

To find over half of an ecumenical sample agreeing on a doctrinal point is only a dream for many church leaders. While there was less consensus on the question of salvation than there was on the Bible in this sample (with 53.5% believing that God only saves those who have been "born again"), this conservative position was by far the preferred choice among five options in every grouping. Still, variations occurred (Table 3.3).

Table 3.2 **Percent responding affirmatively to the statement, "The Bible is the actual word of God and should be taken literally"**

	Percent	(n)
Total Sample	72.1	(1078)
Denomination (*)		
Traditional AA	77.4	(887)
Mainline Protestant	54.7	(191)
Occupation		
Professional	70.9	(326)
Non-Professional	72.7	(752)
Education (*)		
High School	76.8	(562)
Post High School	68.8	(481)
Income		
Low	70.3	(166)
High	71.1	(328)
Proximity to church (***)		
Walkers	69.6	(160)
Commuters	72.6	(918)
Affiliation with P.I.A.		
Affiliated	73.3	(450)
Non-affiliated	71.3	(628)

(*) indicates significant difference at the <.01 level
(***) indicates significant difference at the <.05 level

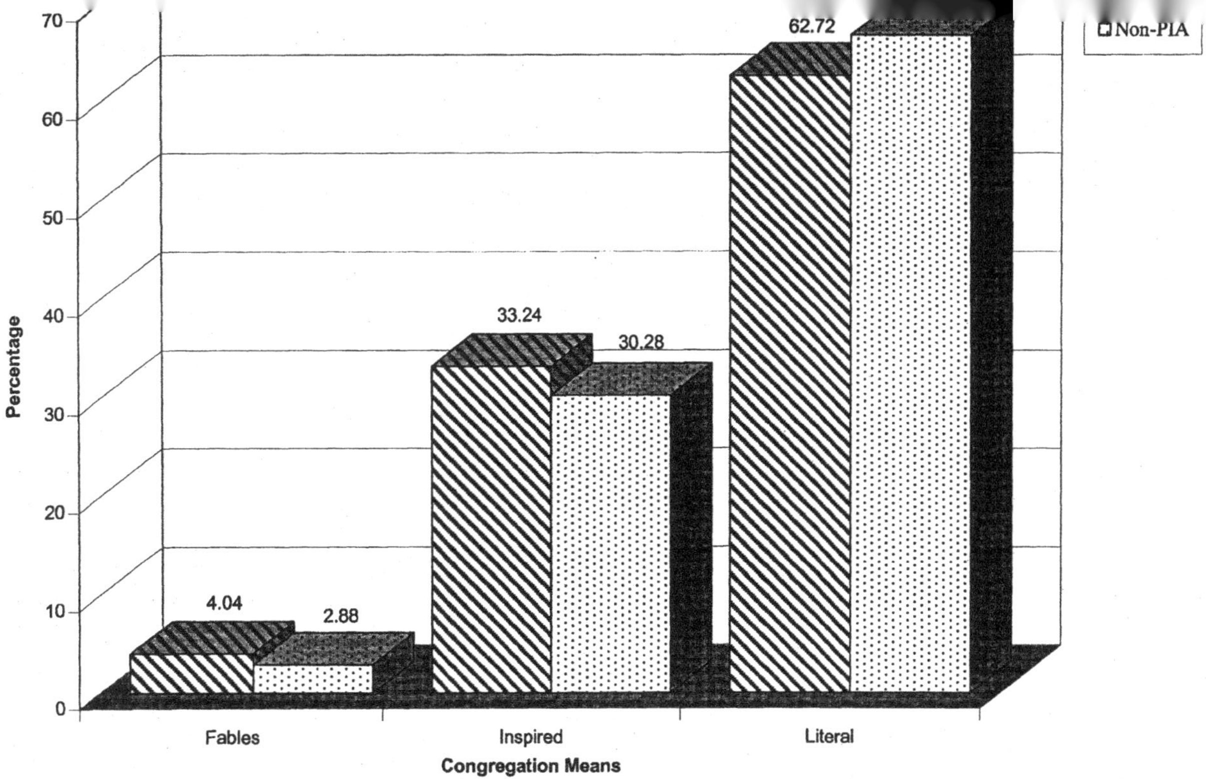

Chart 3.6 Religious Beliefs: Views on the Bible

Table 3.3 Percent responding affirmatively to the statement, "Only those who have been born again are saved by God"

	Percent	(n)
Total Sample	53.5	(787)
Denomination (*)		
Traditional African American	57.2	(641)
Mainline Protestant	41.7	(146)
Occupation (*)		
Professional	59.1	(266)
Non-Professional	51.0	(521)
Education (*)		
High School	48.4	(344)
Post High School	59.5	(413)
Income (*)		
Low	43.9	(101)
High	59.1	(269)
Proximity to church (*)		
Walkers	44.3	(101)
Commuters	55.2	(686)
P.I.A. (*)		
Affiliated	59.3	(357)
Non-affiliated	49.4	(429)

(*) indicates significant difference at the <.01 level
(***) indicates significant difference at the <.05 level

Here there are differences between the indicators of socio-economic class. Those who are professionals, the commuters, and those with higher levels of education and living in more affluent areas are significantly more likely to take the more conservative view on salvation, as are the P.I.A. affiliates. Again, denomination also had the strongest effect, as those of the African American traditions believed more strongly in the need for a born again experience than their sisters and brothers in the mainline Protestant congregations. There was also a broad range by congregation as was seen in the previous question with only 5.3% of the Episcopal members choosing the "born again" option, compared to 82% of those in the Pentecostal church.

It is interesting to note that "all true believers, of any religion" came in a strong second and "all those who have been baptized" made a very poor showing. The rite of baptism is not the ultimate determinant of salvation for most respondents. Rather, the responses indicate that acceptance by God is a matter of personal experience and belief.

Here is an instance where the individual and aggregated data differ (Chart 3.7). Whereas 59.3% of the individual members of P.I.A. churches chose the "born again" response, the congregations had a sample mean of 46.26% which did not differ significantly from the mean from non-P.I.A. churches. Once again the data analysis by congregation demonstrates parallel belief patterns between the two sets of churches.

Theological Self-identification

Respondents were asked to identify themselves theologically with the label with which they were most comfortable. Generally, people preferred to call themselves "moderate" (35.6%). About one in five chose to identify with the "conservative" (22.4%) and "liberal" (20.9) labels. Only 9.1% of the whole sample considered themselves to be "fundamentalist," and 12% chose "other," often writing in "Child of God" or "Believer."

These results do not correspond with their responses on the previous two questions. Those who responded with the most conservative views on the Bible and salvation were recoded into a single category which accounted for 40.1% of the population. Since a literalist view of the Bible and exclusivist view on salvation (*vis a vis* the born again experience) are considered the distinguishing beliefs of Christian fundamentalism, it is interesting to note that this sample of African American Christians did not identify with the fundamentalist label. Even when just looking at the responses of the 40% who held fundamentalist positions, only 12% claimed the label.

The question about self-identification, therefore, does not pass the test of validity: it is not an accurate indicator of where, in fact, a believer might fall on the theological spectrum. What is a fairly

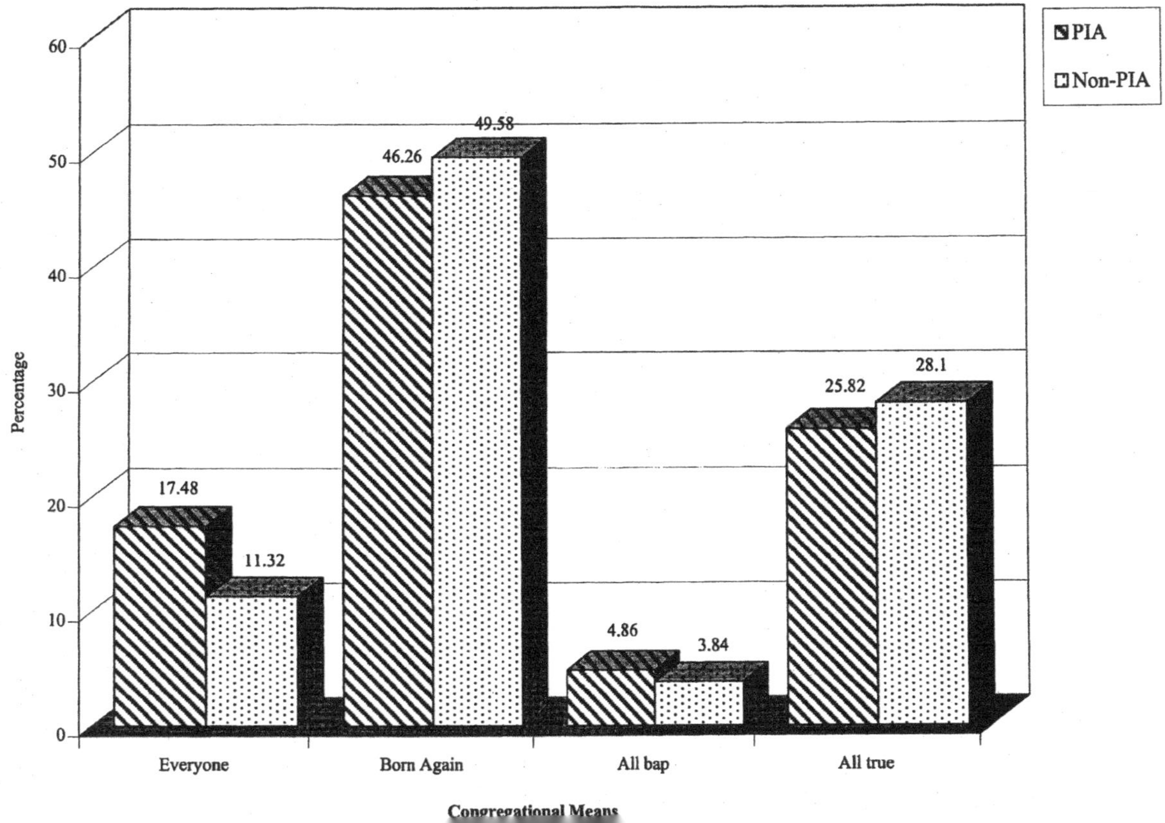

PIA
Non-PIA
60
50
40
30
20
10
0
Percentage
17.48
11.32
46.26
49.58
4.86
3.84
25.82
28.1
Everyone
Born Again
All bap
All true
Congregational Means

standard categorization of theological perspectives (fundamentalist/ conservative/moderate/liberal), showing up frequently on religious surveys, was not a helpful indicator among this population. What is interesting is why this might be the case. Does "fundamentalist" sound pejorative? Does it connote whiteness or even racism, as often communicated through the media? Does holding more progressive views in other areas, coexistent with conservative theology, serve to moderate one's view of oneself? Or are these labels simply not as meaningful to this population as they are in other sectors of the Christian community? How African American Protestants construct their own self-identities as Christians is a broader question beyond the scope of this research.

To summarize the patterns of religious belief: denominational affiliation is related to differences in theological orientation, with the traditional African American churches demonstrating more conservative stances. There are also some indications that differences exist along socio-economic lines, with a more conservative bent being observed among those of a higher socio-economic status (especially on the understanding of salvation). Those members from P.I.A. churches had belief patterns which followed those of the higher s.e.s., though less strongly.

Socio-economic Status

In order to look more closely at the demographic profile of the sample, indices of socio-economic status were selected to see what variations existed within the sample. First, the proportion of those with post-high school academic training were compared within denominational groups (traditional African American and Euro-American Protestant bodies), theological orientations (conservative, moderately conservative, and non-conservative), proximity to the church (walkers and commuters), and affiliation with P.I.A (Table 3.4). Once again, there was a difference seen in the denominational categories: members of mainline Protestant denominations had significantly higher levels of education. When looking at specific levels by congregation, indeed the mainline Protestant congregations had proportions of members with graduate degrees ranging from 10.3%-25%. The traditional churches ranked below that, with 9.8%

down to 2.8% holding graduate degrees. But the greatest discrepancy in education levels was seen in the comparison between walkers and commuters, a difference of almost 16 percentage points.

Higher levels of education existed among the most and the least conservative theological orientations, although the difference was not significant. Nor was there significant difference in educational levels among those in P.I.A.-affiliated congregations compared to the non-affiliates.

In looking at the percentages of congregants who identify their occupations in the professional and managerial categories, it seems that the class difference between denominational groups, as suggested by the educational levels, disappears. Those in the historically Black traditions do not differ so much from those affiliated with predominantly Anglo denominations. However, when all of the occupational frequencies are reviewed, differences do emerge. The African American traditions have about twice the proportion of workers in the clerical (17.2% versus 7.4%) and service categories (11.7% versus 6.2%). However, the most dramatic difference exists in the proportion of retired workers: 33% those in the mainline Protestant congregations are retired compared to 9.9% of those in the African American traditions. Congregations varied widely in their proportion of retired workers, with one mainline Protestant congregation having 42.3% of its membership retired, down to 3.4% in an independent Baptist church. The mainline Protestant congregations have larger proportions of older members. Their higher education levels suggest that many of these workers have retired from professional-managerial occupations, which explains why the proportion of those identifying their occupation as professional was not higher. It also explains why the proportion of full time workers is comparatively low (71.3%) for the mainline Protestant groups and perhaps why their income levels are lower.

When considering theological orientation, there is a relationship between conservatism and employment: a significantly higher proportion of conservatives has professional/managerial employment status and more are working full-time. However, the non-conservatives are more likely found in the mainline Protestant churches and thus, are more likely to be retired. This would moderate the differences between theological groups; if retired professionals could be counted, the differences in occupational status and full-time work would probably even out.

The most dramatic class differences can be seen when comparing the walkers and the commuters. The latter group has significantly higher levels of education and income and are more likely to be professionals and full time workers.

To summarize class stratification does exist in this sample along denominational lines, as in earlier studies (Niebuhr, 1938; Roof and McKinney, 1988). There is also a relationship between theological orientation and s.e.s with conservatives having higher income and occupational status. Congregations themselves reflect internal stratification, with those living closer to the churches having levels of education, occupation and income which are clearly lower than those of their brothers and sisters who commute to church.

The class indices among the P.I.A. members were not as clear. Affiliates and non-affiliates had similar levels of education, professional status and full-time work. Yet a significantly higher percentage of those in P.I.A. churches came from more affluent tracts (80.7% compared to 57.8% for non-affiliates). This provides a challenge to more Weberian assumptions about the predominance of economic self-interest -- the goals and tactics of community organizing for CED do not always represent or protect the interest of those with higher socio-economic status. Why would they be affiliated with churches working for community development through the often-controversial tactics of community organizing?

Beliefs about Poverty

Causes of Poverty

In turning to opinions about poverty, one is struck by a resilient consensus on the issue, no matter how the data is approached (Table 3.5). Roughly one-third of those sampled believed that poverty is caused primarily by "inadequate government support and services." The structural causes of "racism/discrimination in hiring" and "unavailability of good jobs"were selected by one in five respondents

Table 3.4 Indices of Social Class Location: Percentages of those with Post High School Education, Professional Occupation, Working Full-Time, High Incomes

	Post H.S.	Professional	Full-Time	High Income
Total Sample	48.6%	31.3%	82.5%	66.0%
	(728)	(465)	(876)	(476)
Denomination	(***)		(*)	(*)
African American Traditional	47.1%	30.7%	84.9%	69.7%
	(543)	(372)	(737)	(368)
Mainline Protestant	53.9%	28.0%	71.3%	56.2%
	(185)	(105)	(139)	(109)
Theology		(***)		(***)
Conservative	52.1%	33.9%	84.3%	72.7%
	(297)	(200)	(370)	(197)
Moderate Conservative	45.5%	28.0%	82.3%	63.0%
	(300)	(192)	(368)	(203)
Non-conservative	49.1%	27.2%	78%	59.7%
	(131)	(85)	(138)	(77)
Proximity	(*)	(*)		(*)
Walkers	35.2%	15.7%	77.3%	40.7%
	(81)	(36)	(116)	(50)
Commuters	51.1%	29.1%	83.2%	71.3%
	(647)	(365)	(760)	(369)
P.I.A.				(*)
Affiliate	48.1%	33.2%	82%	80.7%
	(296)	(203)	(377)	(209)
Non-Affiliate	49.1%	30%	82.9%	57.8%
	(432)	(262)	(499)	(267)

(*) indicates significant difference at the <.01 level
(***) indicates significant difference at the <.05 level

each. Relatively few (16.1%) attributed poverty to individual "laziness, lack of motivation." Far fewer were fatalistic about poverty, with less than 1% holding "bad luck" responsible.

Some of the variations within the sample were interesting, however. Again denomination had an effect. Mainline Protestants did not hold government as responsible for causing poverty, but felt more strongly than the traditional African American members that poverty did have structural causes (namely, racism, and availability of jobs).

Interestingly enough, the churches affiliated with the mainline denominations (which historically have taken liberal stances) exhibited a slightly higher willingness to blame individual laziness for one's poverty.

Education seemed to have the effect of dissuading respondents from the dominant ideology of individualism, making them more aware of how racism operates. However, those with higher levels of education also held the public sector more responsible and the private sector less responsible for poverty than did those without education beyond high school.

Occupational status did not make a significant difference in the interpretation of poverty. Professionals were slightly more individualistic (choosing laziness), and more aware of racism than those in other occupational categories. But they were also less structural in that they were less willing to hold government or the economy responsible for creating poverty.

Income followed similar patterns. It did not make a great difference in beliefs about poverty, but those from more affluent areas also attributed racism more than those from lower income tracts. Like the mainline Protestants and the professionals, they held government less accountable; with the professional group they were less willing to blame poverty on the unavailability of jobs.

These results correspond to findings in an earlier study on perceptions of wealth and poverty (Kluegel and Smith, 1986). The researchers found that the effects of education on the perceptions of economic justice were ambivalent: while academia provides the opportunity for challenging the dominant ideology of individualism, it

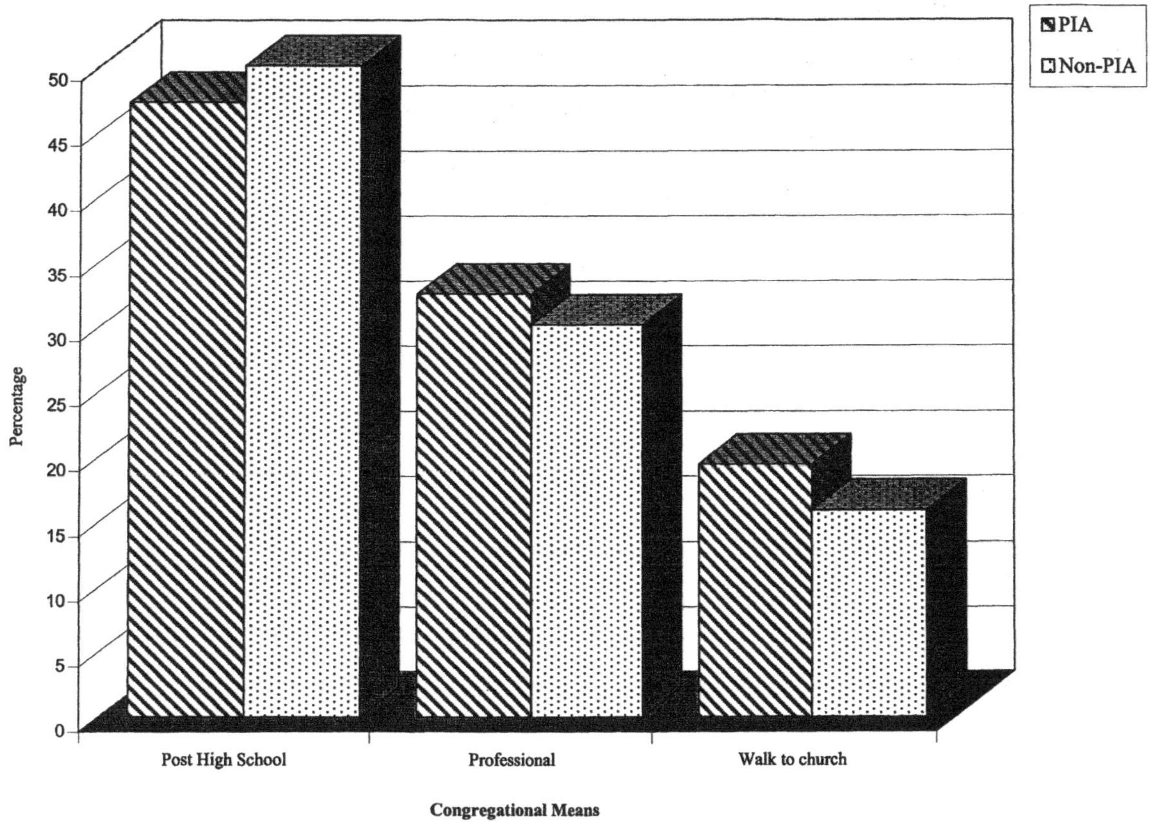
PIA
Non-PIA
Percentage
50
45
40
35
30
25
20
15
10
5
0
Post High School
Professional
Walk to church
Congregational Means

Table 3.5 Responses on the sentence completion, "I believe that poverty is caused primarily by..."

	Laziness	Bad Luck	Racism	Govt.	Jobs
Total Sample	**16.1% (241)**	**.6% (9)**	**18.2% (273)**	**32.7% (489)**	**21.7% (325)**
Denomination (*)					
African American Tradition	15.9% (182)	.6% (7)	17.8% (203)	33.6% (384)	20.3% (232)
Mainline Protestant	16.7% (59)	.6% (2)	19.8% (70)	29.7% (105)	26.3% (93)
Theology					
Conservative	15.7% (88)	.2% (1)	18.2% (102)	34% (191)	20.7% (116)
Moderate Conservative	15.9% (104)	.5% (3)	18.1% (118)	34.3% (224)	21.7% (142)
Non-Conservative	17.4% (49)	1.8% (5)	18.8% (53)	26.2% (74)	23.8% (67)
Education(*)					
High School	19.9% (147)	.5% (4)	16.5% (122)	31.1% (230)	22.3% (165)
Post H.S.	12.3% (85)	.6% (4)	20.1% (139)	35.2% (243)	20.4% (141)
Occupation					
Prof./Manager	16.6% (75)	.4% (2)	19.4% (88)	30.5% (138)	20.5% (93)
Other	15.9% (166)	.7% (7)	17.7% (185)	33.7% (351)	22.2% (232)
Income					
Low	15.2% (36)	.8% (2)	18.6% (44)	35.4% (84)	21.9% (52)
High	14.6% (67)	.7% (3)	21.5% (99)	32.6% (150)	18.9% (87)

Table 3.5 Continued

	Laziness	Bad Luck	Racism	Govt.	Jobs
Proximity(***)					
Walkers	13.2%	2.2%	17.6%	35.7%	19.8%
	(30)	(5)	(40)	(81)	(45)
Commuters	16.6%	.3%	18.4%	32.2%	22.1%
	(211)	(4)	(233)	(408)	(280)
P.I.A.					
Affiliate	16.9%	.3%	15.7%	32.1%	21.8%
	(103)	(2)	(96)	(196)	(133)
Non-affiliate	15.6%	.8%	20%	33.1%	21.6%
	(138)	(7)	(177)	(293)	(191)

* indicates significant variation at the <.01 level

*** indicates significant variation at the <.05 level

also aids social mobility. "Most people are cross-pressured, having reasons to maintain both structural and individual explanations (of wealth and poverty) by reason of their diverse group memberships" (Kluegel and Smith, p. 94).

Higher socio-economic status, *vis a vis* academic training, income and professional status, might liberalize individualistic views about poverty and raise consciousness around issues of race, but it does not necessarily translate into a structural understanding of poverty, especially one which might lead to an economic critique or commitment to social change.

Whether one lived in the relatively poorer neighborhoods around the churches and walked to worship, or commuted to church does make a significant difference in perspective, but not as strongly as might be anticipated. The commuters did feel more strongly than the walkers that individual laziness and the unavailability of jobs were to blame for poverty. This is interesting to note, considering the higher rate of unemployment among the walkers. A higher proportion of walkers held government responsible for poverty than in any categorization of the sample.

Perhaps the most interesting thing about the function of theological orientation is that those with radically different (and often mutually exclusive) faith perspectives do not vary significantly in their perspectives on poverty. Theological differences did not matter at all in the designation of racism as the cause of poverty, for example.

To summarize: denomination and education have the greatest effect on the interpretation of poverty. Mainline Protestants chose the structural explanation of **job availability** as the cause of poverty in the highest proportion. Education is responsible for the greatest difference in an **individualistic** interpretation. Indicators of higher socio-economic status (education, professional occupation, income, affiliation with mainline Protestant churches) felt more strongly that **racism** causes poverty. Those holding the **government** most responsible were more likely theological conservatives or moderate conservatives, from the African American traditional churches, walkers, those with post-high school education, yet from poorer tracts and non-professional-managerial occupations.

Finally, when looking at the opinions of those within P.I.A. churches compared to the non-affiliates, there is no statistically significant difference in both the individual data and congregational means (Chart 3.9). Those involved in community organizing do not exhibit less individualistic, more structuralist interpretations of poverty, as might be expected.

<u>Responsibility for Ending Poverty</u>

Perspectives on the solutions to the problem of poverty paralleled those on the analysis of it (Table 3.6). Generally, the population sampled held the government even more responsible for ending poverty (47.3%) than they did for causing it (32.7%). Similarly, a smaller proportion (6.2%) held individuals responsible for resolving their impoverishment than the number who blamed the individuals for their situation (16.1%). Further, the respondents expressed more faith in the "third sector" than they did theprivate sector for eliminating poverty: 11.4% looked to the Church, 10.5% to community organizing and only 6.8% to businesses and banks. These general contours held through all categorizations within the sample, with the variables related to differences in **intensity** of perspective, rather than altogether different ones.

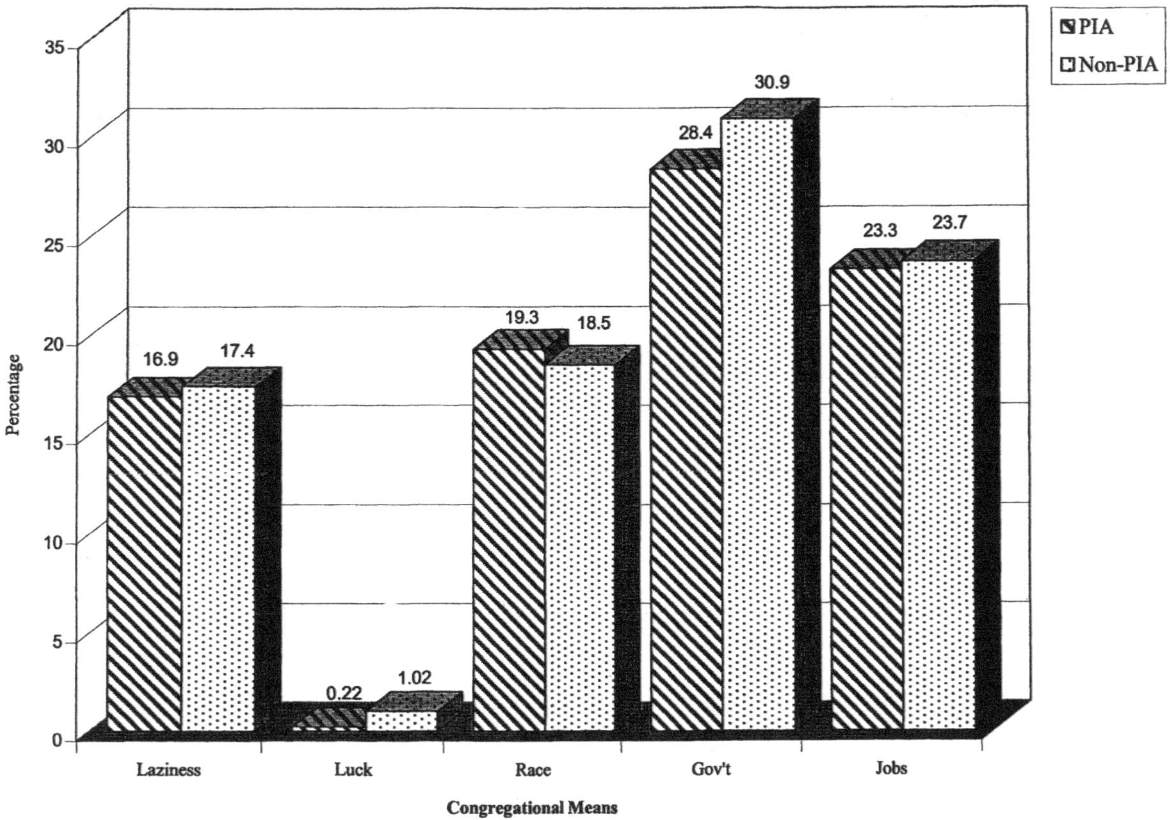
PIA
Non-PIA
Percentage
35
30
25
20
15
10
5
0
16.9
17.4
0.22
1.02
19.3
18.5
28.4
30.9
23.3
23.7
Laziness
Luck
Race
Gov't
Jobs
Congregational Means

Denomination made a significant difference in perspectives on ending poverty, with mainline Protestants being the only grouping which believed more in the private sector (businesses and banks) than in the church as an agent for change. This pattern was followed by the theological non-conservatives. However, the links between denomination and theology are not always so predictable: mainline Protestants favored a stronger government role than did those from African American denominations, but non-conservatives were weaker on government than the two more conservative groups.

Education and occupation demonstrated significant variation. For example, those with **lower** education and occupational status believed in a **stronger** role for government. It is interesting to note that income and residential context (proximity) did not make a significant difference in shaping perspectives on whom is most accountable for addressing poverty.

It is difficult to understand from this question what relationships might exist between political opinion and the choice of affiliating with a community organization, a primary goal of which is to address the suffering of the poor. "Community organization" was favored to a greater degree as a strategy for ending poverty by the more theologically liberal, those with lower education and occupation levels, and those who walked to church. This is understandable. While affiliation with P.I.A. did make a significant difference in perspectives on this question, there was clearly little difference between members and non-members in looking toward community organizing. Where the variation existed was on the role of government and the church: P.I.A. affiliates tended to follow the belief patterns of those of higher class status and the traditional African American denominations in believing **less** in government. However, with the traditional denominations, theological conservatives, and those walking to church they shared a stronger belief in the role of the church to bring about an end to poverty.

These same patterns were reflected in the congregational means, but when compared statistically, no significant differences exist. P.I.A. churches share the same political perspectives as do those opting for a more traditional approach to CED.

Table 3.6 **Responses on the sentence completion, "Those most responsible for ending poverty are":**

	Individual	Bus/ Bank	Govt.	Church	Comm.Orgs
Total Sample	**6.2%** **(92)**	**6.8%** **(101)**	**43.7%** **(651)**	**11.4%** **(170)**	**10.5%** **(157)**
Denomination (*)					
African American Tradition	5.7% (65)	6.2% (71)	42.9% (490)	12.4% (142)	10.5% (120)
Mainline Protestant	7.7% (27)	8.6% (30)	46.1% (161)	8.0% (28)	10.6% (37)
Theology (***)					
Conservative	6.9% (39)	5.2% (29)	43.0% (242)	13.3% (75)	8.9% (50)
Moderate Conservative	5.1% (33)	7.9% (51)	45.3% (293)	11.4% (74)	9.9% (64)
Non-Conservative	7.1% (20)	7.5% (21)	41.4% (116)	7.5% (21)	15.4% (43)
Education (*)					
High School	4.8% (35)	6.6% (48)	48.5% (353)	11.7% (85)	12.2% (89)
Post H.S.	6.7% (47)	7.0% (49)	40.1% (280)	11.2% (78)	8.3% (58)
Occupation (*)					
Prof./Mgr.	6.1% (28)	8.5% (39)	37.9% (173)	11.8% (54)	7.9% (36)
Other	6.2% (64)	6.0% (62)	46.3% (478)	11.2% (116)	11.7% (121)

Table 3.6 Continued

	Individual	Bus/ Bank	Govt.	Church	Comm.Orgs
Income					
Low	7.2%	5.1%	51.1%	10.5%	8.4%
	(17)	(12)	(121)	(25)	(20)
High	4.6%	7.0%	45.2%	9.6%	7.8%
	(21)	(32)	(208)	(44)	(36)
Proximity					
Walkers	4.4%	4.8%	42.3%	14.5%	13.7%
	(10)	(11)	(96)	(33)	(31)
Commuters	6.5%	7.1%	43.9%	10.8%	10.0%
	(82)	(90)	(555)	(137)	(126)
P.I.A. (***)					
Affiliate	5.8%	6.7%	40.4%	13.3%	10.9%
	(36)	(41)	(249)	(82)	(67)
Non-affiliate	6.4%	6.9%	46.0%	10.1%	10.3%
	(56)	(60)	(402)	(88)	(90)

(*) indicates significant variation at the <.01 level
(***) indicates significant variation at the <.05 level

Beliefs about the System in Relation to Poverty

The survey contained two questions which focused on the perceived need for political and economic change in addressing the issues of poverty. To the first, respondents were asked to indicate their level of agreement or disagreement with the statement: "It is the responsibility of government to reduce the difference in income between people with high incomes and those with low incomes." Over 37% agreed or strongly agreed -- indicating that this sample of African American church-goers felt more positively toward government intervention in income redistribution than was the case in the general population -- 32.9% agreed to the same statement (NORC, 1990) (Table 3.7).

Within the sample significant differences did not exist between the denominational groupings. Theological orientation did make a significant difference, with conservatives indicating weaker conviction

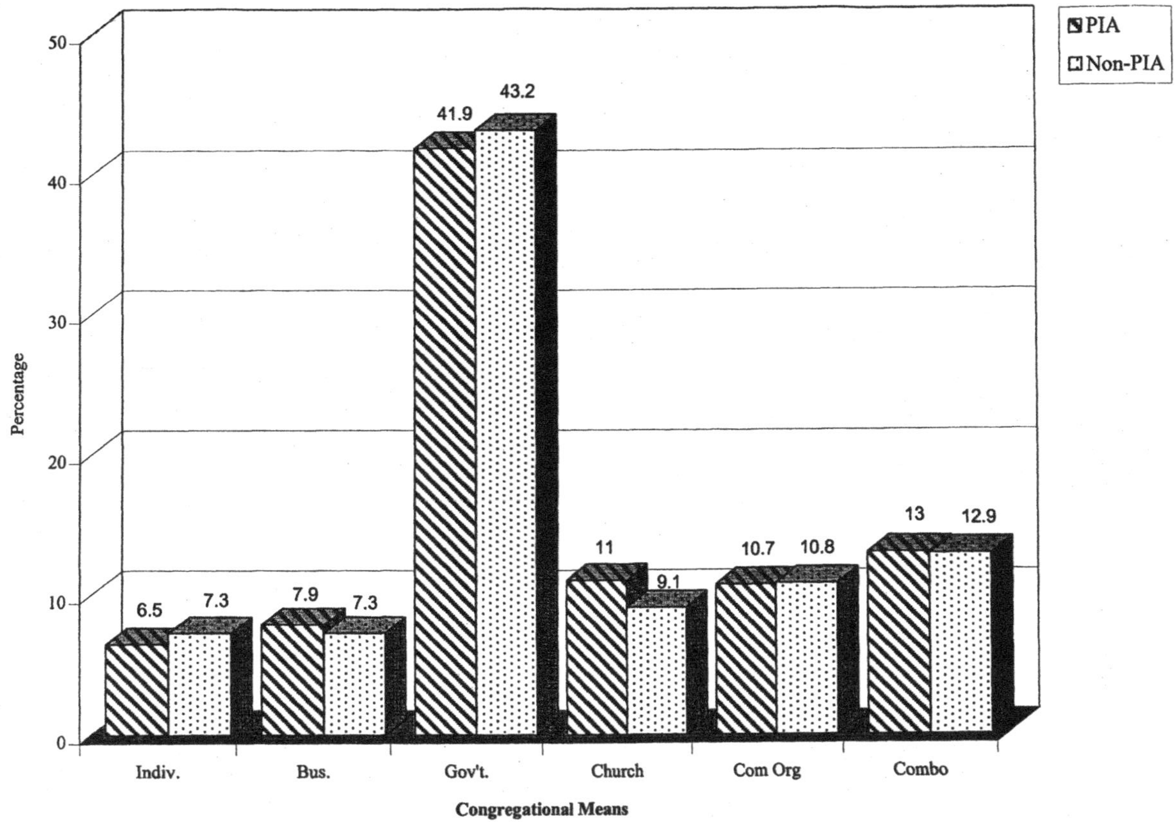
PIA
Non-PIA
Percentage
50
40
30
20
10
0
6.5
7.3
7.9
7.3
41.9
43.2
11
9.1
10.7
10.8
13
12.9
Indiv.
Bus.
Gov't.
Church
Com Org
Combo
Congregational Means

Table 3.7 Beliefs about structural change: Percentages agreeing/strongly agreeing that the government should be involved in reducing the gaps in income distribution (GAP) and that the economic system is in need of major change if poverty is to end (CHANGE).

	GAP	CHANGE
Total Sample	**37.8% (566)**	**83.2% (1262)**
Denomination		(*)
African American Tradition	37.2% (428)	84.9% (987)
Mainline Protestant	39.4% (138)	77.7% (276)
Theology	(*)	
Conservative	36.7% (207)	86.1% (494)
Moderate Conservative	37.4% (246)	81.8% (543)
Non-Conservative	40.6% (113)	80.7% (226)
Education	(*)	
High School	41.3% (308)	84.4% (637)
Post H.S.	34.3% (242)	82.6% (590)
Occupation	(*)	(*)
Prof./Manager	33.2% (155)	82.6% (388)
Other	39.9% (411)	83.5% (875)
Income		
Low	42.7% (99)	85.0% (204)
High	33.4% (156)	82.9% (388)

Table 3.7 Continued

	GAP	CHANGE
Proximity	(***)	
Walkers	46.2%	86.9%
	(105)	(200)
Commuters	36.2%	82.6%
	(461)	(1063)
P.I.A.	(***)	
Affiliate	36.4%	83.2%
	(225)	(521)
Non-affiliate	38.8%	83.1%
	(341)	(741)

(*) indicates significant difference at the <.01 level
(***) indicates significant difference at the <.05 level

than their theologically more progressive counterparts in this type of role for the government. There were more distinctive trends along the class indices. Those with lower education and occupational levels once again felt the government should take a stronger role in alleviating poverty. This was also true of the walkers. Such a position would, of course, be in their interest. P.I.A. affiliation was related to opinions on this question; members did not feel as strongly that government should be involved in income distribution. However, when comparing congregational means, significant differences dissolve (Chart 3.11).

There was a remarkably high level of consensus on the next question, with 83.2% indicating agreement with the statement, "In order to bring poverty to an end, there will have to be major changes in our economic system." Interestingly enough, class effects were minimal on this question; rather, denomination was related to differences in opinion.

African American traditional church members felt more strongly than the mainline Protestants that economic change was necessary (84.9% versus 77.7%). Here is an instance where conservative theology is related to a more liberal position on an economic issue. Even when controlling for education as a proxy for class, theological conservatives were more progressive in their opinions about economic change. It could be speculated that the eschatological themes in conservative Christian theology highlight consistently a utopic vision of an egalitarian "new heaven and new earth" which is the ultimate standard against which contemporary reality is judged.

There was no significant difference between the P.I.A. affiliates and the non-affiliates in either the individual or congregational analyses (Chart 3.11). If this question is any indicator if dissatisfaction, it can only be said that the level of dissatisfaction was high throughout the sample, and a different degree of dissatisfaction does not correlate with those who are in churches which choose to pursue social change through community organizing.

Beliefs about Social Change

Strategies for Social Change

When given six different strategies for social change (in addition to "don't know," "other" or indicating a combination), by far the preferred option was "spiritual conversion" (45.9% of the whole sample). It is unknown whether respondents meant that everyone needs to experience a spiritual conversion or if they had the perpetrators of evil particularly in mind. Nevertheless, when approaching social change, there was a definite orientation, or worldview, operating for more people which is individualistic and spiritual. Spiritual conversion does not necessarily connote a passive approach to social change, however. The least-favored options were those which betrayed a more passive orientation, whether secular or spiritual: "leave it to the experts" (.5%) and "wait for God to act" (3.3%).

While "to join with others and organize protests" suggests an empowered posture, this option was chosen by only 8.2% as the best way to bring about social change. More mainstream strategies of "electing better officials" and "for individuals to speak up" were preferred over protests (13.5% and 11.2%)

This question brought about a significant degree of variation (Table 3.8). Traditional denominations, post high school education, professional-managerial occupational status and conservative theology were all positively related to the choice of strategy, with these groups

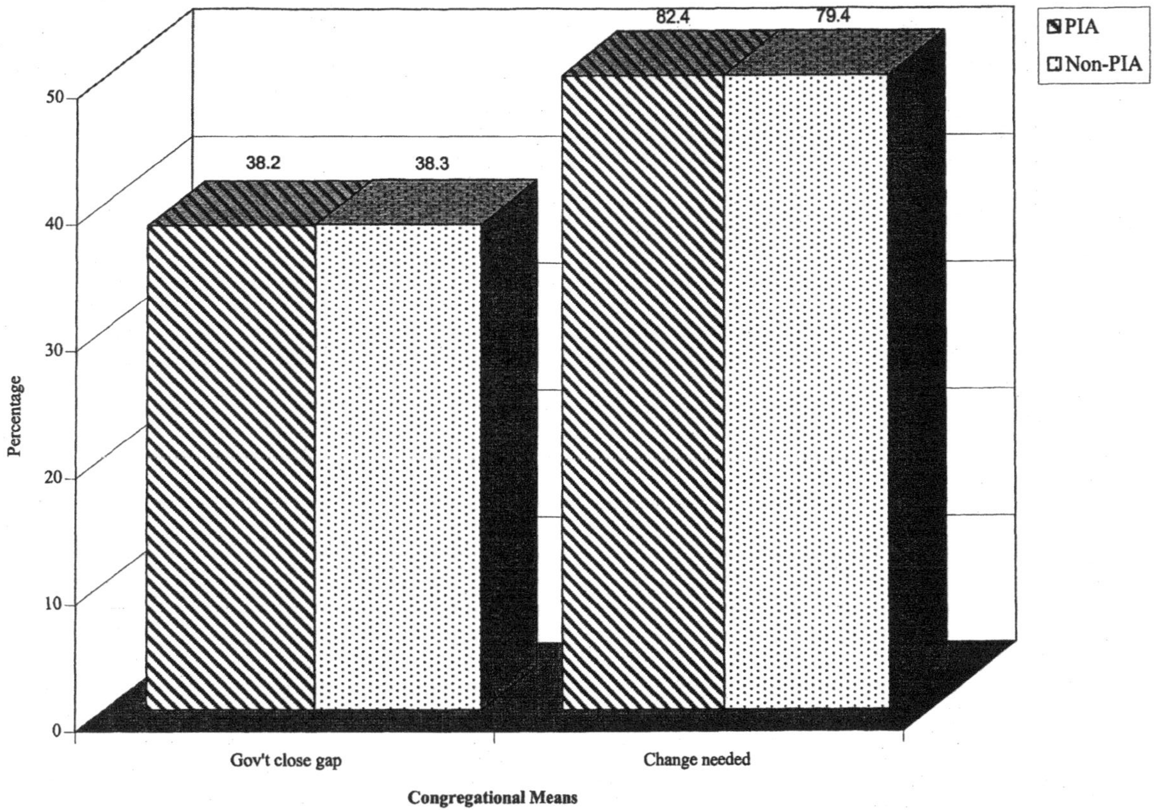
50
40
30
20
10
0
Percentage
38.2
38.3
82.4
79.4
PIA
Non-PIA
Gov't close gap
Change needed
Congregational Means

Table 3.8 Responses on the sentence completion, "The best way to change society is:"

	Spiritual Conversion	Electing Officials	Leave to Experts	Org. Protests	Indiv. Speak	Wait-God
Total Sample	**45.9% (688)**	**13.5% (203)**	**5% (7)**	**8.2% (123)**	**11.2% (168)**	**3.3% (49)**
Denomination (*)						
African American Trad.	48.7% (563)	12.3% (142)	.3% (4)	7.0% (81)	9.8% (113)	3.5% (41)
Mainline Protestant	36.4% (126)	17.6% (61)	.9% (3)	12.1% (42)	15.9% (55)	2.3% (8)
Theology (*)						
Conservative	56.0% (321)	11.0% (63)	.3% (2)	3.8% (22)	8.7% (50)	3.5% (20)
Moderate Conservative	42.6% (278)	14.3% (93)	.6% (4)	8.3% (54)	14.0% (91)	3.2% (21)
Non-Conservative	32.6% (90)	17.0% (47)	.4% (1)	17.0% (47)	9 .8% (27)	2.9% (8)
Education (*)						
High School	42.9% (321)	16.0% (120)	.5% (4)	8.8% (66)	11.4% (85)	.9% (29)
Post High School	48.9% (347)	10.7% (76)	.4% (3)	7.9% (56)	11.3% (80)	2.0% (14)

Table 3.8 Continued

	Spiritual Conversion	Electing Officials	Leave to Experts	Org. Protests	Indiv. Speak	Wait-God
Occupation (*)						
Prof./Mgr.	52.1%	10.2%	.4%	7.8%	10.5%	.7%
	(239)	(47)	(2)	(36)	(48)	(3)
Other	43.2%	15.0%	.5%	8.3%	11.5%	4.4%
	(450)	(156)	(5)	(87)	(120)	(46)
Income						
Low	47.9%	13.2%	.4%	9.4%	8.5%	1.7%
	(112)	(31)	(1)	(22)	(20)	(4)
High	43.4%	13.5%	.4%	7.5%	12.5%	3.2%
	(202)	(63)	(2)	(35)	(58)	(15)
Proximity						
Walkers	45.5%	10.8%	–	8.2%	9.5%	6.1%
	(105)	(25)		(19)	(22)	(14)
Commuters	46.0%	14.0%	.6%	8.2%	11.5%	2.8%
	(584)	(178)	(7)	(104)	(146)	(35)
P.I.A. (*)						
Affiliate	46.8%	11.0%	.3%	7.8%	9.7%	5.3%
	(294)	(69)	(2)	(49)	(61)	(33)
Non-affiliate	45.2%	15.4%	.6%	8.5%	12.3%	1.8%
	(394)	(134)	(5)	(74)	(107)	(16)

(*) indicates significant difference at the <.01 level

more strongly favoring spiritual conversion. However, proximity to the church and income had no significant effect on this choice. It is interesting to note that while P.I.A. affiliation did make a difference in the individual data, it did not effect the choice of spiritual conversion; rather, differences are found in the other response options.

Mainline Protestants and those more liberal in their theology still opted for spiritual conversion, but to a lesser degree; they indicated more faith in both electoral and protest politics, and in the effectiveness of individuals speaking up to bring about change.

Class trends were not clear. Those with less education and lower occupational status were more positive about electing better officials, which is the opposite of what might be expected.

Among the more interesting results were the findings that those commuting to church from outside the neighborhood, and those in congregations not affiliated with P.I.A. were more likely to prefer electoral politics and organizing protests as the means to social change. While P.I.A. is adamantly non-partisan (and does not get involved in electoral politics at all), they do deal with officials quite a bit. Their tactics have the effect of exposing the weaknesses of officials and suggesting where change of personnel might be needed. Further, they rely on organized assemblies and public protests in demonstrating their power for bringing about change at the local level. Yet members of P.I.A. churches are less open to these strategies than their counterparts. And they believe just as strongly in the possibilities of spiritual conversion.

Again, when comparing congregational means, the null hypothesis is not disproven. Congregations are remarkably similar in their opinions about strategy, despite the course taken by their own church.

<u>The Church and Social Change</u>

There was a high degree of consensus of agreement on the statement: "Working for change in society is an important part of the mission of the church" (85.8%) (Table 3.9). While those outside the religious establishment might assume such an attitude is basic to faith communities, this is not the case. Many congregations, from separatist-fundamentalists to the most establishment groups, do not believe that the church should involve itself in social change. This is a dramatic consensus, although it should be kept in mind that the ten churches in this sample have a demonstrated commitment to community betterment.

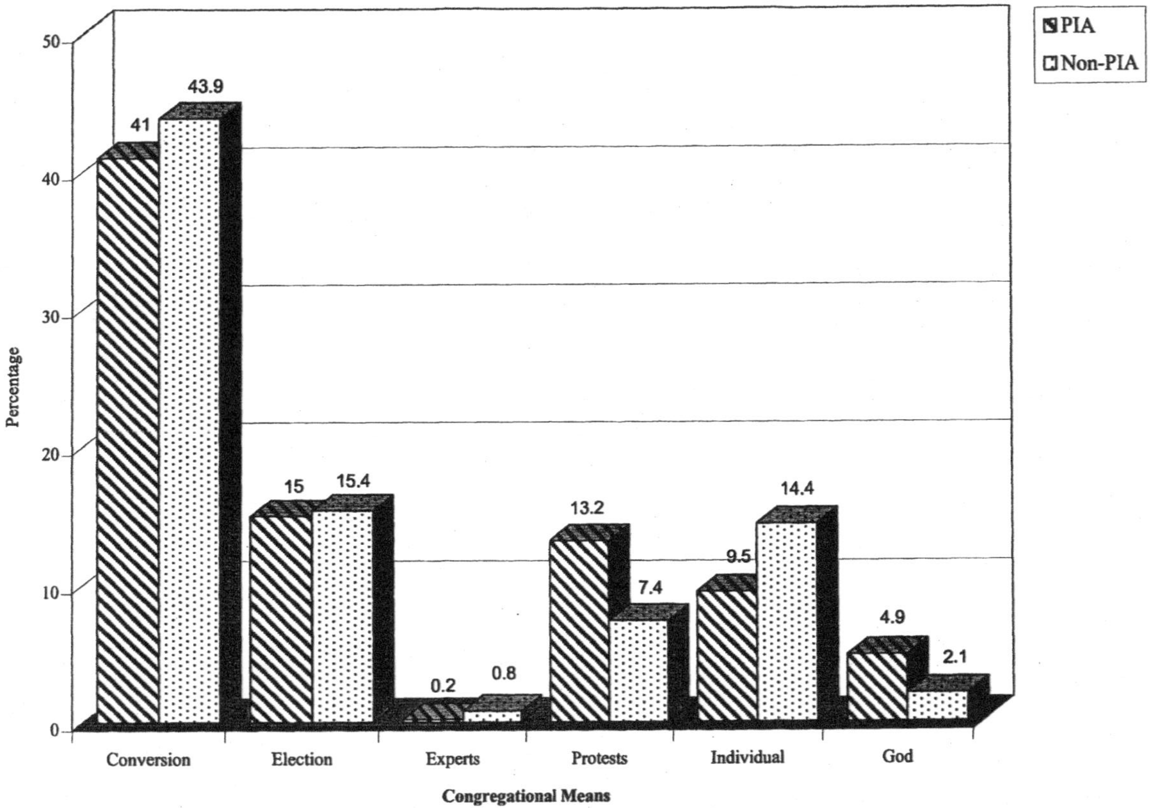

PIA
Non-PIA
Percentage
50
40
30
20
10
0
41
43.9
15
15.4
0.2
0.8
13.2
7.4
9.5
14.4
4.9
2.1
Conversion
Election
Experts
Protests
Individual
God
Congregational Means

The respondents were not as convinced that the pastor should be involved in the public arena. Only 52.1% expressed agreement to the statement: "he pastor of a congregation should be involved in politics and issues of public concern."

Theological orientation had a significant relationship to perspectives on the role of the church. Conservatives believed more strongly than liberals (i.e., non-conservatives) in the public mission of the church (89.8% versus 80.5%). There was no significant difference in opinions regarding the pastor, along theological lines. However, denomination did not play a role in support of either the church or clergy in social change.

Higher levels of education and professional-managerial occupational status were significantly related to higher agreement on the public mission of the church and its pastor. (Those living in more affluent areas were more likely to support the idea of pastoral leadership than those from poor neighborhoods (57.2%/47.3%) although income was not a significant factor in the range of responses.)

Again, residential context and P.I.A. affiliation did not make a difference in perspective on the church and social change. One might expect that there would be higher levels of agreement among P.I.A. members on both questions, as affiliation with the community organization necessitates an activist role for both the congregation and the clergy. While there was not significant difference when comparing the congregational means (Chart 3.13), the range among churches on the question on pastoral involvement is striking: there was a high level of support of 68.5% and a low of 39.7%. Both of these congregations are members of P.I.A. and both clergy have high profiles in community leadership.[9] This suggests that for those congregations with low levels of support for the idea of clergy involvement in public issues either: a) there is dissatisfaction with the pastor's activities, b) the pastors are involved in spite of the opinion of the congregation or c) the congregations somehow do not understand this activity to be outside of the spiritual duties of the pastor. The ethnographic material should shed some light on this question.

Table 3.9 The Church and Social Change: Percentages who agree/strongly agree that the church should be involved in social change and that the pastor should be involved in politics and public issues.

	CHURCH	PASTOR
Total Sample	**85.8% (754)**	**52.1% (778)**
Denomination		
African American Tradition	86.7% (1009)	52.0% (601)
Mainline Protestant	82.6% (290)	52.5% (178)
Theology	(***)	
Conservative	89.8% (516)	50.0% (285)
Moderate Conservative	84.5% (560)	52.3% (345)
Non-Conservative	80.5% (223)	56.0% (149)
Education		
High School	82.9% * (631)	51.0% * (385)
Post H.S.	89.1% (637)	53.5% (384)
Occupation		
Prof./Manager	89.6% * (424)	55.2% * (260)
Other	83.9% (875)	50.6% (519)
Income		
Low	88.4% (212)	47.3% (113)
High	88.1% (417)	57.2% (267)

Table 3.9 Continued

	CHURCH	PASTOR
Proximity		
Walkers	86.0%	50.0%
	(197)	(114)
Commuters	85.6%	52.5%
	(1102)	(665)
P.I.A.		
Affiliate	86.1%	51.8%
	(544)	(318)
Non-affiliate	85.4%	52.3%
	(754)	(460)

(*) indicates significant difference at the < .01 level
(***) indicates significant difference at the < .05 level

Discussion

Most striking about the survey results is the strong consensus of opinion which resists the pulls of theological and socio-economic diversity. There is a broad spectrum of theological perspectives represented which is closely identified with denominational affiliation. The sample also drew responses from those with low levels of education, non-professional jobs, living in the poorest of neighborhoods, as well as those commuting to church from much more affluent areas who hold educational credentials and high-level positions, and many in-between. There was some stratification by denominational groupings, with those in the predominantly white denomination-affiliated churches associated with more upward mobility. (This could be a short-lived phenomenon, as these churches also had congregations which had higher proportions of retired members.)

These differences tended to produce variations in the intensity of opinions (as measured by the percentages choosing a particular response) as well as some predictable trends, but did not drive great dissension. For example, in following the opinions of those with professional-managerial status and higher educational levels, it was found:

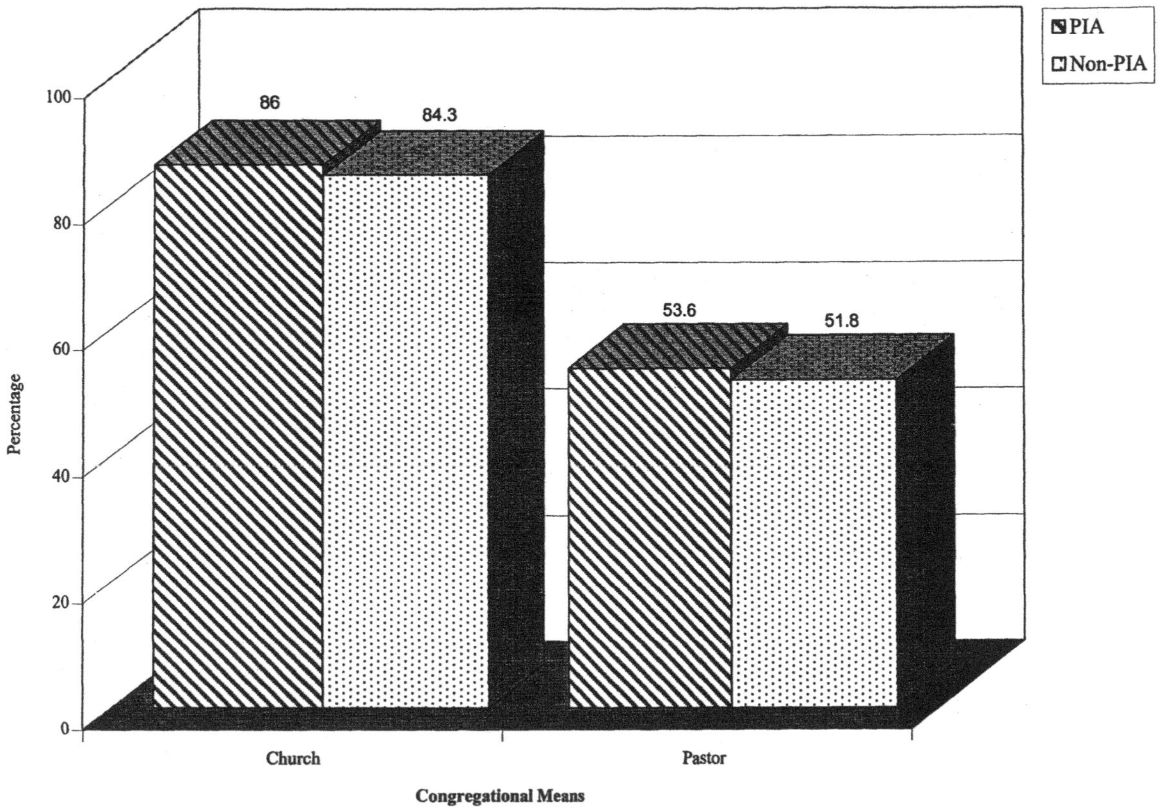
PIA
Non-PIA
100
80
60
40
20
0
Percentage
86
84.3
53.6
51.8
Church
Pastor
Congregational Means

A. They tended to have more conservative theological stands and believed more strongly in the effectiveness of spiritual conversion in changing society, both of which suggest a more individualistic orientation. Yet education and occupation levels operated independently, and ambiguously in individualistic interpretations of poverty. Those with more education blamed individuals less for their poverty, yet they held them more responsible for ending it when compared to both those with less education and with professional-managerial occupational status. This represents a tension of consciousness and self-interest which is not easily resolved for upwardly-mobile African Americans who in many ways have "made it," yet continue to choose to participate in a Black congregation which is investing human and financial capital in the local community.

B. Those with higher levels of s.e.s. were consistently less enthusiastic about government intervention in ending poverty, yet were just as convinced that major economic change was necessary. Again, here is evidence of political perspectives which are related to both class status and identification with the larger community.

Similarly, denominational affiliation and theological perspective were often related to each other, but did not always function in predictable ways. Those coming from the African American traditional churches were more likely to blame government for creating poverty, yet less likely than mainline Protestants and non-conservatives to look to government to end poverty or to redistribute income. Yet more felt that economic change was necessary. The traditionalists/conservatives felt, to a greater degree, that the church should involve itself in social change, and chose spiritual conversion as the best strategy. The mainline Protestants/non-conservatives exhibited more individualistic orientations on one question (ending poverty) and more structural perspectives in their other responses (cause of poverty, income redistribution, social change).

Those who walked to church were from very different socio-economic circumstances than their fellow parishioners. Coming from a more economically disadvantaged perspective, they were more likely than the commuters to blame government for poverty, to look to government to close the income gap, and believed more strongly in the need for economic change. However, they did not vary significantly in their preference for spiritual conversion for social change or the importance of church and pastoral involvement. More walkers did feel that it was best to just "wait for God to act" than did any other grouping. Still, the percentage was relatively small (6.1%).

While class, proximity and faith perspectives did not radically alter opinions, some trends were seen and their influence was demonstrated.

Despite the different effects of theology and social location on the opinions expressed, those affiliated with P.I.A. churches did not look, think, or act distinctly. While P.I.A. affiliates tended toward theological conservatism, they did not follow the opinion patterns of the theological conservatives, for the most part. If P.I.A. affiliation was driven by conservative theology, one would expect to find high correlations between membership in the organization and agreement on spiritual conversion for social change, and the need for economic change (as was exhibited by the theological conservatives). However, this was not the case. Chart 3.14 illustrates the point. When comparing congregational means on two points of doctrine (the literal interpretation of the Bible and necessity to be born again), and two political perspectives (the need for economic change and conversion as the preferred strategy for social change) there is no significant difference between the P.I.A. and non-P.I.A. churches. Yet when churches are clustered by denomination -- Mainline Protestant and Traditional African American -- significant differences do exist.

While the socio-economic profile of the P.I.A. did not differ greatly from that of the whole sample, there was a slightly higher proportion of professionals (3.2%) in the P.I.A. group, hardly enough to expect class interest to drive affiliation. Indeed, there was little evidence that opinion patterns followed the class trends. The professionals tended not to lean as heavily as those in the other occupational categories on government as the cause or cure of poverty. While those in the P.I.A. churches did not hold government as responsible for ending poverty, they did not shy away from government as the major cause of poverty or as needing to play a role in income redistribution. Further, while professionals believed more strongly in spiritual conversion for social change, and less in the need "to wait for God to act," P.I.A. affiliates did not differ from the

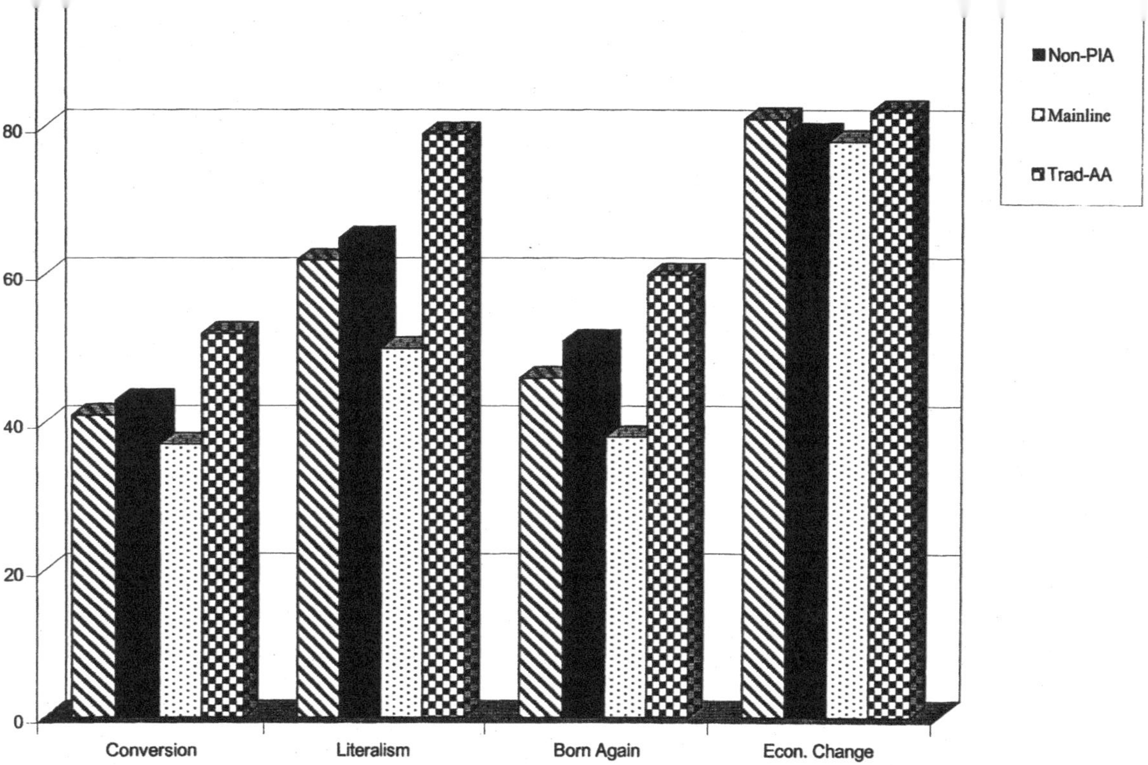

Chart 3.14 When Denomination Makes a Difference: Comparison of Means

norm on spiritual conversion but did believe more strongly in God's action for social change. Moreover, the liberalizing effects of education (which blames the individual less but racism more for poverty) were not felt in the P.I.A. group.

There was some commonality of belief with the walkers, particularly on the question of social change (with both groups believing less in electoral politics and more in divine intervention) and ending poverty (both held individuals and the government less responsible, but looked more to the church). It could be speculated that here might be a link: P.I.A. church members identify more with the concerns of those in the local neighborhood, which is the focus of their CED activity. However, when it came to income redistribution and economic change, the walkers were much more anxious for structural change than the P.I.A. group or any other category within the sample.

Clearly there is not an ideological affinity between the P.I.A. group and theological conservatives, the professional-managerial class or those living closest to the churches, in impoverished neighborhoods, although the interests of all these groups are represented in the churches which join the community organization.

Relationships aside, it might be expected that congregations come into P.I.A. with members who see poverty in more structural terms (i.e., as a result of economic realities or public policies) and less individualistically. While this was the general opinion of the whole sample, the P.I.A. members did not distinguish themselves from the sample in intensity of belief. In addressing poverty, P.I.A. members did not hold the individual or the government as responsible as the non-P.I.A. group did; in fact, they looked more to the church. This might be expected. However, they did not vary in the proportion which put their hope in community organizations. In fact, while one might expect P.I.A. members to be less enthusiastic about electoral politics or individual spokespersons (which they were), but they also had less faith in the tactics of organizing protests. Moreover, the P.I.A. members did not bring to the organization a stronger sense of vocation to social change on the part of the congregation or its clergy. As a precedent to activism, we might look for clues of higher levels of dissatisfaction with economic realities. Again, the P.I.A. members did not distinguish themselves from others in the already high level of belief that major economic change is needed.

As discussed in Chapter 2, there were two churches in the sample which were somewhat atypical: one in the P.I.A. group which participated to a lesser degree in the coalition than the other P.I.A. churches in the study, and a non-P.I.A. church which had "flirted" with affiliation. In order to test the validity of the results, all the cross-tabs presented were re-run while eliminating these two churches. On every question the response patterns remained the same; the only differences which emerged were in intensity. For example, in the larger sample, 73.3% of P.I.A. affiliates favored a literalist interpretation of the Bible, compared to 71.3% of non-affiliates. When eliminating the more atypical churches, the pattern persisted but the gap widened: 72.1% versus 62.4%. Similarly, although .1% separated the two groups on the question of economic change, the distinction became more clear in the sub-set, with 6.2% more of the P.I.A. group agreeing. In other words, differences were more apparent when looking at the "true believers": those more committed to community organization. However, not all who join coalitions become highly involved. The two churches in question are somewhat atypical to their cohorts in this study, but are not atypical of the ways that some churches participate in community organizations.

To summarize: there are no distinctive opinion patterns among individual members of P.I.A. churches which precede or could predict involvement with the organization. While there are some belief patterns related to class (education and occupation), proximity to the church, and along theological and denominational lines, these are not related to P.I.A. membership. When comparing congregations, even the few differences found in the individual data disappear: there were no significant differences on any question between P.I.A. and non-P.I.A. churches. The null hypothesis is completely unchallenged.

Yet, the two approaches to CED represent both philosophical, as well as strategic, differences and make very different demands on congregations. When looking at individual churches, there is certainly evidence of distinctiveness. Congregations take on unique features, if not personalities, which certainly lead them into strategies which "make sense" within their subculture. If there are commonalities among the congregations which join the coalition (as well as those which do not), they cannot be located in the class, religious beliefs or political opinions of the members.

For example, two of the congregations most widely divergent from one another in religious beliefs and political opinions are among the leading congregations in P.I.A. (with both pastors having served on the leadership board). They were the subjects of the ethnographic research reported in Chapter 6. Similarly, the two non-P.I.A. congregations described in Chapter 5 have very different demographic profiles, religious and political perspectives.

In examining how congregations end up affiliating with the city-wide coalition with its often confrontational tactics, we next turn to the pastors. Acting as spiritual leaders, interpreters of reality and gate-keepers of congregational commitments, their role is critical in the decision to become involved in community organizing.

---

[1] This figure does not include those with vocational training, some of whom probably received their training after completion of high school.

[2] Of respondents living in Philadelphia (87.7% of the sample), 55.4% could be matched with census tracts based on intersections indicated.

[3] Conservatives are defined as those who both believe the Bible should be taken literally <u>and</u> that only those who are born again will be saved. Moderate conservatives responded thusly on question A <u>or</u> question B. Non-conservatives chose other, generally more liberal, responses to both questions.

[4] Those identifying themselves as professionals or managers were put into the first category; all other occupational groups were put into the second group.

[5] Those indicating that they had done academic work beyond high school were categorized as "high". Those with vocational training were included in the "low education" group, as this type of training is often received within, or in lieu of, a high school curriculum.

[6] For those who could be matched with census data, tracts with median incomes above the citywide median were labeled as "high," and those below as "low."

[7] Those who indicated they walked to church comprised one category; drivers and those taking public transportation were categorized as commuters.

[8] Four independent Baptist and one Church of God in Christ were included in the "traditional" category; the Presbyterian, Episcopal, United Methodist and American Baptist congregations were labeled "mainline Protestant."

[9] These were also the same two churches on each end of the spectrum of those favoring spiritual conversion for social change, with a high of 59.5% and a low

of 23.7%. Again, both are P.I.A. members. The church which believes that the pastor should not be involved in the public arena, also looks to him to convert the unsaved. They maintained a strong belief in the church's mission to change society.

Chapter 4

Leading the Flock: The Role of the Pastors in Social Change

Introduction

The pastors of African American churches historically have had a strong role in their congregations and communities. They have oftentimes been the spokespersons for people with little public voice. Black pastors have inspired their flocks through the hardships of poverty, injustice, and racism; they have interpreted reality when the folks were immersed in senseless physical and social suffering and helped them to find strength for survival and more -- "abundant living." In so doing, their authority has been more secure, by and large, and their status more symbolically elevated within their constituencies than that of their brothers and sisters of European descent in ministry.

It is not surprising, therefore, that in the African American churches in this study, the role of the pastor emerged as a more critical factor in shaping the outreach ministries of the church than the beliefs, opinions, and class location and interests of the congregation itself. Lincoln and Mamiya found the political consciousness of African American clergy to be related to the community involvement of their churches: those with higher levels of racial consciousness were more likely to be involved in the community, particularly around advocacy for civil rights and through ecumenical collaboration (1990, p. 189). It is to the clergy of the ten churches in the sample that we now direct our focus, as the interpreters of social realities and brokers of strategies for their congregations.

The question becomes how particular strategies for CED are constructed out of the consciousness of these African American clergy. All the clergy in the sample would have been effected by the political opportunities created by the deterioration of the Black power structure in government and through the Black Clergy Association. (Although they may not have all interpreted this change as opportunity.) Still, different tactics toward development goals evolved. What factors had the greatest weight in moving some towards, and others away from, church-based community organizing? In the interviews with the clergy the effects of social location, their contexts/relationships in the church and community, self-identification, and perceptions were analyzed so that the formulation of strategies might be better understood.

Demographic Factors

Age

The clergy of the P.I.A.-related congregations were somewhat younger than their brothers in the non-affiliated churches. (The mean age was 53.6 years, compared to 57.8 years.) This corresponds to the Lincoln and Mamiya study which found that age was correlated with increased political consciousness, with higher consciousness expressed among younger clergy. (1990, pp. 179, 185) While "black consciousness" is not to be equated with the choice for community organizing here, both are more progressive orientations for social change.

Both groups had relatively long tenures at their churches, with the P.I.A. clergy having somewhat shorter stays in their present positions (18.8 compared to 20.6 years). This could be explained by the difference in age.

Education

Unlike Lincoln and Mamiya's findings on the relationship between education and Black consciousness, the clergy involved in community organizing had lower levels of education than their brothers pursuing less aggressive means of social change (1990, p. 185) In the P.I.A. group, two of the clergy had had no formal theological training, while three did have the M.Div. as their terminal degree. In contrast, not only did all the non-P.I.A. affiliated group have M.Div.'s, but four clergy had doctorates (two were earned, two had honorary degrees).

Church Size

The younger, less-credentialed P.I.A. clergy served noticeably smaller congregations. The average attendance at their churches was 390; for the non-P.I.A. churches it was 515. (A statistical comparison of means showed that they did not differ significantly, however.)

Lincoln and Mamiya found that congregational size was highly related to community involvement (1990, p. 188). However, in their study, it was the **larger** churches which were more involved in community ministries. While in this sample congregations of all sizes are involved in such ministry, one might also expect to find the larger churches being more drawn into community organization. After all, affiliation with P.I.A. involves a larger number of congregation members in CED (and other) activities. Such was not the case.

Social Location

Only one of the ten pastors lives in the neighborhood in which the church is located. (He is not a member of P.I.A.). Six live in other areas of Philadelphia, two reside in the Philadelphia suburbs and one commutes from New Jersey.

Examination of the census data from the tracks in which they reside show an interesting pattern (Table 4.1). All of the pastors live in tracts which are more affluent than the citywide means. However, the P.I.A. clergy live in areas with statistically significant higher household incomes and lower percentages in poverty than the non-P.I.A. clergy. (This is especially interesting in light of the higher levels of education of the non-P.I.A. group.)

Further, the P.I.A. clergy live in areas which have lower proportions of African Americans than either the citywide mean or the residential tracts of the non-P.I.A. clergy. That is to say, the non-P.I.A. clergy live in communities more solidly Black; the P.I.A. clergy go home to predominantly Anglo neighborhoods. Again, a comparison means showed the difference to be significant.

Table 4.1 Demographics of Census Tracts in which Clergy Reside

Mean	P.I.A.	Non-P.I.A.	City
% Latino	3.29%	1.54%	5.4%
% Black	11.27%	55.47%	39.5%
Poverty Rate	14.05%	21.37%	20.3%
Income	$37,936	$29,955	$25,287

Political Consciousness and Activism

The Black Consciousness Scale administered in the Lincoln and Mamiya study was not given to the clergy in this sample. However, if their findings are consistent with this sample we would expect that the more educated clergy serving larger congregations (as is descriptive of the non-P.I.A. pastors) would have higher levels of racial consciousness. It should be noted that all of the non-P.I.A. clergy had undergraduate degrees from Black colleges; by contrast, four of the five P.I.A. clergy attended integrated schools. Would attendance at African American schools have contributed to shaping more issue-based (racially-oriented), rather than mass-based activism?

For the most part, the clergy in this sample had been only moderately involved in the civil rights movement. Only two spoke of a strong activist history in civil rights -- one was a P.I.A. member and one was not. More typical of their self-descriptions were:

I'm really not a joiner. I always felt one step behind politically. (P.I.A.-1)

I went on some marches, but I was not a militant. (non-P.I.A.-4)

I always supported the cause, but for some reason I just never got around to being involved. (P.I.A.-4)

Most of the pastors had been involved in electoral politics, with candidates being welcome to speak during worship services. Two had worked full-time (while pastoring their churches) in politics: one with a congressional staff (non-P.I.A.) and one P.I.A. member having headed the O.I.C. (Leon Sullivan's organization which is dedicated to economic development in the African American community through advocacy and training.)

If there was higher level of racial consciousness among the non-P.I.A. clergy, this did not manifest itself in distinct histories of political activism. However, a heightened racial consciousness -- in which political consciousness is largely shaped by a strong sense of African American identity -- might have contributed to an aversion toward bi-racial coalitions, or at least established a habit of organizing only in the Black community.

Community Economic Development Projects

A large portion of the interviews was devoted to the pastors' description of their community economic development projects: how they were developed, the strategies used, the goals set, and the value commitments which they saw as relevant to the projects. While the physical projects of the two groups of clergy were very similar, there were differences in the ways in which they conceptualized and acted which corresponded to the choice of strategy.

Most of the clergy (9 out of 10) had worked, or were working, in the development of housing for low and moderate income people. This included a federally-funded high-rise for elderly (called "202 projects"), and several homeless shelters as well as tracts of rehabbed or new-construction housing units being worked on by all nine. Three CDC's (community development corporations) had been formed by the churches (two by P.I.A. churches). A non-affiliated church had organized the oldest church-based credit union in the city, and another had been instrumental in developing United Bank (a local African American institution).

Two clergy had been involved in commercial developments -- small shopping centers in North Philadelphia which will (when the second is completed) generate several hundred jobs. Commercial development is arguably more complex a process than housing development, as it brings together capital from the government, corporate investors, and financial institutions. It relies more upon accessing power than empowerment of the grassroots constituency. The two clergy involved in this enterprise are those whose participation in P.I.A. has been more ambiguous -- neither strongly in nor outside of the organization, although one is technically a member.

Among the ten churches, eight have bricks and mortar to show for their efforts. Two of the churches -- one in P.I.A. and one not affiliated -- are still in the planning and organizational stages.

In terms of the CED projects of the two groups, there is little difference. The P.I.A. clergy, as well as their unaffiliated counterparts, can point to impressive track records of housing units created, people sheltered, jobs generated, and capital organized. The P.I.A. clergy were already involved in these activities prior to joining the coalition. Now they continue to pursue the goals of economic development, but through a very different strategy.

Frames for Action

There were clear differences in the ways in which the clergy had pursued their CED goals which were closely related to how they interpreted their political context, understood the resources available and how to best utilize them, and conceptualized their roles as agents of change. Interviews were analyz in light of the four polar tensions outlined in Chapter 1: clerical versus shared leadership, parochial versus coalitional organization, accessing power versus empowerment, and accommodation versus social change.

<u>Clerical versus Shared Leadership</u>

All of the pastors in the P.I.A.-affiliated churches could be considered strong leaders. They do not manage democratically-run congregations where the majority determines the direction in which the church will go out of frequent plebiscites. Rather, the pastors exercise power in all aspects of congregational life, including the decision to join P.I.A. (which puts significant demands on the budget and participation of laypeople).

Even so, four of the five clergy in the P.I.A. group articulated a philosophy of leadership in which power was shared with laypeople and had, particularly in their CED activities, acted accordingly. For example, one pastor, as founder of his church, is unquestionably its patriarch. Despite numerous invitations to speak around the country and a staff of 12 assistants, he preaches a minimum of 40 Sundays out of each year. "My people need to touch me.." he explained (P.I.A.-4). Major decisions about the church's program have come directly out of his spiritual experiences. He felt God told him to buy a building which he drove past one day; an interaction with a homeless person which had particularly moved him ultimately resulted in the congregation's developing a shelter for homeless men. In explaining his security in his role he said simply, "No one else is called to be pastor of this church." Still, when it comes to CED activities he defers quickly to those with more expertise. While attending a workshop on packaging proposals for federal funding, he hired one of the social workers in attendance on the spot after realizing he did not have the technical skills to broker public funding.

This pastor adamantly opposes the ordination of women. However, he encourages both men and women to take leadership in outreach ministries as part of their Christian "discipleship." This has included P.I.A. Members of his congregation have attended the 10-day training, which encourages attendees to "do actions" upon their return, not only on City Hall, but even within their own churches. This pastor does not seem threatened by this, nor is he uncomfortable with the leadership structure of P.I.A. in which power is shared among a representative team of men and women, clergy and laypeople, Catholics, Jews as well as Protestants, and African Americans as well as those of European descent.

His strong leadership is tempered by his own self-critique. "Ego can kill a church." Later, in discussing his understanding that leadership should be shared, at least outside of spiritual matters, he said, "So much could be accomplished if we didn't care who gets the credit, because really, Jesus should."

Three of the other P.I.A. pastors also reflected perspectives which preserved the unique authority of the pastor while seeking to develop leadership from within the congregation to be major actors in CED activities. One saw himself as a "cheerleader" and "networker," rather than an administrator (P.I.A.-2). In his church, the leaders of CED projects are frequently recognized and asked to speak. Another admitted that he was "90% of the driving force behind (my church's) involvement in P.I.A." (P.I.A.-1) Still, he was trying to cultivate a "remnant" of leaders within the congregation who could share the leadership. Another said that "It's not difficult to get people involved in P.I.A. There's no great leadership here. All you have to do is to tell them what's going on (regarding public issues)." (P.I.A.-3)

For some, involvement in P.I.A. has had a transforming effect on their understanding of leadership, moving them away from sole authority to shared leadership. One pastor admitted that initially his congregation's P.I.A. membership came solely out of his leadership, but:

> I was into my power mode then. I didn't understand. In the Baptist system you spend a number of years fighting to get power. Then your ministry expands and you have all this additional activity as well as

> keeping the church going. I was scared not to be doing everything. I didn't trust people to take leadership. Then I realized we have a lot of talented leadership around here. Now, since ten-day training, things are different. It has really impacted my leadership. For example, I don't have to chair every meeting. I don't want to. We rotate chairs, and that person is responsible for the agenda and the whole meeting. We research issues, then vote on them, hold people accountable to carry them out, just like in P.I.A. This has been an easy transition for me because I was tired -- I was doing too much. I was doing everything! I was moving in this direction (of shared leadership) before the training, but I didn't have a language for it. Now I'm where Moses was in Numbers: I'm trying to find my 70 leaders. (P.I.A.-3)

The exception in the P.I.A. clergy was the pastor of the church which is on the fringe of the coalition (P.I.A.-5). In describing the church's extensive history of CED activity, he did not mention any leadership, or even involvement, beyond himself. Throughout the narrative of commercial development, he presented himself as the sole broker of "five funding streams" for the project. He described his leadership style as quietly aggressive: "I don't make a lot of noise, but things happen because you make them happen." He hopes that his congregation will become more involved in P.I.A. as one of several projects he is pursuing now. But he did not anticipate lay people taking the initiative: "Any community concern comes from me."

The non-P.I.A. clergy group reflected views on leadership which were similar to this anomalous P.I.A. pastor. Four of the five had closely guarded their pastoral leadership not only in the spiritual domain but in CED activities as well, bringing housing and commercial development projects into being almost single-handedly. One is working with a small coalition of other African American clergy in developing 15 housing units. Two others brokered millions of dollars from federal and private sources working only with a fiscal agent who was not a member of the congregation. Another had organized a Model Cities housing development program and co-chaired it with a community member. The congregations supported these efforts, gave financial support, and often became involved in their management boards upon completion.

The pastor-as-solo-actor was rooted in understandings about leadership expressed in the interviews.

The project (202 housing) was worthy, and was needed. That's what drove me. Part of my job is to get everything in line. (non-P.I.A.-1)

> In the Black church, the pastor is the C.E.O. There is not as much lay leadership as in European congregations. A dominant pastor (model) works...Lay people don't have the time or the commitment to do what the pastor does, and pastors won't be laity-led....Its from the African chieftain: the pastor as chief of the tribe. (non-P.I.A.-4)

This particular pastor has a relatively high proportion of professionals in his congregation. Still, as he goes about his work of developing housing in a clergy-only coalition, he believes it is important to report to the congregation, but not to involve them in the project. "Laypeople don't have the time or the interest to meet with politicians."

Another pastor described the authority granted to him. "Sometimes I'm frightened by the power. There is a tremendous amount of loyalty and trust in me. They (the members of his church) don't challenge me." He felt that it was important to educate the congregation about the role of the pastor, as both prophet and priest. He felt that it was important to empower laypeople to take over some of the religious activities. "You can spend all your time in the priestly function. Its not productive. I train others to do this so I'm free to do other things. Anybody can do a wedding or a baptism!" (non-P.I.A.-1)

This pastor described his role as "advocate" or "representative" of the congregation. As such, the "other things" he was "free to do" included complex negotiations in developing elder housing, working with an exclusive group in founding a Black bank, and amassing enough political capital to be considered in many circles -- political as well as ecclesiastical -- somewhat of a Dean of African American churches in Philadelphia.

The two groups of pastors in the study brought different understandings about leadership, and different modes of operating as leaders to their decisions regarding P.I.A. membership. Four of the five P.I.A. affiliates expressed a commitment to sharing leadership with their members not only in CED activities, but in other aspects of the church's program as well. In contrast, the non-P.I.A. clergy and the pastor of the P.I.A. church which is less involved in the organization described their leadership style differently: they were more comfortable operating independently and not sharing responsibility for the direction and implementation of programs with their membership. This came out of an assumption that either laypeople were not interested or capable of taking leadership in CED and/or an understanding of the African American pastor as leader who singularly takes responsibility, acting as representative of the congregation in the public arena.

It is interesting to note that in the history of P.I.A. in Philadelphia, it was precisely around the issue of clerical versus shared leadership that some clergy were dissuaded from affiliating. A small group of African American clergy (who had actually been instrumental in making the initial overture to the Industrial Areas Foundation) challenged the commitment of the parent organization to sharing leadership among clergy and non-ordained members. When the word came back that this was a non-negotiable tenet of the organization, those who had issued the challenge backed off from involvement with P.I.A.

Parochial versus Coalitional Organizing

In many ways, the choice to organize solely from the base of one's congregation rather than to join in a coalition is an extension of the orientations toward leadership. The six pastors most comfortable with elitist (clerical) leadership had developed projects in which their church was the only, or at least the major, player. (The one exception to this was the pastor who collaborated only as far as working with two other clergy in developing housing.) Again, the distinctions between the P.I.A. and the non-P.I.A. clergy were clear. However in this case, the rationales given were framed more in pragmatic, rather than theoretical, language.

The same four P.I.A. clergy who preferred to share leadership in CED projects were also convinced that participation in a coalition would increase their effectiveness.

Diversity strengthens our efforts. The Civil Rights Movement was too dependent on personalities. (P.I.A.-1)

> A coalitions can have a major impact. An ecumenical, multi-racial coalition has more political and economic clout. The mayor doesn't want to fight the whole religious community. (P.I.A.-3)

Pastors who had become involved with P.I.A. saw membership to be in their own self interest. They had no doubt but that eventually the power of the coalition would focus on the issues literally closest to home -- creating housing, addressing blight, and directing public resources to their neighborhood. "Citywide strategy translates into block strategy," one explained. In several cases, CED projects begun by a congregation were deferred so that energy could be directed to city-wide issues through coalition activism.

Working in coalition has stretched the sensibilities of many of the P.I.A. pastors. For example, there was a struggle within the organization after a synagogue joined about addressing Jesus in the prayers at their meetings. A compromise was struck, but the issue was not resolved at a personal level for some. Still, there was a willingness to transcend religious differences to focus on the common goals of change in Philadelphia.

The non-P.I.A. clergy were also operating out of pragmatic concerns yet had chosen more parochial strategies. While several offered visions of how at least several churches could work together, they had not pursued it -- there was an expressed assumption that joining a coalition might dilute the effort. Their development projects were usually very close to the church building. This preserved an intense geographical focus to the church's ministry, even when a majority of members commuted to church from outside the neighborhood. Despite the criticisms of outsiders that the parochially-oriented pastors were egotistical, competitive, or engaging in empire building, this was not apparent in their own articulation of their rationale. In explaining why he chose to put his time and energy into housing development in the neighborhood rather than participating in a coalition, one pastor explained: "We're more effective than groups like B.C.A. (Black Clergy Association). They are too broad, too regional in their focus. They don't have zeal for particular parts of the city." (non-P.I.A.-4)

Another pastor was not concerned by the fact that three other Baptist churches within four blocks were also working on CED projects in the neighborhood they shared. For him, coalitions (even small ones) required too much time. He felt that he "walks a tight rope" when participating in outside groups, because he is always looking out for his congregation's interest -- wanting to direct resources to his church and its immediate neighborhood. (non-P.I.A.-1)

A large church pastor involved in a major commercial development project couched his explanation of parochial strategy in the language of self-help. "Now in Philadelphia we have got to do things for ourselves.

We need a moral revolution, a revival, and we need to develop economic self-help. We have got to get people saved and safe." His church was working intensely on both fronts in their corner of the city. While only 18.8% of his congregation walked to church in this densely populated neighborhood, there was a geographical focus to the ministry that might be compromised by bringing in other partners and/or expanding the service area. (non-P.I.A.-3)

He was one of several pastors who said, "If the Black church doesn't do it for the folks, it won't get done." All of the pastors in the study articulated a common concern for pragmatism -- "What is the best way of achieving our goals?". For some, working alone and in the local neighborhood best served the congregation's interest and was the more viable option -- they chose not to join P.I.A. For the P.I.A.-affiliated clergy, the increased power of a coalition seemed a more effective route of improving the quality of life, locally as well as regionally.

Power: Accessing or Empowerment

As pragmatists seeking very tangible changes for the poor, all ten pastors in the study had ventured into secular politics and had highly developed understandings of power. They harbored few illusions about human nature. Although power -- of the divine and transmitted to the believer -- is at the very core of Christian theology and ministry, seldom was it referred to in the interviews except in the most concrete terms.

There was a clear distinction between two general approaches to power: **accessing established power** or **empowering** (politically activating) the "grassroots" through organization. All of the non-P.I.A. clergy and the one P.I.A. clergy who has remained on the fringe of the organization described strategies of bringing about economic development which were largely dependent on their personal contacts with those in power. There was a sense of pride that they were part of the power structure: several maintained that they were among a small group of clergy the Mayor might personally call. Others spoke of important relationships with judges, politicians at the federal and state level, and powerful actors within the financial community. While one pastor admitted feeling like "we're the 'house folks' to these people," there was a sense of reality to this strategy: this is how the game is played. "There are four things that control our destiny," explained one pastor. "Insurance, money, real estate, and education. In order to get ahead, we (African Americans) need to get a whole lot more of all of these." He had pursued these four resources through developing contacts and sitting on several corporate Boards. (P.I.A.-5)

It was interesting to note how the institution of Temple University had affected several of the churches in the study, and the neighborhoods in which they sit. Three out of the five non-P.I.A. clergy had organizational connections with the university and talked about working with its president and provost in the context of their CED activities. One had worked with the president in the incorporation of the church-based C.D.C. Another was on a special committee with the provost to facilitate relationships between the neighborhood and the university. Yet another had a long history of negotiating an agreement (called a "*charette*") in 1970 which set down principles for neighborhood participation in Temple's expansion in the community. He is also on a board sponsored by a program of the university. The president attended his anniversary banquet. These pastors were somewhat wary of the power of the university to shape the future of their neighborhoods; yet they had been co-opted into the structure enough that they felt that they were in partnership with the institution, rather than in an adversarial relationship. They felt uniquely positioned to understand the workings of the university and to defend the interests of their churches and immediate neighborhoods.

Accessing power had often meant personal compromise. Those utilizing this approach described the cost of protecting their hard-won political capital. "We need to subjugate our anger," one pastor explained in describing how he sought change through cultivating relationships with those in power. (P.I.A.-5) Another spoke of maintaining his relationship at the expense of his sense what should be done:

> I've been out front so long, I don't need to sit on stage (referring to P.I.A. assemblies to which politicians are invited and often challenged.) But I've told the people on the stage to be careful...Someone needs to confront (Mayor) Rendell. It won't be me. I'll publicly support him. Let someone else confront him. (P.I.A.-5)

Four of the P.I.A. clergy spoke of power in very different terms. In describing how they pursued their CED goals, they spoke little about their individual contacts with those in the power structure. (The only name dropped as being a "friend," was that of Marian Wright Edelman.) Through coalition activism, these pastors had developed heightened public profiles. This could have put them in the position to cultivate such personal relationships with those in the power structure, but they had not pursued them. In the course of working with P.I.A. they had had encounters with the Mayor, administrative officials, and powerful players within the financial sector both in public forums and closed door meetings. Still, they operated as representatives of the coalition, not as individuals. Because they were not previously enmeshed in the power structure, there was no personal political capital to protect, no need to subjugate their frustrations. Acting on behalf of grassroots constituents, they could maintain independence in their relationships with those in power, free to either collaborate or criticize.

The strategic approach to power as articulated by the P.I.A. clergy focused on organizing people (for public protests, small group "house meetings," or ongoing work groups) and pooling resources to which they had access (particularly denominational funding). Not only was this seen as being more effective for bringing about change, but also related to the institutional interests of the church. "If the church doesn't deal with power, it won't attract young people. The church needs to be about power if it is going to attract men." (P.I.A.-2)

The grassroots empowerment approach as articulated in the interviews was more accommodating of confrontation compared to the access-to-power orientation:

> We want enough power to oppose policy makers, to address injustice and corruption, 'by any means necessary,' like Malcolm said. (P.I.A.-1)

> We need to fight the establishment, to bring tension to a head. If the heat's too much, then get out of the kitchen. (P.I.A.-4)

The four P.I.A. pastors espousing the empowerment approach had found an ideological resonance in the coalition for pre-existing ideas about the role of the church in society and a suspicion toward the power structure. This was reinforced through participation in the coalition, and particularly through the training. The approach taken by I.A.F. toward power and social change was different from that of their seminary training. "P.I.A. is not afraid of power, but the church is...P.I.A. is helping me to understand power theologically," one pastor said. (P.I.A.-1)

They also expressed appreciation of the availability of training for their laypeople. It should be recalled from the survey results that the P.I.A. congregants had only slightly less faith in the government to end poverty and in elected officials to bring change. The congregations, therefore, did not exhibit a strong ideological bias that drove affiliation membership. The pastors were not conforming to their congregations' perspectives on power; rather it was their own views which found a home in the orientation of the I.A.F.

For four of the P.I.A. clergy, their empowerment perspective resulted more from experience, rather than theoretical commitment. When evaluating the role of African American churches in social change, they concluded that accessing power had not gotten their constituent communities very far down the path of economic development. They were demoralized by the poverty and discrimination which had persisted despite the gains which resulted from the Civil Rights Movement. More African Americans were in the power structure, yet resources were not trickling down.

Yet the access-to-power position was articulated by those who still truly believed that it was the most viable and realistic way to broker enough political power to bring resources to their development goals. They felt that clergy could only gain enough status to negotiate with those in power by representing a large, if silent, mass base who could be depended upon at election time. "We need to be able to deliver votes," one pastor explained. (non-P.I.A.-1) Another went farther and had made a sizable contribution to the Mayor's campaign:

> I haven't given up on City Hall. But I want to bring power to the table, and not come begging. There is a new movement of Black power: and that is when churches buy power. (non-P.I.A.-3)

Those representing the empowerment position do not believe that one campaign contribution or delivering a block of votes on Election Day is enough. They are much more concerned with the process of governing between elections. It is not so important who is in office; their focus is on expanding the numbers of those who can articulate a community's concern, and to "hold officials accountable" in the public forum. The "show of strength" of a large and diverse group of people in a public action which provides face-to-face interaction with those in the power elite is more effective, they believe, than a disembodied number of votes every four years.

What became a "defining moment" in the life of P.I.A. was an assembly attended by 330+ (including the four P.I.A. pastors who expressed the empowerment position) in which a city housing official was enthusiastically applauded when he announced the city's commitment of $4.5 million toward the construction of Nehemiah Housing. The District Attorney was just as enthusiastically booed out of the meeting when she attempted to bypass the agenda and speak from the floor. She had been taken off the agenda earlier in the week when she did not comply with P.I.A. demands in her policy on crack houses.

Power is defined in the P.I.A. as "the ability to get things done," resulting from "organized people and organized money" (two frequently heard tenets of the I.A.F.) For four of the member pastors, the type of grassroots empowerment described above was perceived as being a more effective means of change. It is too soon in the life of the organization to measure effectiveness in quantitative terms, such as the number of housing units constructed. It should also be kept in mind that for the members of P.I.A., development projects do not represent an end in themselves, as they do for those utilizing the access-to-power strategy. For the community organizing coalition, empowerment is the ultimate goal. Development projects are secondary goals and, as educational opportunities, the means through which the larger goal is approximated.

The Goals of CED: Accommodation or Change

The language of change was the most difficult to analyze. All the pastors reflected both social and individual dimensions in their interpretive paradigms of what creates problems and the strategies needed for addressing them. Not even the most individualistically-oriented pastor could have his position simply reduced to accommodationism -- that is, that it is entirely the responsibility of individuals to conform to the system (considered fair or neutral) in order to benefit from it. None of the pastors was uncritical of the system; and all affirmed individual agency in economic distress. Still, there were paradigms which emerged in which the individual or the system were weighted more or less heavily in both the social analysis and perspective on strategy. For example, from one P.I.A.-related pastor:

> I think poverty is caused by our capitalist system which creates a heart for injustice, rather than community. I also think that sin is at work in personal choices, like the single-parent homes. I agreed with (former Vice President) Quayle's analysis of the family. The problem was that he had the power to change the situation but he didn't use it. Government is hypocritical because it influences the deterioration of the family. I'm opposed to welfare (which he described as 'institutional slavery') but I'm more opposed to starving. (P.I.A.-3)

For this pastor there was a dialectical relationship between individual and social sources of evil. The economic system influences the individual, and the individuals are often sinful in their choices. While the individual is responsible for their behavior, the government is responsible for their welfare -- making sure basic human needs are met and supporting the family structure. The government or system are not morally neutral, but becomes responsible and accountable as it becomes an agent of destructive social trends.

In the pulpit this pastor almost exclusively stressed personal spiritual change and growth. However, when working on economic development he sought to change the policies and processes for allocation of public resources rather than trying to shape individuals to fit into the system.

This paradigm -- of giving systemic analysis and social change more weight than concentration on the individual in their public ministry -- was shared by three other of his fellow P.I.A.-related clergy. One pastor said of the church's mission: "We have to find ways of being nurturing **while also** being prophetic and seeking social change. Otherwise, we're just holding hands in the darkness." (P.I.A.-2)

Another reported that involvement in community organizing had helped him "to look at the church with new eyes", that is, more as part of the system which needs to be changed. He said "In trying to understand why things happen (i.e., social problems) I'm finding that the church and the city will be changed simultaneously. And so a goal has become to change the church too -- to decolonize it." (P.I.A.-1)

For four of the non-P.I.A. clergy and the one pastor in the P.I.A. group who has consistently expressed views different than his fellow affiliates, the individual became the focus of economic development efforts. There was little tampering with the system which, they would admit, had not been fair to African Americans.

Stress was frequently placed on education -- motivating individuals to pursue it as well as making it more accessible. One pastors said of his own personal history,

> I was immersed in getting an education instead of civil rights. My goal has been to become more self-directing so that I can change the system from within. If I do a better job, you'll respect me. (non-P.I.A.-4)

This pastor was involved in leveraging public and corporate investment in housing in North Philadelphia. He hoped to continue in this vein until "all of North Philadelphia is redeveloped." His education and contacts had enabled him to do this work. Throughout his narrative, there was no criticism of institutional or social factors which might have contributed to the deplorable housing conditions, nor of a need for systemic change. It was the responsibility of individuals within the economically disadvantaged community (in this case, a few pastors) to figure out how to work the system to get what is needed.

Another pastor spoke of "needing to work within the system." (non-P.I.A.-3) However, for him this came out of realism, for he was not uncritical of the system. He felt that while flawed, it was too difficult to change it. He had been heavily involved in the Civil Rights Movement yet had become discouraged. "After Martin King, things are no better. There are more Black politicians, but there is no improvement in the system. We are still in great need of spiritual and economic liberation." He explained that as administrations change, the rules change. It is up to the African American community to learn the new rules, and it is up to the church to provide spiritual support and leadership in working the system for so that self-help is possible. Finally, if individual African Americans "make it," it might be through the system or in spite of it. However cynically the system is viewed, this pastor thought energy could be better spent learning to work within it, rather than to challenging it.

Another non-P.I.A. clergy rooted his approach more philosophically. "Good public policy begins at the local level." (non-P.I.A.-1) What he meant by this was that as individuals were spiritually changed, there would be a "ripple effect," which would eventuate into improved quality of life, and perhaps public policies. He had had a long history of public involvement, and had been approached about running for public office. While deciding that there was more freedom in pastoral work, he maintained that it is important for pastors to "work with the comfort level of politicians." There are a lot of good people in politics, he believed; however, without input from clergy they can "lose their vision of what is possible." It is through these interpersonal relationships (access-to-power) that the church can have some input into influencing the system. However, this pastor also stopped short of discussing essential changes in the system.

A current example of his own public ministry has been in his work on local education. He has had a highly publicized and almost single-handed program to escort children to and from a school that is located in what has been a dangerous area. However, in developing this approach, he has chosen not to put his energy into challenging the police or education departments for better services.

One P.I.A. pastor had only been attracted to the organization because it could mobilize more people in his congregation. (P.I.A.-5) Otherwise, as previously described, he remained somewhat skeptical and ambivalent toward the coalition. His priority for outreach had been education, although he had also been involved in housing, commercial development, and job training. This stated priority was rooted in a perspective on the government and economic system which, while critical, resists strategies directed at changing it. At a pragmatic level, he was concerned that African Americans re-direct their energy and anger into working their way into the system.

> We (African Americans) need to get rid of all the obstacles that keep us seeing things differently. We need to appreciate who we are, but also who others are...We can't let the truth (about racism) create evil in us -- anger and violence. (P.I.A.-5)

Once again, the pastors moved toward two different poles in their perspectives on change: those who felt that it was more important to equip the African American community to "play the game" and those who wanted to see the rules of the game changed. But as with their views on power, this was rooted in pragmatism. For those who moved toward accommodationism, there was not a sense that the system of distribution was fair and not in need of change. They were often as sensitive to institutionalized injustice as their brothers who articulated the "change" position. However, they finally did not feel that change was **viable**; i.e., energy expended on changing the system was energy wasted. Better to put that energy toward preparing people to participate in the system, and hope that through infiltration the system would eventually be changed.

Discussion

As the pastors approached a decision (or more accurately a series of decisions) on the strategies to employ in working toward their CED goals, advantages and disadvantages were weighed. Is confrontation with City Hall and the change it might bring in policy worth risking hard-earned political capital? Is the investment of energy in working on citywide issues going to benefit the neighborhood in which the church sits and to which it ministers? These are complex questions which do not lend themselves to formulaic cost/benefit analysis.

Nor are the decision-making processes simple; they are not disembodied, purely rational choices. Rather, there is much that is brought into the decision: the pastor's past experience, social location, congregation, and consciousness. All of this shapes what is finally seen as being viable and in the best collective (congregational) interest.

There is much that was shared by the pastors. Almost all were theologically conservative and well-educated. They shared a commitment to improving the physical, as well as the spiritual, well-being of both their congregants and their neighbors. They saw the discrepancies in opportunities between races and classes, and acted in the ways they felt would be most effective in bringing change.

While there were personal benefits attached to either strategy, to be sure, the overriding interest was consistently interpreted collectively in all the interviews. Solidarity with the congregation in deciding strategy was exhibited in concerns about the church's survival, constraints on budget, use of the pastor's time, etc. Solidarity with the community was apparent in directing the attention and resources of largely commuting congregations (by mostly commuting pastors) to the needs of the local neighborhood. This corresponds to the definition of loyalty offered by A.O. Hirschman (1970) as being evident when a "group member is continuing to care about the activities and output of the organization even after one has left it."

At this point, the differences begin to emerge. There were two different paradigms operating in the construction of strategies for change. On the one hand, those who had chosen to affiliate with P.I.A. gravitated toward strategies which were broadly coalitional, had shared leadership, sought to empower the grassroots and sought change not only in individuals and policies, but in the very systems which formulate those policies. Those clergy who had opted not to join P.I.A. on the other hand, generally preferred strategies for CED which were clergy-led, parochial (i.e., usually only involving their church), relied on accessing those in power and not challenging what is admittedly an often-unjust system.

While there has been some transformation and intensification of paradigm after participating in the P.I.A., these are characteristics of the consciousness brought into the decision to affiliate by these pastors. P.I.A. pastors had a shared language of community organizing, often heard at the meetings including, "accountability," "one-on-ones," *, "doing an action." Only three of the pastors had been to the intensive 10-day training and one chose afterwards not to affiliate. For the most part, exposure to the organization on a day-to-day basis corresponded to pre-existing orientations and commitments of the pastors.

A striking difference between the P.I.A. clergy and the non-P.I.A. group was the metaphorical language they employed in communicating their views. The P.I.A. group utilized images of morality and conflict: justice, war, sin, evil, the devil, holy power. For example, one pastor used war imagery in responding to a question about the possibility of neighborhood revitalization:

> Only if we identify the enemy and go to war. Everything else must be postponed. There is no volunteer army, so we need to draft soldiers. But it is the difficult things that God does best. And there is always a remnant. (P.I.A.-1)

In contrast, non-P.I.A. clergy borrowed language from the corporate world in their narratives. The church as "entrepreneur" was offered as a model by several. Others spoke about "negotiation," "leadership," "integrity," and "realism." The church was perceived more as an institution and its pastor as C.E.O., and less as embattled warriors.

---

*This refers to meetings between two people to get to know one another, share concerns, etc. This is understood in the I.A.F. as the basic unit of organizing -- building personal relationships.

The metaphorical language betrays the deeply-held views of how the pastors interpreted their place in the world. P.I.A. clergy perceived themselves to be on a quest: there was a sense of imperative. Further, there was an expectation of succeeding. The non-P.I.A. clergy did not see the system as being so alienating. Nor did they hold as high expectations for change.

The pastor as actor in social movements comes as one who is "embedded" in their culture, history, and social networks, all of which shapes consciousness and action. The contextual differences between the two groups were striking. Those who had chosen to work parochially were older, more educated, from larger congregations and more integrated into existing power structures. This may have contributed to a strong sense of personal security and autonomy from other clergy. For the most part, the non-P.I.A. pastors communicated that did not feel like they needed to work in coalition -- they had the personal and institutional resources and connections to effect the change they sought by working alone.

In contrast, those who chose to join P.I.A. had more to gain in working through a coalition. There churches were smaller and they were not entrenched in the power structure. They were eager to learn new skills and increase their power base.

The P.I.A. clergy also had more exposure to multicultural educational and residential contexts. The non-P.I.A. clergy had trained, worked and lived in overwhelming African American contexts. Their leadership style corresponded more toward the traditional expectations of the preacher's role in the Black community. There is also the possibility of suspicion in working across cultures and faith traditions, or at least the learned habit of working monoculturally. It is clear that their power base is in the African American community; perhaps there is an assumption that moving outside of that at all might compromise that base, and hence, one's power.

To summarize: the choice of strategy was predominantly a matter of pragmatism and not ideology. The pastors generally shared theological and political viewpoints as well as a grim diagnosis of the realities faced by urban African Americans. Yet in shaping their strategies, different consciousness was at work in defining what course was finally viable in the collective interest. This was influenced most by personal history, professional status, social class, and status, and access to existing power structures.

The dynamics between the pastor and congregation also has to be taken into consideration. It is, after all, in the local church that the pastor is most deeply embedded and socially rewarded.

Chapter 5

"The Extension of our Dreams"

Introduction

One could infer from the questionnaires and the interviews with the pastors that the congregations had nothing to do with the development of the CED strategies and the clergy had everything to do with it. Yet pastors are very much embedded in the subcultures of the churches they serve. Ethnographic research was conducted in four congregations which explored this context more fully. How does the relationship between the pastor and his people affect the approach to CED he will employ? How do the cultural dynamics shape the nature of their outreach to their community, as they define it?

This chapter describes two very different congregations neither of which had not affiliated with P.I.A. However, as will be seen, both have made important contributions to economic development in North Philadelphia. The first case, Grace Memorial Baptist Church, was the site of more extensive ethnographic research. The study of Knox Presbyterian was more limited. However, it served as an important point of comparison to Grace; despite their differences, common themes emerged.

Grace Memorial Baptist Church

In an unmerciful heatwave in July, the air-conditioned sanctuary of Grace Memorial Baptist Church provided an oasis from the baking city streets on this Sunday morning. Neither weather nor vacation schedules had kept the 500+ worshippers from crowding into the worn stone structure at the corner of 14th and Foster Streets. The harsh poverty of this neighborhood was certainly not reflected in the elegant dress of so many of the women. For nearly three hours, the congregation "had church" -- that is, participated enthusiastically with body and soul as they communed with God, preacher, and each other.

Whether intentional or not, a recurring theme throughout the service was **water**, a metaphor of catastrophe, strength, salvation, and celebration. Within the prayer circle, God was called upon to aid flood victims, as well as to save drug dealers, bring wisdom to City Hall, help members with personal problems, and deliver them safely to their heavenly home.

Later in the service, as one of the four choirs performing that day was returning to their pews, several women and one man went into an ecstatic dance. Other members formed circles around them so that they might safely and freely praise God in what appeared to be a trance. As they began to calm down, glasses of water were passed through the congregation for them. Pastor Joseph Johnson patiently waited for almost 15 minutes for the "shower of the spirit" to subside. Clearly this was not interpreted as a disruption but a spiritual refreshment for the whole congregation.

The sermon was loosely based on a reference in the Hebrew Scriptures which likens God to a river. Hence, the word about water this day was one of comfort and strength -- the water quenches thirsts and cleanses unrighteousness. It connects people to God: "The river runs to your heart, to my heart, from the heart of God." Believers are protected from being dominated by unspecified hostile forces.

> The river is your strength. The Enemy (Satan) can't see your source of supply. The Enemy can't find or control your inner strength. The river is secret and mysterious...So come to the source. Come to have your thirsts quenched. Come to be cleansed. Come to the river.

The sermon ended with the traditional "call and response" -- an emotional dialogue within which the pastor chants a phrase of encouragement or celebration and the congregation responds, urging him on. The preacher then made a transition into inviting individuals to come forward if they would like to respond to the message. Five people walked down the aisle. After embracing the preacher, they were escorted out of the church by a Deacon. Later in the service they were introduced. At the end of the month they would be immersed in another "river" as 30 new members in robes were individually baptized in the tank which remained hidden in the chancel three out of four Sundays.

As stimulating as the service might have been, it was not unique in the long line of Sunday morning services since the congregation was founded in 1915. It also reflected the larger traditions of the National Baptist Convention and the history of Black Baptists, rooted in the South and now also entrenched in urban areas.

Walking out of the church, one sees the cityscape which represents a once-working class, rowhouse neighborhood that is now struggling to survive. Grassy lots are interspersed with two-story homes, some of which are boarded up, some newly renovated, others immaculately maintained. Sitting on a triangular lot next to the church, and looking conspicuously modern and institutional, is the Joseph Johnson Manor -- a federally subsidized housing project (202), opened in 1991 which is now home to 60 older people. Rev. Johnson seemed to enjoy telling the story of how Johnson Manor came into being:

> It all started about 10-12 years ago. The vision (for Johnson Manor) came out of an experience with an older member of the congregation. She was living in sub-standard housing, and had agreed to move into senior citizen housing but never did. Later, her house caught on fire and the woman died. At that point, I vowed that no senior citizen should have to live in sub-standard housing.

After deciding to pursue 202 housing, he became a man with a mission, a quest. He sent a proposal to HUD (Department of Housing and Urban Development) which was rejected "five or six times." In the process he learned that "The need and value of the project had nothing to do with it. It was all about politics."

Despite all the problems with HUD, Rev. Johnson remained optimistic. " I just felt that it would happen...you need someone with vision. A leader needs to instill hope." The sponsorship of the congregation was not hard to get. They originally put in $10,000. By the time the project was complete, Grace Memorial "had a total of $250,000 tied up in it."

Sitting in his office (the walls of which are filled with awards and framed photographs of Rev. Johnson with public officials), the entrepreneurial pastor said that he realized two things in his struggle to make the vision a reality: "First, that you don't get anything out of the government without persistence," and that he needed to use his connections to access power. "So I called on people with whom I had a relationship...(Then Congressman) Bill Gray took a personal interest in the project and brought his power to bear[1]...Everyone I needed, all the connections, were there." Besides Gray, the regional director of HUD went to bat for them, as did their state representative. They got some money from a local non-profit investment corporation, as well as from the state and federal governments.

The $4.4 million project is now governed by the Grace Memorial Non-Profit Development Corporation. Although a separate entity from the church, the Board is comprised mainly of church leaders and there is certainly an attempt to involve residents in the life of the church. It was the Board which decided to honor Rev. Johnson by naming the new housing development after him. While Board members are now boosters of the project, this was not always the case:

> I came to the project biased against government projects. I'm still ambivalent. I hate government hassles and I got discouraged...**What drove the project was Rev. Johnson, on the front line, fighting, and negotiating.** - Male church leader, Vice-President of Grace Church CDC

> Everyone had given up except (the HUD Regional Director), the architect, and the construction company. They believed in Pastor Johnson....So he just kept contacting HUD. He was the best spearhead because he had the contacts and he had the time. He saw it as one of his ministries, and we were is assistants. But that's how we see it now. Before you always heard, "He wants us to do (the project), he wants us to do." After Johnson Manor was built you heard, "We did it! We did it!" It became the church's vision. Now community development is our vision. - Female church leader, Secretary/Treasurer of Grace Church CDC

Despite the church's outward support of the project (as evidenced by financial contributions), most members harbored serious doubts. They had a different vision of the role of the church and its preacher. Their support slowly evolved:

At first I was negative. We were going to build a new church on that property...But I was finally persuaded out of self-interest. There is a need (for elder housing) and I could need housing when I get old. - Female church leader

> The greatest accomplishment has been Johnson Manor...Its helped me to see that it is possible to improve the neighborhood...We now have hope for the neighborhood..I used to think that (CED activity) was just his (Rev. Johnson's) ministry. Now I see that we can benefit. Maybe he'll be the person who will make a difference. - Female active member, choir member

> after the fire, Rev. Johnson had a vision for the empty lot. He stayed with that vision. He gets things done and with this project he set a precedent: we realized, "hey, we can do that!" **Rev. Johnson is the extension of our dreams**. - Female church leader

As Rev. Johnson and members of the congregation recounted the process which led from a tragic fire and and an empty lot to the four story structure which now provides safe, affordable housing for older people, there are several interpretive layers within the oral history. Embedded in the story are the values which have been woven into the social construction of Rev. Johnson's authority. Further, this narrative, which is so important for the congregation, offers glimpses into the meaning of leadership at Grace Church. That is to say, the action frames described in the last chapter which characterize the consciousness of the preachers[2] are not simply the products of individual personality, philosophy, and history; rather, they are part of an ongoing social reality. To greater or lesser extents, these action frames simultaneously shape and are shaped by the consciousness of the congregation. Analyzing this dynamic, it becomes apparent in the case of Grace Memorial why Rev. Johnson chose not to affiliate with the community organization, P.I.A.

The Pastor as Hero

In the accounts of the development of Johnson Manor, Rev. Johnson is cast as a classic hero reminiscent of Greek mythology. Out of a tragedy (the fire) comes a moral commitment to rescue those who are vulnerable (older people living in sub-standard housing). On a quest, the hero encounters obstacles along the way, from the lack of support of HUD to negativism among his followers. Yet he continues to fight alone, persistently. The struggle costs him, not blood, but energy and political capital. He utilizes methods not at the disposal of his membership; watching him somewhat at a distance they are mystified by his power and abilities. Finally, he triumphs -- the vulnerable are "saved" and he is rewarded. Now his followers reaffirm their loyalty to him and share in the glory of his accomplishments; what was "his ministry" is now "our ministry". Johnson Manor was a defining moment in the life of the congregation. Rev. Johnson's status was elevated and the congregation's identity was enlarged by him.

Grace Memorial has continued to pursue ambitious CED projects. Once Johnson Manor was in operation, Rev. Johnson contracted with a community development agency to do a feasibility study of the area surrounding the church. Out of this has come a 15 year redevelopment project in four phases, which includes developing Section VIII (subsidized) housing, some new construction, as well as rehabbing existing homes. (The church will function as both landowner and facilitator of redevelopment.) While systems improvement is part of the plan, commercial strip development was discounted as "too ambitious." The first phase begins with the building of a new church structure. The goal of the whole effort, according to Rev. Johnson is to "redevelop a triangle here, with Grace as the anchor. We want to stabilize the community from further deterioration and attract middle class people back to the neighborhood." From all indications, the project will be pursued in much the same way as was Johnson Manor, with Rev. Johnson leading the effort. While he expresses a passionate commitment to this corner of North Philadelphia, there has been little effort to involve the neighborhood itself in its own redevelopment, apart from the church members who live there.

Certainly this is a context where heroes are welcomed and ambitious visions are needed. Of the ten North Philadelphia churches in the study, congregational demographics showed that Grace Memorial had a relatively high percentage of members who walked to church (25%, well above the mean for the study, 15.5%). The congregation as a whole was distinctive in the sample, drawing its membership from tracts with the lowest income levels and the highest levels of poverty, female-headed households and racial segregation (Charts 3.1, 3.2, 3.3, 3.4, 3.5). Rev. Johnson is also the only clergyperson in the study to live within his area of ministry -- he lives across the street from the church.

Not only is the context ripe for heroes, but such status is conferred onto those deemed as deserving. Even beyond the church walls, in broader ecumenical circles and the African American community, Rev. Johnson is also cast in heroic terms, if more tempered. For example, his "safe corridor" program was featured on the front page of The Philadelphia Inquirer. Three pictures and much of the copy focused on his central role as organizer and participant in a program which patrols the major walking route for students to a nearby middle school.

> Every Monday since early November, Mr. Johnson, pastor of Grace Memorial Baptist Church, has kept watch over the children walking to and from Vaux along the torturous Master Street corridor in North Philadelphia, making sure that no one harms them. (Philadelphia Inquirer, 2/1/94, p. A 1)

To summarize: a hero is a social construction, a status subliminally negotiated in a context where people and leader understand that heroic measures are needed to bring about change. Although poverty certainly contributes to this possibility, it is not simply a function of poverty: there are other congregations in impoverished contexts where the style of leadership developed by the clergy is not that of hero (as will be seen in the next chapter).

In the case of Grace Memorial, pastor-as-hero corresponds both to the personal style of Rev. Johnson as well as the expectations of the congregation. Both are steeped in the Southern African American Baptist traditions, which is referenced more often as their great tradition than is the northern urban experience. (This is reinforced each year when members of the congregation journey by bus to his family's hometown in North Carolina.) In this cultural context, the preacher transcends the congregation as its **representative** to the outside world and internally as **benevolent patriarch**.

While there is not an identification of the preacher as being God, there is a divine dimension to this role. Therefore, a woman in the congregation who is a strong leader can say, "Whatever assignment Rev. Johnson gives me I know is from God." The preacher himself is less mystical in explaining the divine aura surrounding his role: "There is so much deference given to ministers because the minister represents God." The identification of the preacher with a special vocation, if not power, from the divine is conducive to enlarging the symbol of leader to that of hero. He is, and needs to be, super-human. He is uniquely God's agent for his people.

The Pastor as Benevolent Patriarch

As well as being admired and respected as hero, it is also clear from interviews and observations that Rev. Johnson is well-loved. He is often described by members in sacred and relational terms as "spiritual leader," "friend," "mentor," and "visionary." His familiar style and self-deprecating humor in the pulpit elicit response and represent a comfortable intimacy between pastor and people. This familiarity does not compromise, but seems to contribute to, his authority within the congregation.

Members often mention Rev. Johnson's capacity to listen to their ideas or complaints as a source for their trust and loyalty to him.

> If you wanted to start a new project, first you'd go to the Pastor...He can always find time to talk to you and to be very positive. - Active female member, Sunday School Teacher

> We have few confrontations, no churchwide problems or fights. If there is a disagreement with the Deacons or trustees, Rev. Johnson more often wins. But he won't end a meeting with someone being upset. He listens to things he doesn't want to hear. I left my former church because the pastor didn't listen to the young people. - Female Trustee

Even though Rev. Johnson almost always prevails in situations of disagreement, members feel has if they have been heard and taken seriously. This contributes further to his political capital within the congregation and has the effect of making the decision-making of the church appear more democratic than, perhaps, it really is. While many leading members talked about "confronting" the pastor, or "being outspoken," they also spoke of being won over by him on a particular issue, as was seen with Johnson Manor. Despite the anecdotes of confrontation, Rev. Johnson, in his 18th year as pastor, considered his leadership largely unchallenged by the 800+ active members.

With his position of authority secure, Rev. Johnson readily delegates responsibilities, but does not share the power of his position. For example, on one Sunday morning when he was scheduled to preach, an assistant appeared to lead worship without explanation. Despite his clerical robe and theological training he began his 50 minute sermon with a disqualifier: "I want to bring you the word this morning since Rev. Johnson can't be here. But don't worry, I know my place!"

The singular, unchallenged locus of leadership and the personal style of Rev. Johnson which is endearing of congregational loyalty, is consistent with the narrative and identity of the church. The written history of the church opens with the following dedication which displays their understanding of the primacy of the clerical leadership:

> The early church was very simple in its organizational structure. There was only pastor and people. Thus the success of any church depends upon the proper relationship between pastor and people. Because our church is successful, we dedicate this book to the pastors and people who have served and are serving God through Grace Memorial Baptist Church. (Reflections, Grace Memorial Baptist Church, 1978)

The former patriarch of Grace was Rev. Allen Dixon, also a Southerner, whose tenure lasted from 1938-1970. He led the church through times of membership growth, capital expansion, and the tragedy of a devastating fire. Designated as Pastor for Life, Dixon was also deeply loved and highly revered. Upon Dixon's death, the congregation called a native son to be its pastor; he died after only three years. In 1974 a young preacher from the South was again called to the pulpit, thus beginng what is referred to in the congregation's history as "The Johnson Era."

Rev. Johnson continues in the historical momentum of Black Southern Baptists, and more particularly of this congregation, in assuming the role of benevolent patriarch. The paradox of the social construction of the pastor's leadership role is that the overwhelming majority of church members are women. Many of the most dedicated lay leaders are articulate, strong-willed women. Yet this would not be recognized simply by observing worship services. In keeping with the Baptist tradition, all of the lifetime Deacons are men -- highly visible sitting on the dais around the pulpit each Sunday. Seated on the front pew are the Deaconesses (generally the wives of the Deacons). On the pew behind them are seated the pastor's wife, the nurses, missionaries, and other prominent women in the congregation (or researchers, escorted up from the back pew, where they might have tried to remain unnoticed!)

Recognizing the importance of committed, talented women in the congregation, the obvious question becomes how such a reality exists in a strongly patriarchal context. For women in their 20's, 30's and 40's who are leaders in the congregation, life outside of Grace Memorial is often spent in demanding jobs in administration, medicine, and education. They express a confidence in their skills and an expectation that their authority will be recognized on the job. Consistent among this group were "modern" views on women in the church -- specifically that women could and should be pastors. (One of the women had felt "called to be a preacher" since she was a little girl. A lifelong member, she was now in her early 50's.) They also express an appreciation for the Baptist tradition and "realistic" perspectives on the likelihood of change. Even so, these women profess a genuine loyalty to Rev. Johnson which seems uncomplicated by resentment, anger, or a sense of diminishment.

In speaking of their pastor, these women often begin by describing his capacity to listen and to take seriously the issues they raise. This is reinforced for them by his trust in their leadership in the congregation. There are also signs of change, which give them hope.

One woman in her early 40's (a nursing home administrator) spoke about becoming the second woman to serve as a trustee of the congregation: "Rev. Johnson is a visionary...and he knows where his assets are. It's the women."

Another initiative of Johnson's was to create the Commission on Leadership, a board comprised of representatives and officers of every organization in the church (there are about 40). This enables women who are barred from the Board of Deacons and largely from the Trustees to be able to participate in an upper level board. While the Commission on Leadership has more of a symbolic rather than an administrative function, it was clearly important to the women who were the only ones to mention it in the interviews.

Even Charlotte, called to preach at the age of 7, saw a future in which women could have more authority. It was this hope which held her at Grace as an active member and forceful leader.

> My call was a burden. It was eating me alive. I spoke at different clubs and was told I could be an evangelist, but I wasn't satisfied. I was angry that no one seemed to understand my call. I started taking courses at a Bible college and my husband got worried. Rev. Johnson even counseled us. Finally, I told him (Rev. Johnson) that I had to leave the church. Then his attitude started to change, and finally he supported me...(In three years) I'll get ordained. I want to stay at Grace and minister to the new group spawned by the new church building. I'll be in the trenches. I want to be part of the William B. Johnson team...I want to be a model for other women. Maybe my role is to break the mold and pass the baton.

Rev. Johnson represents a new style of patriarch. He is able to simultaneously fulfill the role expectations of the traditionalist older members as well as to relate to younger people who can appreciate a father figure, yet live in a culture where social relationships are changing. His congregation members have the sense that they are taken seriously by him, even when voicing opposition; still his authority is unquestionably intact.

<u>The Pastor as Representative of the People</u>

If pastors relate to their congregations as patriarch in the African American Baptist tradition, they are further expected to function as the congregation's representative to those outside the church. This has its roots in the 19th century congregations where preachers often had more education than their congregants who were motivated to provide them, when possible, with some of the accoutrements of higher class status -- such as cars, higher salaries, and honorary distinctions -- not only out of respect, but that they might better represent their people in the dominant culture. Within the congregational history of Grace this expectation of the pastor as representative voice is expressed. In describing the clerical role in the 19th century the history reads:

> Rev. Paul and other black pastors were natural leaders, because their support came from the people. Therefore, the black pastor was in a position to speak frankly. Unlike other black leaders, the pastor's job did not require that he have the good will of the white community. (Reflections, p. 4)

Consistent with this heritage, members regard Rev. Johnson as their representative beyond their corner of North Central Philadelphia. They are proud that he is known, respected and listened to in "other worlds," such as the African American religious community, in the multi-cultural religious community of Philadelphia, and in the political spheres of City Hall, Harrisburg, and even Washington. Not only is there a sense that they benefit from reflected glory, but that he can, and does, effectively advocate in their behalf. Knowing that his absences mean that he is working in their interest, they are willing to "let him go."

> Well, we have some problems with Rev. Johnson being away, but there's no problem with his role -- he is our representative, even when he's working with a project we're not directly involved with. - Head Deacon

> We need to be able to not be selfish about his time. There should be no grumbling about that. I want a pastor to go beyond the congregation. He has his ministry, which is God's ministry. This is not the congregation's ministry. And he is growing. - Female life-long member

> Rev. Johnson is uniquely gifted with leadership...All this work in politics, with Bill Grey, that's an extension of his ministry...His influence will trickle down. - Female church leader

Johnson Manor is but one example of his effective advocacy. His high public profile has also been associated with other development projects, such as a Black bank (Unity Bank). Politically, it was during his presidency of Black Clergy of Philadelphia and Vicinity that W. Wilson Goode was elected to two controversial terms as the first African American mayor of Philadelphia. Analysts credit that organization's endorsement and the solid support of Black churches in large measure for Goode's successful campaigns. It was Johnson's role as Co-Chairman of the Billy Graham Crusade that earned him credibility within the well-resourced white Evangelical establishment.

Rev. Johnson can effectively move in many different circles. He is often called upon to speak in ecumenical gatherings as a representative of African American churches. He is a polished and effective speaker. His language and style are distinctly that of a Baptist from the South, but not to the degree of alienating those from other communities. (For example, he has been involved in organizations seeking to "build bridges" between his constituency and the Jewish and Korean communities.) In interviews and observations in a variety of these contexts there were no hints that Rev. Johnson had any enemies. While this is surprising for such a public figure, it is finally testimony to his conciliatory style.

Politically, Rev. Johnson has been able to translate his role as representative into political capital. He explained: "In order to relate to politicians you need to do things. You have to work within their comfort level and you have to be able to deliver votes." One result of his political currency was an invitation by the local Democratic leadership to challenge John Street, a powerful City Council representative of the district.

As Rev. Johnson considered the prospects of electoral politics, and the rumors began to fly, there was almost universal resistance on the part of his congregation. While some cited concern for his health, or an unwillingness to "share the pastor," most members were clear that they did not want to lose Rev. Johnson as their representative and advocate.

Johnson himself agrees -- he sees himself as one who could better serve as a representative who can **access power**. Something would be lost if he made a transition to becoming part of the power structure.

> I have more freedom as a pastor (than a politician). I don't like the fact that you can't choose your friends, you can't choose the issues when you're in office...There are a lot of good people in public office, but politicians lose their vision of what's possible...I'm connected to the public, connected to reality. I could be honest with Bill Gray...But my first accountability is to God.

Finally, Rev. Johnson decided not to run. The church is a base from which he can preserve a measure of security and freedom to speak as his conscience and the needs of his constituencies might prompt. His ability to do so depends on the links to power he has cultivated. Despite changes in the political landscape after Goode and Gray left office, Johnson considers that "I still have a good relationship to the mayor and the governor. It's just quieter."

The decision about public office was a definitive moment for both Rev. Johnson and the people of Grace, which served to clarify the appropriate role of the pastor and to reinforce their sense of boundaries. The result was a renewed commitment for Rev. Johnson to be primarily identified with this congregation, making forays into the public as their representative, and accessing power on behalf of the congregation and the people of that section of North Philadelphia.

The Pastoral Role and the Construction of Strategy

Accessing power

This strategic approach to social change, accessing power, flows out of the social construction of the pastor's role as hero, patriarch and representative. While in a certain sense the congregation's identity is enhanced by the pastor's public presence and access to power, they themselves are not "empowered" or encouraged to participate directly in engaging the power structure. In fact, the need for a representative to access power depends on the congregation not being empowered. They only need a representative if they do not feel that they can be advocates for themselves.

A familiar saying within the congregation was "If the Black church doesn't do it, it won't get done." But as the meaning became articulated in the interviews it was clear that if "it" was social change involving engagement with the power structure, that is a clercial duty. When "it" refers to delivering social services within the immediate community, the rank and file become involved.

Mr. Oscar Jenkins is one such member, hard at work in the community. A retired school teacher, he has moved out of the city, but maintains a passionate concern for the children and teens in the immediate area around Grace. Having served as a trustee and church treasurer, he spends most of his time now teaching Sunday School, running a summer program for kids, and in the public school adoption program. He is active and skilled in this "hands on" work with young people, yet recognizes how the programs could be strengthened through community organization. He articulated his vision of building coalitions between churches and with community groups, of shared leadership, of empowerment of local people to force more focus on North Philadelphia from City Hall, and of finally bringing about systemic change. Yet he thought he was probably unique in his views and anyway, did not know how to get started in pursuing such a strategy. Individual egos, he felt, prevented collaboration between churches. Thinking hard about how such an approach might be developed, he finally deferred to Rev. Johnson's capabilities to access resources and the power structure.

Mr. Jenkins had never heard of P.I.A. (nor had any others who were interviewed informally or in more depth) despite the fact that the philosophy and *modus operandi* of the organization is consonant with the vision for change Mr. Jenkins had expressed. This is particularly significant given Rev. Johnson's involvement with the organization. He had been among the original group which had initiated contact with I.A.F. and had later gone to their 10-day training. He had served on the Sponsoring Committee for almost 4 years (1989-92), which preceded the actual birthing of the organization. Rev. Johnson even spoke at the Opening Assembly of the organization in February of 1992, although there were no other representatives from Grace[3].

Not only had Rev. Johnson decided that Grace should not join P.I.A. but he had not communicated to the congregation that the organization existed. As early as 1990, soon after he had been to the training, he acknowledged that I.A.F. represented a different approach to social change.

> The difference between I.A.F.'s strategy and ours (Black Clergy, Inc.) is that they put more emphasis on training and we work more through the clergy...There are different strategies for moving people -- in the board rooms or on the streets.

The crux of the issue, for Johnson, was the choice between accessing power or empowerment -- they could neither coexist or be mixed. For him, the strategy of accessing power was inextricably rooted in the traditions of the Black church.

> The result of (I.A.F.'s training) is identifying more power brokers. But in the Black church, the pastor has more power. People see their hopes and aspirations in the pastor. They are his invisible cheering squad. I act vicariously for them as their representative and advocate.

To have opted for the I.A.F. strategy of empowerment would have meant not only changing a personal style, but going against the grain of the religious and cultural traditions as received and interpreted in his congregation which had resulted in the construction of an accessing power approach.

Clerical leadership

Similarly, the cultural streams which fed the making of Rev. Johnson as patriarch and hero would have to have been dammed in order to accommodate a strategy which stressed shared, as opposed to clerical leadership. He was among the signatories on a 1990 letter to the national director of I.A.F. asking for a variance in their policies which would exempt Philadelphia's chapter from shared leadership. (I.A.F. responded that they would not allow exclusive clergy leadership in one of their chapters.) The role of hero/patriarch which is so central to life at Grace Memorial is incompatible with decentralized leadership which is represented by I.A.F. This is not to say that responsibilities are not shared or that leadership skills are not valued at Grace. The opposite is very much in evidence. Nor is it to say that leadership is oppressive; again, this was not heard in any of the interviews. But it was important to Rev. Johnson and to other clergy that the centralized authority of the preacher be preserved both in the congregation and in any corporate body which would represent the interests of church people. Judging from both quantitative and qualitative data, the people of Grace support this understanding of strong, centralized leadership.[4]

Parochialism

While the pastor is supported, and indeed expected, to relate to a broader context, finally the benefits of his representation are just as equally expected to trickle back to the Grace Memorial and its immediate context. Despite the fact that 75% of the congregation drives in or takes public transportation to church from around and outside of Philadelphia, there is an intense geographic focus in their understanding of their mission. There is not much interest in effecting life beyond the immediate area of the church on the part of preacher or parishioners.

The process of adopting the four-phase redevelopment plan (which begins with the construction of a new church building to "anchor the triangle") reinforced this collective sense of parameters as well as their definition of the change which is needed. A subtext in the discourse about the plan is the choice not to relocate, not to flee the complexity of issues. Having then committed themselves to a place, their vision of change is also embodied in their interpretation of the plan. The transformation they envisage in the clearly defined area of North Philadelphia to which they feel responsible is at once spiritual and physical.

> The reality is that where the church is located defines the playing field..The goal (in the redevelopment plan) is to stabilize the community from further deterioration, and to attract middle class people back to the neighborhood, in the $35,000-$40,000 range. - Rev. Johnson

> We can't sit on that corner and not get involved with the neighborhood. If not us, then who? - Chairman of the Deacons

> The goal of plan is to redevelop houses, and bring up the neighborhood. We need to eliminate crime here and get people to come to church...Now we're working with ex-drug abusers. But we need to transform the environment, not just the individuals...Actually, I'd like to put the neighborhood development first. But it is a distant second after our three year capital campaign. - Male church leader

> I have hope for the neighborhood, if we could just show more love for the neighbors. I want the community to see Christ in us, then they could be saved through our witness. - Young female choir member

The definition of parameters is driven not only by the location of the church, but in relation to other churches nearby. Sharing space in a troubling urban neighborhood does not translate into collaboration among the 5-6 churches close by, some of which have demonstrated strong commitments to CED and responding to social problems. Rather there is an awareness of "turf" and an undercurrent of competition expressed in interviews with members.

> No, there we haven't really collaborated with other churches (on CED), although Pastor R. was on the non-profit board for a while to help out, and I think Rev. Johnson served on National Temple's board. - Female church leader

> I'd love to get the churches around us together so we could pool our resources, but its too hard. It's even easier to work with the government than getting the churches together. - Male church leader

> What's Deliverance (Evangelistic Church) doing that we can't do? Why should we let National Temple do all the outreach? We've got to do for ourselves. - Female church leader

The parochialism which so clearly defines space and regards other churches as competitors further fuels a concern for institutional survival. If the neighborhood is deteriorating, and other churches have a stronger appeal, what is the future of Grace? The altruistic vision of transforming their "triangle" in North Central is consciously related to their institutional concerns. After all, by not relocating, and by seeing their future within the local population, they are taking a risk. Put in market terms, their investment must produce sufficient dividends or they will be out of business.

> I'd like to see more community development -- building up the neighborhood, rebuilding houses. We need to stabilize the neighborhood so that when we build our new church there will be people who can support it. - Female church leader

> There is revitalization happening in North Central Philadelphia, so we need to stake our claim in community development. - Male church leader

There were differing perspectives on whether or not the immediate neighbors were attracted to the church. Some optimistically saw the growth in the church rolls as representing local pull. Most, however, felt that locals were not coming into the Church and that attempts at outreach would need to be stepped up dramatically.

> If we have a new building, nice facilities, accessible, a strong education program, its all to God's glory. Because when others see that the Lord rewards faithfulness, maybe the neighbors will look inward. Right now, we don't have enough draw with the local community. We've got to have a wholistic ministry. We've got to reach out, go to them. When we redevelop the neighborhood, then we'll have credibility (with their message). - Female church leader

The parochialism which focuses on **this** space and **this** institution rather than identifying with broader issues finds fertile cultural ground in more highly individualistic religiosity (Bellah, et al., 1983). It is, in essence, an extension of individualism. While there is a shared historical and cultural experience among African Americans which contributes to a more collective consciousness, there can, and often does, co-exist a well-articulated individualism, particularly in the churches.

The individualism at Grace is evident in how both threat and change are understood. It is clear from sermons, prayers and conversation that the primary perceived threat to human well-being are assaults by demonic forces. The forms which evil takes are both personal (drugs, crime, unbelief) and systemic (poverty, racism). However, the only real hope for transformation is at the individual level, through religious conversion.

> We do evangelism on 17th St, to tell people they don't have to live burndened down lives, unloved, addicted, living in sin, living like dogs, and hogs...We need to reach out to the youth and develop an awareness of their need for the church. They need life goals, so they know they can make it through hard work. I'd like to reshape the minds of young people so they know that you can be whatever you want if you have Christ. - Female church leader

Rev. Johnson did not discuss his decision not to affiliate with P.I.A. except to say that he could not afford the time. Given the time and attention he had spent in responding to other questions, as well as the significant investment of time he had made in the I.A.F., his answer was curiously short. It was also clear that follow-up questions would not coax him to elaborate.

What Rev. Johnson did elaborate on, however, was his renewed commitment to focus on his local CED efforts, the capital campaign, and his work among the congregation. He related this to the changing political landscape which had weakened the power of the African American community. Still, his parochialism was not newly-found but newly-intensified, and corresponded to that of the congregation. P.I.A.'s strategy would present a direct challenge to such a parochialism which maintained exclusive geographic focus, and non-collaborative. A city-wide focus and coalitional organization could certainly dilute their efforts. Whether the institutional self-interest and individualistic dimensions of their parochialism would be incompatible with P.I.A. cannot be known.

Supporting the status quo

The pastor and people of Grace dreamed of a future in which their corner of North Philadelphia would be home for working and middle class African Americans. Empty lots would be filled with new "townhouses" and a few green spaces. Existing rowhouses would be restored to their original Victorian charm, appreciated particularly by young urban professionals. The streets would be safe, free from drug dealers and abusers. All of this would be in the shadow of a modern church building: Grace would function as the social and spiritual center of the neighborhood.

While the people of Grace recognized that some of the obstacles which stood between the vision and the current reality were systemic, they did not pursue strategies to change the systems. Systemic change was not perceived as being viable. Instead Grace Memorial assumed responsibility for creating a new reality, leaving the unjust systems intact. For example, the Chairman of the Deacons quickly diagnosed a cause of urban decay and offered his prescription: "You know there's still redlining. Well, we have to get involved. The banks won't change. Only the church can get stuff done." Challenging the banks was not an option, because that was a losing battle; rather, through creating independent financing, housing development, and management, the church could make housing affordable, if only for a small section of the city.

For others in the congregation, systemic problems were interpreted as being spiritual or at least psychological. One church leader, who is a strong booster of the redevelopment plan, analyzed the program goals this way:

> The goal of our outreach, to me, is to reinstitute values and the work ethic, to re-establish community here so people won't move out.

In so doing, he attributed the causes of neighborhood deterioration (e.g., poverty and unemployment) to weakened values. Here, the church could make a difference.

Neither the preacher nor the people of Grace felt drawn into battles for social change. An overwhelming percentage (87.2%) had agreed that "working for change in society is an important part of the mission of the church." But as their understanding of change was articulated in the interviews, the transformation they sought was in the quality of life in one section of the city and in the lives of individuals who lived there, not in the policies and systems which contributed to or even created the social conditions which exist there. The battles to be fought with the system were to get resources out of it, not to attack the system itself.

This is not to say that public policy would remain unaffected by the mission of Grace Memorial Baptist Church. "Good public policy begins at the local level," Rev. Johnson believed. Local initiatives such as neighborhood redevelopment could have a "ripple effect," raising the expectations of others for higher quality of community life. This could translate into better policies.

Change could also result from two other sources according to Rev. Johnson. He believed that the spiritual change of people within the power structure would result in better policies. Spiritual conversion was finally the only real hope for social change. Further, as he and other representatives of congregations worked their contacts, positive influence was possible. His role as **patriarch** of his congregation, who **heroically** engaged in battles and **represented** their interests in the secular power structure essentially defined the strategy Grace Memorial Baptist Church pursued in saving the triangle around their intersecting streets. The identity and culture of the congregation consistently reinforced Rev. Johnson's own pragmatism which had led him to opt out of P.I.A.

Knox Presbyterian Church

Ten blocks up Broad St. sits the rounded grey stone building which is a familiar ediface on the edge of Temple University. In many ways, Knox Presbyterian Church is the inverse image of Grace Memorial Baptist. Affiliated with a predominantly white "mainline" denomination (Presbyterian Church, U.S.A.) it follows many of the denominational trends identified by the results of the questionnaire (Chapter 3).

While the members of Grace were drawn from the poorest census tracts in the sample, Knox members ranked second among the ten in residential income levels (Chart 3.1). They were by far the congregation with the highest levels of education. Further, there was a higher percentage of professionals and managers at Knox than there was at Grace, and a smaller proportion walked to church from the immediate neighborhood (Chart 5.1).

The Presbyterians differed sharply from the Baptists in their religious beliefs. Overwhelmingly the people of Grace believed that the Bible should be interpreted literally (85.4%), but only about half of Knox's membership held this conservative view (51.9%).

On the question of who God saves, the Baptists again held more conservative beliefs; they were much more likely to affirm that one must be born again (56%) than were their Presbyterian counterparts (36.8%). Not only was the Knox congregation more liberal theologically, there was also more diversity of views represented (Chart 5.2).

Although there was not much distance between the two churches, they saw the world differently. The Presbyterians were more likely to attribute poverty to the structural causes of jobs, racism, and government policies. The Baptists were more individualistic: Grace ranked highest within the sample in the proportion of members who blamed individual laziness for poverty (22.5%) and lowest in blaming government (17.5%) (Chart 5.3).

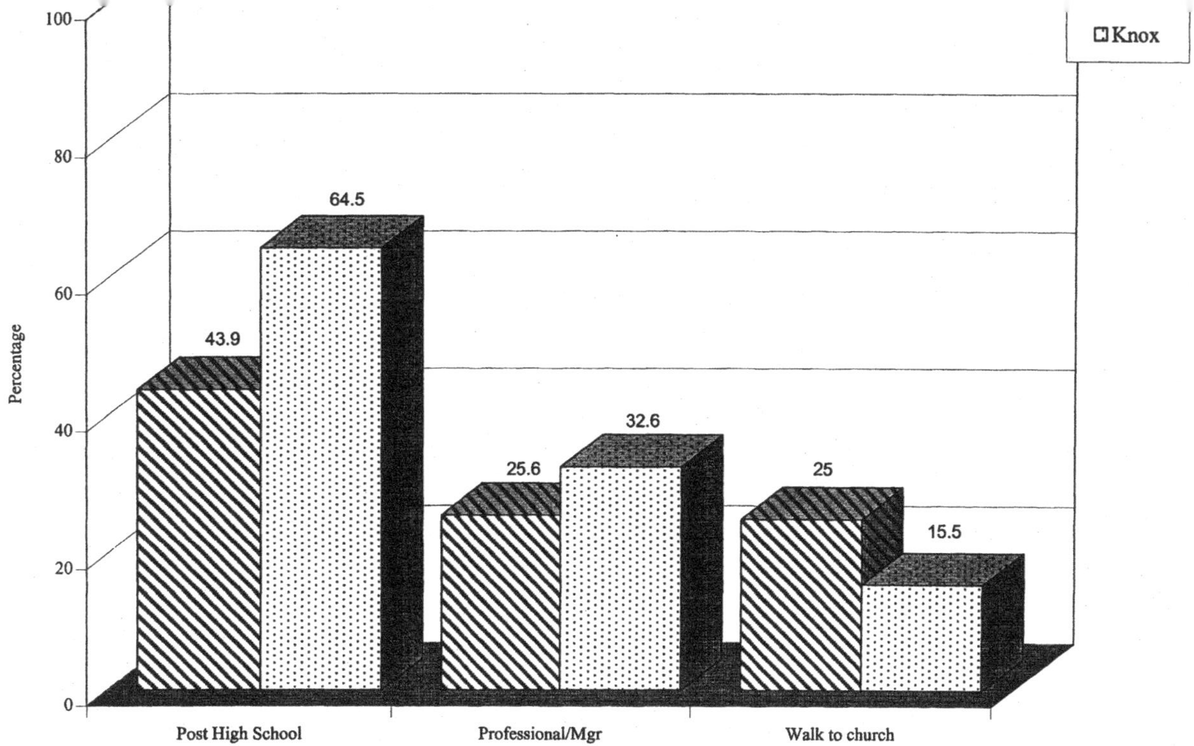

Chart 5.1 Demographic Data: Grace and Knox

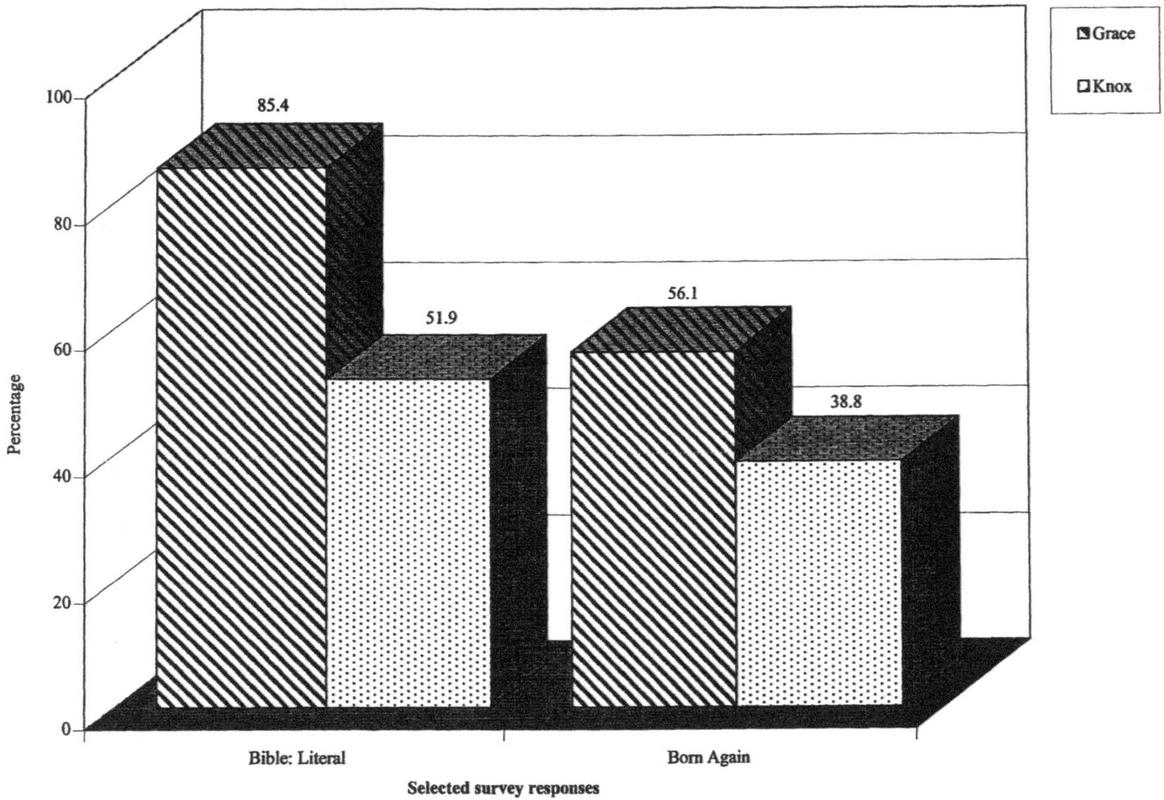
Grace
Knox
85.4
51.9
56.1
38.8
100
80
60
40
20
0
Percentage
Bible: Literal
Born Again
Selected survey responses

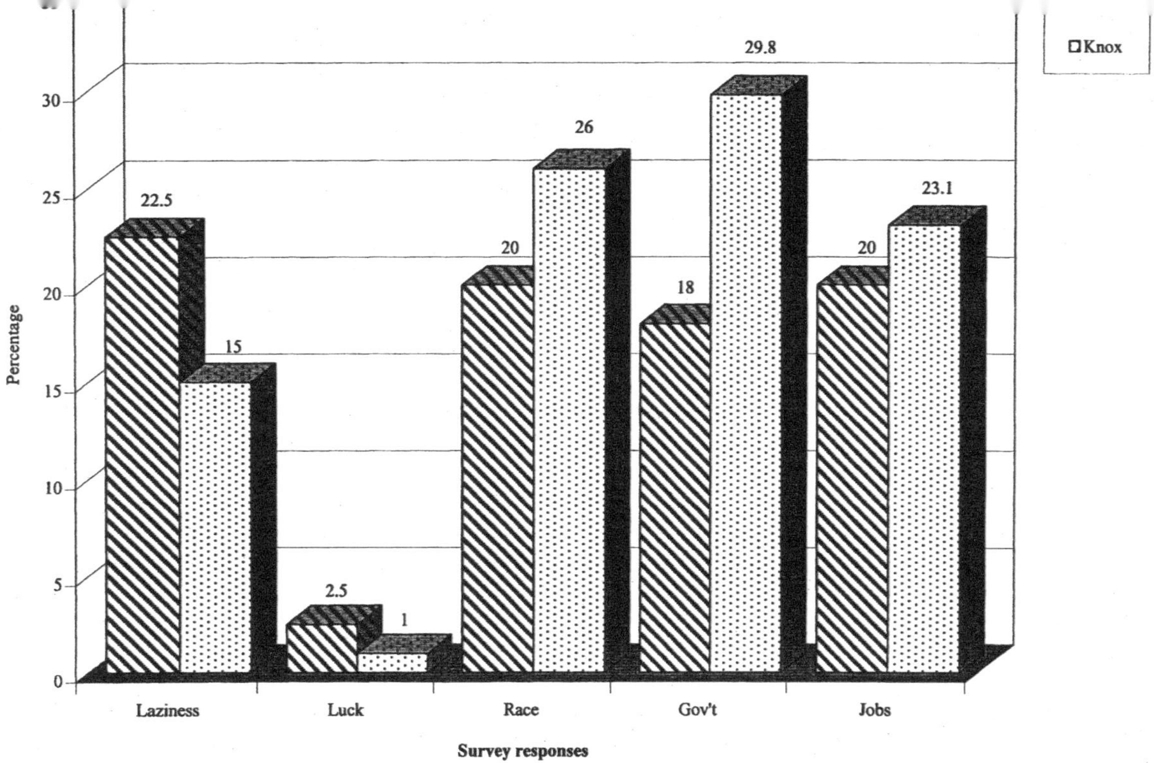

Chart 5.3 Views on Cause of Poverty: Grace and Knox

The same patterns were followed in the congregations' understandings of who was responsible for alleviating poverty, with Knox looking more often to structural solutions. While the members of Grace still looked to the government more (31.6%) and individuals less (10.5%) overall, they were much less supportive of structural solutions and gravitated more toward personalistic ones relative to the other churches (Chart 5.4).

When it came to social change, the Presbyterians and the Baptists followed the trends of their racially-based religious traditions. The members of Knox were more likely to favor protests, electoral politics, and individuals speaking up. Predictably, the Baptists believed to a greater degree that spiritual conversion was the most effective strategy for social change (57.1% compared to 36.5% of Presbyterians) (Chart 5.5).

If differences in class, religious beliefs or political perspectives among congregants drove the construction of their strategies for community development, then different approaches might be expected at Grace and Knox. Yet Knox Presbyterian had also opted not to join with P.I.A. As with Grace, the pastor's leadership is finally definitive in choosing strategies for community development.

Seventy-five housing units near Temple University stand as a monument to the commitment of Knox Presbyterian and the organizing efforts of its pastor of thirty-plus years, Rev. Curtis Smith. "People's Village" was constructed in the late 1960's, a product of both a culture of protest and the federal urban policies at that time. As the story is told by both Rev. Smith and church members, the expansion plans of the university had triggered organized community resistance. The young preacher, literally "the new kid on the block," became a leader in the effort which brought together church and community people in opposition to Temple University's expansion efforts.

Eventually the conflict led to the creation of a *charette*, or "covenanted dialogue" between the two parties. It brought him to the table with the President of the university, Dr. Peter Liacouras. The agreement negotiated included a commitment by Temple University "that they would never go into the community again without the participation of the neighbors, and that Temple would be available to the community as a resource," in the words of Rev. Smith. "Our theme

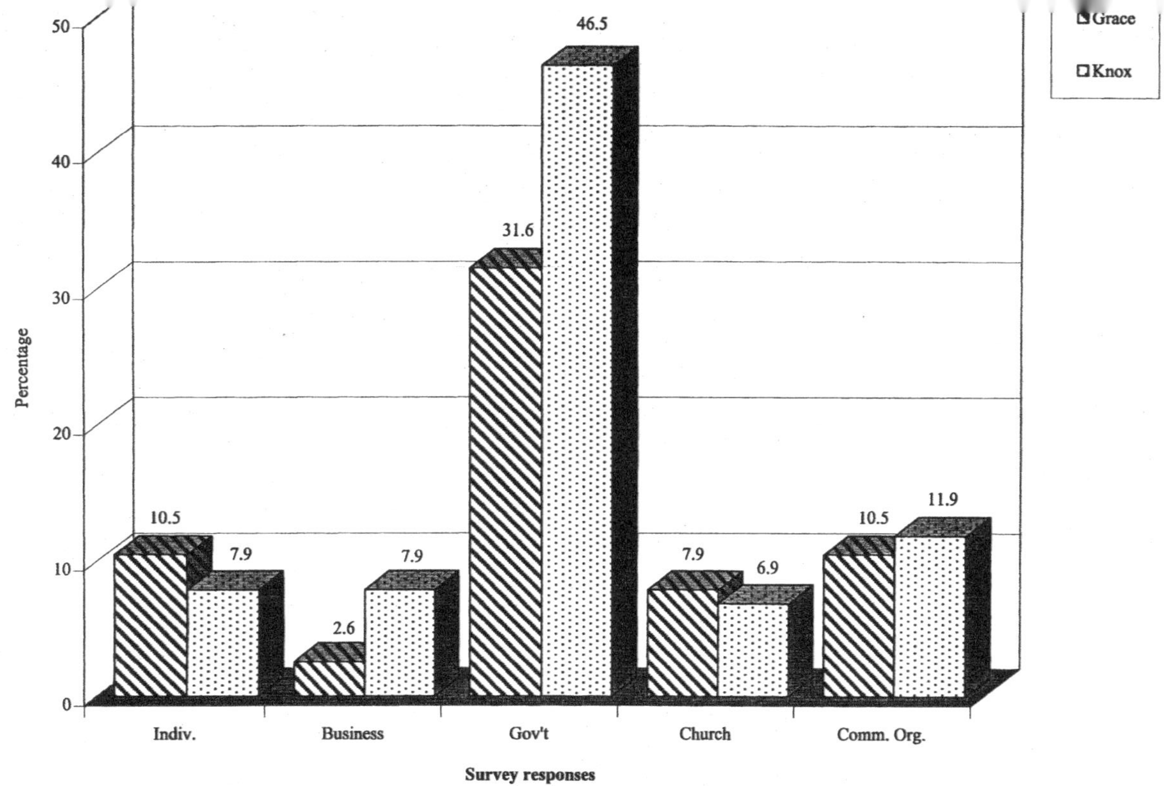

Chart 5.4 Views on Ending Poverty: Grace and Knox

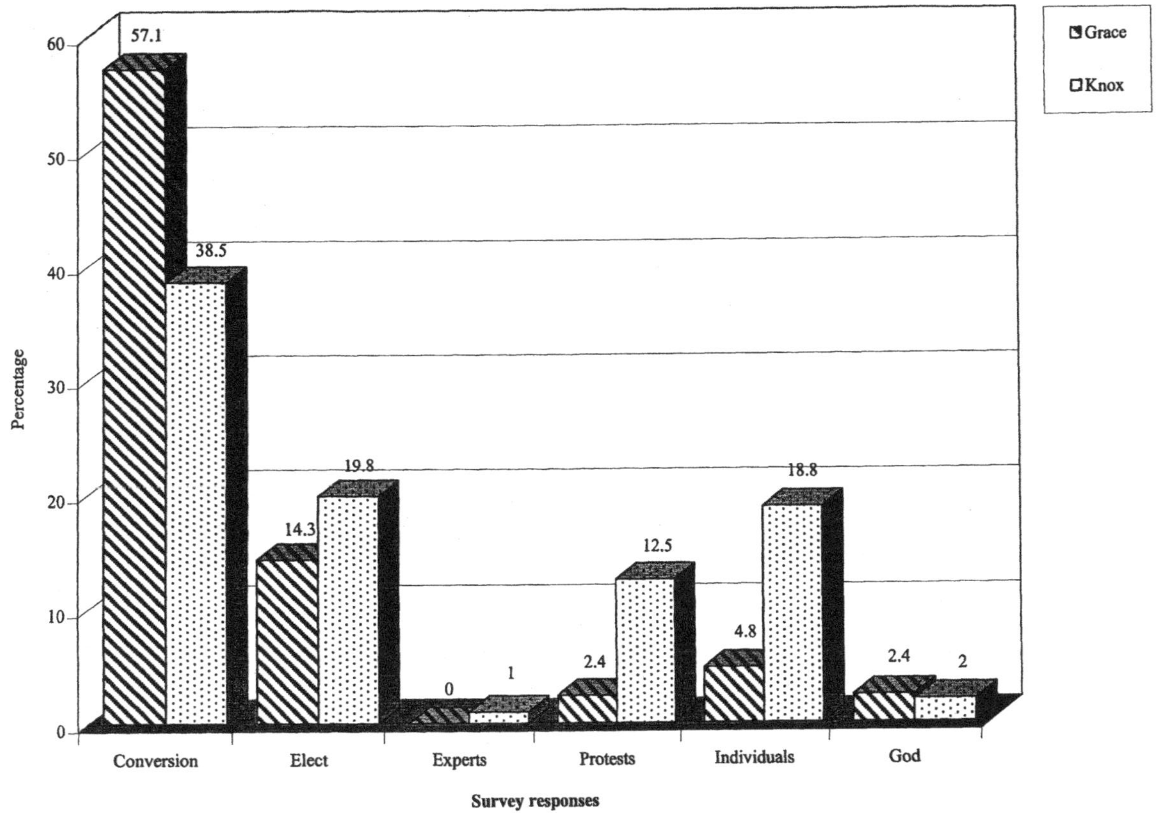
Grace
Knox
57.1
38.5
14.3
19.8
0
1
2.4
12.5
4.8
18.8
2.4
2
60
50
40
30
20
10
0
Percentage
Conversion
Elect
Experts
Protests
Individuals
God
Survey responses

was co-existence. We knew that we had to learn to live together or we would die." The *Charette* of 1970 has endured and Rev. Smith credits it with preventing Temple from leaving the city ten years ago. Currently, he is negotiating with Temple for a parking lot, "as a way to further demonstrate their relationship to the community" although the primary beneficiaries would be the members of Knox.

An immediate result of the *Charette* was Temple's active support of The People's Community Developers Corporation (PCDC), which Rev. Smith served as President. With consulting help from W. Wilson Goode, and participation from the university, land was acquired, federal monies were secured, and the homes were built. Most of the low and moderate income residents were first-time homeowners and the default rate has been quite low. "We proved that when given an opportunity, we can stabilize a neighborhood," said Rev. Smith. Knox brokered the application process for the PCDC, screening, interviewing, and selecting the homeowners. Then having achieved their goals, and aware of a new church-based CDC down Claren Street, the community organization disorganized.

Today, Knox Church continues to be active in the immediate neighborhood, but they have withdrawn from CED activities, instead focusing on social needs. Based in their Community Center, they are involved in feeding the homeless, reaching out to those who are HIV+ and AIDS-infected, and providing a literacy program. Currently they are developing a new program to "support families."

Although these two churches in North Central Philadelphia have both been involved in housing development for economically vulnerable populations, they had utilized different strategies: Knox had worked through grass-roots community organizing in the development of People's Village. As part of a coalition, they had worked to bring change to a system which they felt was unfair.

However, their strategy has evolved into a much more parochial one which was no longer willing to challenge the power structures of City Hall or even Temple University. What contributed to that change? Had the pastor and members burned out? "We couldn't do it now," one church leader said. "The first time around the dream was more exciting. And we were younger."

Another interpretation might be that the group disbanded after having met their goals because they had been co-opted by the university. By everyone's account, the relationship between the two institutions is "harmonious." The university president attended the pastor's anniversary banquet, and Rev. Smith has a seat on the Board of Directors and an honorary doctorate from the institution.

Yet a closer analysis suggests that there was not such a dramatic shift in Knox's organizing paradigm before and after People's Village. The structure of leadership has been constant as the church moved to more parochial and traditional forms of community outreach. Further, there are striking similarities between how leadership has been constructed in the seemingly different congregations of Grace Memorial Baptist and Knox Presbyterian.

Despite its Presbyterian affiliation, worship at Knox is much more like the experience at an African American Baptist church, in both form and content. The two hour service begins with an energetic procession by the choir and congregational leaders. Music is prominent throughout the service, but is drawn from the Gospel music tradition, rather than the more staid Presbyterian sources. Times of prayer are fervent, enthusiastic, and personalistic. The sermon is long and passionate. Rev. Smith occasionally wipes his brow with his hankerchief -- a familiar gesture among preachers in the African American traditions. An "altar call" follows the sermon, in which individuals are invited to come forward if they want to affiliate with the church or want special prayer. Usually 15-20 people end up standing in front of the pulpit. This worship style, which corresponds so closely to that of a Baptist church, is interesting, given the distinctly non-Baptist characteristics of the congregation which became apparent in the survey data.

Like Rev. Johnson, Rev. Smith's patriarchal status is evident as he presides over the worship experience. He interacts with the people in the pews throughout the service with warmth and familiarity. There is also a sense that he suffers for them, bearing the weight of their problems. Rev. Smith is visibly exhausted at the end of the service, having spent his energy in representing God to the people and the concerns of the people to God.

Throughout the service, recurring themes are the faithfulness of God to the people and the need to be faithful, that is, persistent in obeying God and serving God in the world. There is a stress on their distinctiveness as religious people, and the need to resist pressures which would dilute their identity in the world. There is an intentional effort at Knox to reinforce the racial dimension of that identity, as well as the spiritual. African "kente" clothe is worn by choir members as well as many of the women in the congregation. Pictures and biographies of accomplished African Americans are featured in the worship program. Special seminars are offered on Afrocentrism by the Chairperson of the African American Studies Department at Temple. Clearly, the people of Knox are responding to perceived threats not only in matters of conscience/faith but also as people of African American identity. Being in relationship to the institutions of the Presbyterian Church and Temple University, the need to reassert a strong African American identity is understandable.

As people talk about Rev. Smith's leadership in community development, it is evident that, like Rev. Johnson, his public profile took on heroic dimensions through the process of developing housing. While the leadership of PCDC was supposedly shared between the President (Smith) and the Chairperson (Hilda McCoy, a community activist), "he was the force who propelled the whole thing," according to one member who participated in the project. (In fact none of the people interviewed, including the pastor, could remember McCoy's name.) His role, however, was vividly remembered by another informant, a female member who had been active in PCDC:

> In the church, there was only a small group of us really involved, although the whole congregation supported us...It was really Rev. Smith's vision...He had to do things that didn't come easy for him. He was pushing City Council and even went to Washington. He did a lot of things (behind the scenes) that we didn't even know about. - Active church member

Rev. Smith had knowledge and contacts which were not available to the grassroots participants. As their representative, he did battle for them -- the church and neighborhood -- and, as hero, he triumphed. As the struggle is remembered by the former members who participated in

PCDC, they did feel "empowered," doing things they never thought they would or could do to help build houses. Yet they also felt that, in the end, it finally depended on accessing power. As hero and representative, Rev. Smith was able to do that in Washington, at Temple University, and in City Hall. That legacy continues. Almost twenty five years later, both people and pastor refer to the relationships Rev. Smith has with those in power which can be appealed to to bring, or prevent, change: the President of the University, and the President of City Council in particular. He even recently met with President Clinton, as part of a group of African American clergy involved in responding to the AIDS crisis in urban areas. (The exact benefit to their program was not known, but this contact was assumed to have an effect.)

There are parallels between Revs. Johnson and Smith which would give further insight into the strategic approach they have taken in serving their respective areas of North Central Philadelphia. Like his Baptist colleague, Rev. Smith has attained some status beyond his congregation. He is well-known in the regional denominational network and has chaired prominent committees at the national level. He is also invited to participate in ecumenical and civic projects. While receiving recognition outside of the congregation which contributes to his status within the church, Rev. Smith's ultimate focus is Knox and the people who come to their door on corner of Broad and Claren Streets for help.

Both pastors seem satisfied in their positions. Both have relatively long tenures in congregations, which under their leadership, have garnered some prestige in broader circles. Within their congregations they are loved and respected as patriarchs, heroes, and representatives who can access power on behalf of the church. Yet they lead their people into battles which are primarily personal -- fighting assaults on the faith, identity, and well-being of those in and around the church. Both Revs. Smith and Johnson have cultivated some political capital with those in the power structure, and have built housing as a result. But they are not willing to risk their capital in challenging that structure. This reticence is fueled less by ego than it is by the construction of their leadership throughout their tenures which is consistent with the models of ministry handed down from the African American church traditions.

Finally, as the two churches chart their missions, P.I.A. has not been regarded as being necessary or appropriate. In fact, by representing a different set of frames of action, it could interfere with the pursuit of their own goals.

---

[1]Rev. Johnson had served as the Chief of Staff for Congressman Gray's District Office.

[2] clerical versus shared leadership; parochial versus coalitional organizing parameters; empowerment versus access-to-power approaches to power; *status quo* versus social change as organizing goal

[3] It should be noted that at this assembly over 1000 people attended, representing 40 churches and 4 organizations. Of these, 7 were African American Baptist churches.

[4] Grace ranked third in the percentage of members who agreed that "the pastor of a congregation should be involved in politics and issues of public concern," with 54.8% agreeing or strongly agreeing (x=52.1%)

Chapter 6

"A Place to Let my Light Shine"

The Church of the Advocate

Introduction

Four blocks down the street from Knox Presbyterian are the offices of ACDC --Advocate Community Development Corporation -- the organization which by its early success and visibility, prompted the People's Community Developers Corporation to go out of business. The two organizations emerged in similar ways from the same North Philadelphia soil. ACDC had also grown out of a church's ministry, that of Church of the Advocate, the cathedral-like Episcopal church on Diamond Street. Both had gotten consulting help from W. Wilson Goode and ACDC, like PCDC, had been accepted in the Model Cities program. The two programs were born in the cultural context of rage in the late 1960's which had inspired so many "grassroots" people of North Philadelphia into organized response to the injustice they experienced.

While "the Advocate" and its surrounding community are also in the shadow of Temple University, the Episcopalians' involvement in building houses was sparked from a source of pressure other than institutional encroachment: the real estate market for low-income families.

As Christine Washington tells the story of the birth of ACDC, it had its roots in a protest at the Board of Education in 1967 by high school students and their parents who were demanding a stronger Black presence in both the curriculum and personnel. The response by police was so violent that it came to be known as "Black Friday." Out of that event, the Black People's Unity Movement organized a response at the Advocate, the church at which her husband, Rev. Paul Washington, served as priest from 1962-1987. Small groups called "learning centers" were organized. Christine Washington participated in one of these with eleven other mothers who were concerned about public education.

One of the women in the group, a single mother with seven children, was about to be evicted from her home. The other women in the group committed themselves to helping her find adequate housing, a goal which took two full months to realize. Outraged at the paucity of adequate housing available, Mrs. Washington declared to her husband one night that "We're going to have to build houses for our people."

Although she had not been a community leader to that point, she organized her small group through the incorporation process. None of the members of this original board had a college degree or the skills needed to develop real estate. Yet through the resources of the Model Cities Program and eventually the Ford Foundation they "learned by doing." By 1971, fifteen newly-constructed units for welfare families were completed two blocks away from the church. The first-time buyers participated in construction and were given training in home maintenance. Washington herself oversaw the day-to-day construction project, as she and members of ACDC were not satisfied with the work of the contractor.

Since that modest beginning, Christine Washington has continued to serve as Executive Director of ACDC, leading it through efforts which have dramatically changed eighteen blocks along the Diamond Street Corridor. By 1993, they had developed 303 units of housing (both new construction and "rehabs"), with 187 awaiting development. Most of these are for low-income buyers, but some of the developments are targeted for other populations including moderate and mid-income buyers, renters, homeless persons, and the phyically challenged. In addition, they have developed a park and a number of supportive social services for the population. Washington stresses that the goal of all this CED activity is not to attract a higher level population which would displace the poor (gentrification), but to stabilize the neighborhood by providing attractive, affordable housing for the population which currently lives there, is most likely to live there, and who have the fewest options available to them. Hence, only vacant properties are acquired for development.

Although Christine Washington has not strayed from her original goals, the rise of her own learning curve in CED has been remarkable. She is regarded in Philadelphia's non-profit world as having a high level of sophistication in her development skills. In her first twenty-five years on the job, she had put together funding packages totalling $15.5 million from public and private sources, yet she has never accepted a salary. "There are other ways to pay people," she says with a smile.

ACDC is an important part of Advocate's story. Indeed, both Christine and Paul Washington loom large in the oral history and current congregational identity. Any analysis of the Advocate today must begin with a consideration of Father Paul Washington's service there and the indelible print that his legacy has had.

<u>The Washington Years, 1962-1987</u>

Paul Washington was appointed by the Bishop in 1962 to serve as the first African American priest in the North Philadelphia church going through the same racial transition the neighborhood was experiencing. Soon after arriving at his new position, he was confronted by a woman who represented for him all the problems of the inner city -- a homeless single mother. When he tried to offer comfort she challenged him to not just tell her about God's love, but to show it to her. Rev. Washington often refers to this story as being pivotal in how he came to define his tenure at the Advocate.

> I knew from that moment that we had to act out God's love, and it began right there. Christine and I gave her a room in the rectory..Shortly after my encounter with Jackie, I added to the sign on the church's lawn at the corner of 18th and Diamond, 'This church lives the Gospel.' For God does not appear in words, but in action. (Washington and Gracie, 1994)

That commitment to social action led Father Washington "into the streets" of racial politics in Philadelphia in the 1960's. Not only did he become a familiar presence in local demonstrations (such as the protest movement at Girard College in 1965, called "Philadelphia's Selma"), but he became recognized as a compelling speaker on issues of racial justice. Further, many of the significant events of this period were held at the Advocate. The Black Unity Rally was the first such event in 1966; later that year Stokely Carmichael spoke twice at the church. Groups such as the Northern Student Movement, the Student Non-Violent Coordinating Committee (SNCC), the Congress on Racial Equality (CORE), and the Black People's Unity Movement (BPUM) regularly held meetings and rallys there at that time. Two years later, in 1968, almost 8,000 people from around the country came to the Advocate for the Black Power Conference. In 1970, the church hosted 6,000 participants for the Black Panther Convention. The edifice which Father Washington refers to as a castle housed other significant events which had a lower public profile -- a series of meetings between warring gangs of local young people, provision of "sanctuary" for those avoiding legal sanctions and a series of memorial services for those lost in "the struggle." To study the history of this church and its outspoken priest is to study the social history of the Black consciousness movement in Philadelphia in the 1960's and early 1970's. (Washington and Gracie, 1994)

The events based at the Advocate came out of a change in consciousness for Father Washington. He had been highly committed to the non-violent civil rights movement, most clearly represented by Martin Luther King, Jr. However, he came to appreciate the need for a separatist Black Power movement. While never comfortable with the use of physical force in service to social change, he could understand such a strategy. Eventually he publically identified himself with Black nationalism, and learned to live with his own unanswered questions.

> I felt in tune with Martin, but also with Malcolm and the Panthers. For me it became not a matter of one or the other; within my 'one dark body'[1] the two represented what for me was wholeness, even if I could not intellectually resolve all the contradictions they raised. (Washington and Gracie, p. 130)

He began to talk about and preach a "Theology of Black Power," which was political in its articulation. Washington advocated moving beyond integration, but challenging an oppressive system through the power of Black nationalism. His position was clarified through challenges from his own institution (the predominantly Euro-centric and relatively affluent Episcopal Church of America) as well as from Black activists.

Speaking to a group of Episcopalians in the affluent suburbs of Philadelphia in 1968, he developed his central theme: "Integration is not the answer to the racial problem. The black man is developing a heritage of his own through black nationalism." (Washington and Gracie, p. 71). In an interview for the Evening Bulletin he was quoted as saying:

> Riots? You ask why? I don't think the riots today have a calculated aim any longer. People riot, not for the right to get a better job or a better house -- but because they've already found there is not job, there is not house. They've been promised and they believed, and then they found there is nothing. Most white people now fear a real revolt. So, instead of working to elimate the causes, they advocate more police. But the tighter you press the lid down, the greater the explosion. Yes, I think there is a chance (for improving racial relations). Its like the relationship between a man and a woman. You can either have a relationship based on integrity or one based on force. Either you respect her or rape her. Now, black people are not willing to be raped any longer.

Such public statements provoked angry responses, especially from Episcopalians throughout the diocese who questioned why they should support such a priest, such a church. Early threats to the continuation of denominational funding for the Advocate later became well-organized efforts to cut off the support. At a number of points, they might have been successful if he did not have the strong support of the bishop at that time, the Rt. Rev. Robert DeWitt. The irony of being attacked and protected by his religious institution paralleled Washington's own ambivalence in his relationship with the denomination.

His participation in political struggles soon led him into other battles within the church. In 1969 Father Washington was attracted by the moral clarity and urgency of the Black Manifesto, which called on all religious institutions in the country to pay reparations to African Americans totalling $500 million. He soon became allied with Muhammed Kenyatta in Philadelphia in a protracted effort to get reparations from the diocese and then the national church. Disappointed with the results and outraged at the process, Father Washington ended up resigning from the diocesan committee and later, leading African Americans out of the national convention of the Episcopal Church.

The Advocate received a lot of attention in July of 1974 when, in defiance of the policies of the Episcopal church, eleven women were ordained to the priesthood there. Again, Father Washington had been central to this effort of both protest and change. Again, he had risked his own status within the church, and the much-needed financial support of the Advocate.

Washington has continued to be involved in controversial issues. In the late 1970's he formed a relationship with the MOVE community in West Philadelphia, and tried to act as mediator in their confrontation with police. After the "MOVE tragedy" of 1985 he was appointed by Mayor W. Wilson Goode to the investigative commission on the incident. Having been a long-time associate of Goode's, he supported the Commission's findings of "gross negligence" in the Mayor's actions. Although he has been critical of MOVE's ideology and tactics, Washington has nevertheless continued to be an advocate for their just treatment -- not a popular stand in the city of Philadelphia.

Since retiring in 1987, he continues to speak out in the church and and in public on a variety of issues, from gay and lesbian rights to the commutation of the death sentence for Mumia Abu Jamal. Gentle in demeanor and elegant in his presentation, Father Washington at 74 still manages to inspire, provoke, and offend.

<u>The Pastor as Prophet</u>

In his own self-understanding, Paul Washington believes his ministry of working for social change has been driven by his own pursuit of personal integrity. "I've always tried to be on good terms with God," he said in explaining the primacy of conscience over institutional concerns or even personal security. This was tested throughout his career, but an early incident was pivotal in his own formation. In 1966 he was challenged by John Churchill, a young activist on the staff of the Advocate who had been funded to do work with gangs, to throw his full support behind the Black Unity Rally to be held at the church.

> I always had the feeling that John had serious reservations about my sincerity and commitment. He saw my anxiety about what he was asking and he said something to me that I shall never forget. He said, You are an Episcopalian. It is a church that represents the white establishment and racism in its most sophisticated but vicious fashion. You are going to have to make a choice, to fight for the liberation of our people and maybe get kicked out of this church, or you may reach a point where you have to leave.' I felt that I had to prove to both John and myself that I was not a hypocrite. I answered very quietly and simply, "I'm going all the way." (Washington and Gracie, p. 42)

The integrity which "grips" Father Washington has led him into the role of lone **prophet**, the word which is used most often by the members of the current congregation and those who have known him through the years. In honoring him with an honorary doctorate, his alma mater, Philadelphia Divinity School, cited Paul Washington as "a disturbing prophet, a healing priest."

As a prophet, Washington has identified with the needs of the poor and socially marginalized. Consequently, he has interpreted the threats to be addressed as being structural, cultural, material in origin. The battles he has chosen have been waged against enemies such as racism and sexism, particularly as demonstrated by the institutions of the state and religion. He has not interpreted the primary threats to human well-being as spiritual or individual; rather, personal malaise is the consequence of the greater evils.

The prophet does not enjoy the universal accolades bestowed on those we would make our heroes. This prophet's efforts have been more focused on battling the dragons than the more literal rescue of the vulnerable. In so doing, Father Washington is regarded by many as an outlaw. His collaborator described his complex public identity:

> Was this black priest what most white churchmen wanted him to be -- a reconciler, a moderating influence on a community that seemed on the verge of revolt, and a trusted interpreter of the meaning of the social turbulence to members of the white establishment? Or was he himself an agent of revolt, adept at using the established Episcopal Church as a cover and and shelter for movements of black liberation that otherwise might be

isolated and stifled? The truth is that he was both. (Washington and Gracie, p. xviii)

It is important to also recognize the ability this prophet has had to gain access and trust of those in positions of power. While his positions might be threatening, his personal style with people is direct and engaging. One activist who had worked with Father Washington in the black nationalist movement called him their "legitimizer." He lent credibility to their efforts and kept them in dialogue with those they considered part of the oppressive establishment.

Father Washington's independence from institutional partisanship as well as his concern for personal integrity have contributed to his identity as a lone prophet. Although he would never endorse clericalism as a theoretical construction, historically he has acted very much alone. "It means something to see your pastor taking a stand -- people take comfort in that." The series of decisions involving the Advocate in the struggles of the 1960's and 1970's were far from democratic, even in Washington's own analysis. Despite the impact they could and did have on the congregation, the decisions were made unilaterally by the priest. "There was no one I could really consult with. The vestry wasn't where I was -- I was closer to the people of the neighborhood...I was at odds with the class interests of the congregation." Usually, the vestry would just "go along" with their pastor's decisions. Once, they challenged an action he had taken which had supported Black separatism over inclusion of Anglos. Following his conscience, he justified his decision, telling them, "I know what I'm doing," and offered his resignation. The vestry backed down.

Paul Washington has also felt estranged from his fellow clergy: "There was no single minister I could talk to" during his involvement with the Black power movement. "I had no alliances with other Black clergy, the others were not activists." The loneliness of the prophet led him away from ecumenical coalitions and shared leadership. He collaborated with networks outside of the church, hence the title of his autobiography, <u>Other Sheep I Have</u>[2].

The work of Paul and Christine Washington has been, in Paul's words, "interdependent." They have dedicated themselves to seeking change, at both individual and social levels. Despite the fact that he was critical of his denomination for only supporting "safe" economic development projects which did not challenge the political status quo, Father Washington also values the contribution of ACDC has made under Mrs. Washington's leadership. As a project of, by, and for the local Black community, it continues in the spirit of the earlier movement's commitment to self-determination. Through its alliance and identification with the Advocate, ACDC has never been too far removed from social change efforts.

While Christine Washington has worked parochially, Paul Washington worked in coalition, albeit with political groups and not with other churches. The corner of 18th and Diamond has been an island of political activism and a strong center of CED in North Philadelphia.

Both of the Washingtons hope that the outcome of their commitments is that the powerless will become empowered. Yet the success of their own work has depended on their ability to gain access to those in power. Despite the strategy of accessing power, those associated with the Washingtons do not consider that their loyalties have been co-opted or their values compromised by their relationships to those in power. Father Washington believes there "should always exist a tension between ..the establishment and the church." In one of the books on MOVE recently published by a former city official, Washington is described as "a member of the anti-establishment, who was understood and trusted by the establishment." (Bowser, 1989) He has been honored in many ways which reflect his identification with both communities: from the prestigious Philadelphia Award (1986) to the huge mural of him painted on the side of a building in his own neighborhood, Strawberry Mansion.

The very public role of the Washingtons created an image of this small congregation which was larger-than-life. Rev. Washington is proud that his tenure "put the Advocate on the map." Ironically, as his high-profile political activism grew and ACDC continued to develop more housing, membership at the Advocate declined to approximately 100 members. Within that small yet highly visible religious community, the impressions made by Paul and Christine Washington on their culture were signficant during his tenure, and have continued eight years after his retirement.

The Impact of Legacy

Not surprisingly, the congregation experienced a conflict over its identity soon after Rev. Washington left. "There had always been tension between those who were pro-social action and those who were more conservative," one long-time member explained. "They were a silent minority (on the vestry) during Paul Washington's tenure. But the tension re-emerged during the transition." Another church leader described the conservatives as "wanting a more structured middle-class church..a full church." This concern became focused on building preservation and the choice of interim priests to succeed Father Washington. In a dramatic vestry meeting in which a member of the Bishop's staff intervened, four members ended up resigning, three of whom left the church altogether. The struggle over identity came to an end, with an affirmation that the Advocate would continue to be a "service church" in the tradition of Paul Washington.

Despite the consensus on their commitment to social action, another dimension of the corporate identity of the Advocate is the inherent contradictions it embodies. Like the "warring ideals in one dark body" Washington experienced as a Black activist priest in an affluent Euro-centric denomination, the congregation reflects similar constrasts which they seem to relish.

This is physically represented in the building itself, an impressive structure built in the late 19th century. Complete with vaulted ceilings, flying buttresses and gargoyles, it is most often compared to the cathedral at Amiens, France. The sanctuary is grand in Gothic design, yet the art work which surrounding it heightens a sense of contrast. Fourteen large murals, painted by African American artists Walter Edmonds and Richard Watson between 1973-1976, depict the history of their people in this country. The figures are familiar -- Martin Luther King, Malcolm X, Nat Turner, Frederick Douglass, Elijah Muhammed, among them -- and the presentation is dramatic. The murals have been a source of controversy themselves, in form as well as in the sometimes violent content. In short, they are not the sort of art work one would expect to find in such a formal Episcopal church. But neither is the congregation. The building is more often described as an "albatross" and a "drain" than it is considered as a resource. Yet the paintings and all that they represent make the building more comfortable in its irony.

Ideological consensus is high in the congregation: by far the membership of the Advocate was the most theologically liberal congregation in the study, following the trend of other mainline Protestant churches. Yet this church brings together an unlikely group of people, representing different classes and races. For example, while the Advocate had the second-lowest proportion of members with any post-high school education[3], it was the congregation with the highest percentage of members holding graduate degrees.[4] Over one-third are in professional-managerial occupations, yet the Advocate is second only to Grace Memorial Baptist in the low income levels and poverty rates of the tracts represented by the membership. The Advocate also distinguished itself in the study by having the highest proportion of members who walk to church from the neighborhood --35.9%. The data only confirm what is easily observed: published writers, welfare mothers, teachers, homeless persons, administrators and domestic workers all gather together on Sunday mornings. The Rev. Ann Robb Smith, Assistant Rector, believes that the largest draw of this anomoly among religious congregations is the diversity itself. As a WASP, upper class woman who commutes from an affluent suburb, she describes herself as well as many of the professionals in the congregation as having consciously chosen "social dislocation." Other people from higher social classes have been attracted to the Advocate by its diversity, unique history, perspectives and commitments to social action. However, more of those from the professional-managerial class left the church for the same reasons during the Washington years.

For the majority of members who come from lower socio-economic strata, the Advocate is a place where they can get involved in changing the realities of poverty, whether through community organizing for CED or by helping with the 60,000 meals which are served each year in the soup kitchen. One very active church member described her experience this way:

> When my father was dying, he said to me, 'Judith, you've just got to let your light shine'...I was doing a lot of church work (in another congregation) but it wasn't until I came here that I found out what my father meant. My emptiness is lifting. **This is a place I can let my light shine.** - Active church member/leader

Many of those who "chose social dislocation" and wanted to identify with the causes of the urban poor were drawn to the Advocate during the Washington years. But Miss Judith Hansen was "scared of the Advocate when the Black Panthers were meeting here. A lot of people were." She was attracted to the church three years ago by the congregation itself, under the leadership of Washington's successor, Rev. Isaac Miller.

In many ways, "Ike""Miller represents a continuation of Paul Washington's commitments. Like his predecessor, he has been at times in conflict with his denomination and its hierarchy as an African American priest. He too has had a long history of activism, particularly in the Civil Rights movement and in later issues related to racial justice. Rev. Miller came to the Advocate in 1990 at the age 47 following positions in public administration, campus and congregational ministry. His commitment to seeking social change led him to P.I.A. early in his tenure there. The current priest, like the former one, is comfortable with political confrontation in the service of change. He also finds tensions within the congregation to be healthy, particularly the identity struggle around what he calls "the internal vs. the external focus." "The different perceptions reflect the tension with the Black community as a whole, being prophetic vs. the desire of upward mobility."

The affinity between the two clergy is apparent, as is their mutual respect. Indeed, Ike Miller would not be at the Advocate were it not for the legacy of Paul Washington, a legacy of social activism. The elder priest has returned to the congregation since Miller has come and frequently participates in the worship service. This type of collaboration between a pastor and his/her predecessor is unusual in mainline Protestant churches.

Into Shared Leadership

Despite the similarities, Father Miller also represents a different leadership style. He is not the crusading, lone prophet that Father Washington has been. A man of deep conviction, he nonetheless does not function as the solitary voice of conscience in the city. He has developed a different way of relating to the congregation and leading them into CED activity.

Although by everyone's account, Father Miller was instrumental in getting the congregation involved in P.I.A., he was first attracted by "the opportunity to be involved in social issues which was not clergy-led." Miller has been a strong leader within P.I.A., often one of the speakers at their larger rallies. Yet he is committed to **shared leadership**. Despite the fact that he could easily lead the sixty or so worshippers through the Sunday service alone, he usually shares that responsibility with at least two other priests and one or two members themselves. Major decisions are made jointly by the priest and the vestry, a democratic process in the description of all interviewed. "There are few power-mongers around here," concludes the church treasurer.

Father Miller laughs in describing his leadership as "**not** an administrator...but I think I have the ability to keep a kind of vision before people, and to help people plug into that larger vision in a very nuts-and-bolts way."

Further, involvement in P.I.A. is shared within the congregation. Ten people had gone to the 10-day training, a high percentage for such a small congregation. Miller is pleased by the fact that more people from the congregation show up at the P.I.A. rallies than attend worship, reminiscent of the Washington years. Some of the strongest leaders in the citywide organization come from the Advocate, representing both the "socially dislocated" professionals as well as local community folks. Miss Judith Hansen has also been a strong public presence at P.I.A. rallies, making face-to-face demands from Mayor Ed Rendell, and later sitting with him on a tractor for the ground-breaking for the Nehemiah Housing.

Rev. Miller is concerned that the congregation itself function as prophet and advocate, not just himself. He is never far from the membership in his activism. Building relationships and nurturing individuals are key to shared leadership, he feels. Eventually he believes that their involvement in P.I.A. will be what helps the Advocate survive. Leaders will be trained, responsibilities shared, and this will create the "glue" which brings cohesiveness to this small community and attracts others to it. This perspective is shared by the members who equally value the relationships and sense of community within the Advocate as well as its activism.

While the emphasis on shared leadership differs from the style of Washington --who so often felt that he had to act apart from the congregation -- it is a logical extension of his legacy. Many members regard the "irregular" ordination of women as the Advocate's "finest hour." Washington defied not only the denomination but his own bishop in pressing ahead with the effort to include women in church leadership. Many of the women associated with the Advocate (including Barbara Harris, the first woman elected as Bishop in the Episcopal church) attribute their current leadership to the courageous action of Paul Washington. In fact, this small congregation has produced more women priests than any other Episcopal congregation in the country, according to Harris. (Washington and Gracie, 234) The congregation was necessarily involved in this action of bringing those excluded from leadership into positions of power. That first ordination service looms large in the consciousness of the congregation twenty years later, providing inspiration and legitimation for shared leadership between women and men, clergy and laypeople, Episcopalians and those of other faith traditions.

Into Coalitional Organizing

There is a similar dynamic in the affinity for **coalitional** organizing on the part of the current priest and congregation -- drawing on the Washington legacy in moving in a different direction. In their successful CED efforts, the Advocate has been parochial, working locally and not in collaboration with other congregations or groups. Currently within the congregation, members express pride in what ACDC has accomplished in the name of the Advocate. Christine Washington is still highly respected by members. The agency is described as "an extension of our church" or "a satellite of Advocate," yet it is seen as being largely independent of the church at this point. New homeowners have become involved in the management and development decisions of ACDC but so far, have not been attracted to the church itself. Paul Washington serves on the Board of Directors as "Chaplain," and Rev. Ann Robb Smith is a member. Rev. Miller participates in the groundbreakings, usually by offering the opening prayer. Other than historic and symbolic connections, ACDC and Advocate operate separately. This seems to have resulted not from acrimony, but as a natural outcome of ACDC's organizational growth.

The shift from parochial to coalitional organizing for CED seems like a natural evolution to members, rather than a radical change of difection. "Everything P.I.A. stands for corresponds to what Advocate has been about. P.I.A. is doing what Advocate has done, except on a citywide basis," explained one church member. The priorities of P.I.A.-- housing development for low-income people, the reform of public education, the just distribution of municipal resources and pushing the police to become more "neighborhood friendly" -- are all activities which correspond to activities in the history of the Advocate. While historical circumstances have changed, the confrontational tactics sometimes employed by P.I.A. around these issues are reminiscent of the Washington era.

Vulnerability and Empowerment

While Paul Washington was more likely to find political partners in activist groups outside of the church, the Advocate is now linking with other churches in pursuit of parallel goals. The most likely factor driving coalitional organizing is not ideological, but a recognition of their own institutional vulnerability, a realistic appraisal of the political power needed to bring about significant change, and a desire to amplify their own political capital.

The Advocate would be considered at-risk by most church standards. The membership size is small and many cannot contribute much to the Church revenue. The building is in serious need of repair -- between $2.5-$3/5 million, Miller estimates. In July of 1994, the twentieth anniversary service of the ordination of women had to be relocated because the building was judged to be unsafe. Even with 40% of the operating budget coming from the Diocese, those handling the church finances consider the Advocate to be a miracle. The financial warden said, "We're not supposed to be here!" The treasurer echoed his amazement, "Our cash flow is down to zero every month, but somehow we make it. (The Advocate) reminds me of a perennial garden -- it just keeps coming back, it just keeps doing, helping the down and out even when we have so little."

The staff and congregation is very conscious of the seriousness of their institutional dilemma and have launched more intensive membership and revenue drives. In a sermon the week the sanctuary was closed, Rev. Miller said: “"For us, God has been at work this week. We have received a loud, clear, in-your-face wake-up call.”

Despite an acute awareness of their own vulnerability, all but one who were asked had a positive image of what the Advocate might be like in twenty years. They saw a healthy, viable neighborhood and a strong, lively church. The building would be repaired and renovated. The congregation would be larger, representing even more diversity in the church, with more Latino and gay representation. (Several mentioned that there would be same-sex weddings performed as a matter-of-course.) There would be African music in the worship service regularly (a simmering tension in the church over the years.) The Advocate was seen to “still be on the cutting edge politically.” The surrounding neighborhood would see the development of small businesses, a land bank, better schools, and more economic diversity among residents.

The curious coexistence of an awareness of institutional weakness and visions of a utopic future belie an optimism based on a sense of **empowerment** in the subculture which is the Advocate. Despite the formidable obstacles they face, they believe they have the resources to create such a future. They do not look to those in the ecclessiastical or political power structure to save them. Rather they believe the human and material resources needed will come from within. Further, there is an idenfication of their capacity to meet their goals with divine power. From Rev. Miller’s charge to the congregation:

> As a result of the decision to implement our fund raising campaign, our vestry decided that it would be the group to initiate and make decisions regarding the campaign. The hard choices will be the vestry's with every one's input..We need to organize ourselves. We cannot expect others to give to us unless we give ourselves. This is not just about fund raising -- others giving to us -- it is about stewardship -- our reaching into our own pockets...This campaign needs to be staffed. Neither Rev. Ann or I have the time and -- honestly -- I am not the kind of administrative detail person that is necessary for this kind of undertaking...We also need the Spirit's power at work among us because we need more people. We need

> to know that the spirit has the power to raise up sisters and brothers in Christ in this place. We don't need more people for the sake of more money, we simply need more shoulders to lean on in the work to which we are called by the Spirit...It is daunting work to which the Spirit has awakened us, but that's alright.

This articulation of empowerment resonates with how the congregation sees itself. It is difficult to conclude any single source of this can-do attitude. Certainly Paul Washington attracted idealists to the congregation, and Ike Miller's style of shared leadership contributes to the sense of empowerment for many. Less clear is the extent to which P.I.A. has created such empowerment through 10-day training, public rallies, and organizing successes (the most obvious being Nehemiah Housing).

Those most active in P.I.A. from the Advocate do not describe any "conversion experiences," or radical changes in their consciousness as some from other churches have testified. Their experience in P.I.A. has instead confirmed their own perspectives.

> P.I.A. is very much in keeping with our values (at the Advocate). I can now say I have lived to see the day when churches are cooperating along denominational and racial lines and have been meeting with legislators.
> - Father Paul Washington

> Everything P.I.A. stands for corresponds to who we are at the Advocate. - Active church member/leader

> The training was a good experience for me. There was a lot of comraderie and interaction. It didn't change my mind about anything, but it added to my perspective. - Active church member

Despite the church-specific nature of their recent challenges, members of the Advocate have always understood the threats to which they must respond are larger than those faced by individuals or even congregations. "For us to get ahead we have to move a whole nation," according to Father Washington. The Advocate has always been identified with challenging the status quo and seeking social change, and in the mid-1990's, they continue to work on goals which might seem extravagant given the size of the congregation. Economic restructuring to create employment, racial equality and inclusion and justice for gay and lesbian people were the most frequently cited issues on their agenda.

In their efforts over the last three decades the Advocate has been involved in efforts to transcend the normal boundaries which divide people; hence **shared leadership** and **coalition building** are integral to their own history and culture. The affinity with P.I.A. in style as well as content of collective action has seemed like a natural fit. In fact, in some interviews it was clear that there was a high degree of identification of the two.

> What does P.I.A. mean to the Advocate? Advocate **runs** P.I.A.! And there will be pay-off for us when people see that. - Active member (and P.I.A. leader)

To summarize: while measuring the impact of P.I.A. on the Advocate's current sense of empowerment would be impossible, it can be said that the commitments of the I.A.F. and P.I.A. correspond to those of the Advocate, and in this coalition the congregation finds its own culture enhanced. P.I.A. is not saving the Advocate from powerlessness, or transforming an access-to-power frame of action. Rather, as ""a place to let my light shine," the congregation and clergy at the Advocate find that their light is amplified in this coalition, their own experience of power is expanded.

Sanctuary Memorial Baptist Church

Introduction

Rev. Samuel Shipley has been serving as pastor of Sanctuary Baptist Church since 1975, but never met Father Washington, a clerical contemporary. There is not much distance separating the two churches -- one can drive up Broad St. to Sanctuary on Roosevelt Boulevard in about ten minutes. Yet the worlds of the Episcopal and the Baptist churches were vastly different. Nowadays, it would seem that the only thing the two churches have in common is their strong participation in P.I.A. The same might be said of the pastors, Revs. Miller and Shipley, who are now close associates in the coalition.

The structure of Sanctuary dominates the landscape of its immediate neighborhood, not only because of its impressive architecture, but also because the surrounding houses are sinking, with most being abandoned. For some reason, the building which they bought from the Congregationalists in the 1970's is firmly anchored in the otherwise sinking sands of Logan. Its main problem is that on Sundays it can barely hold this energetic and growing congregation, now estimated at 1200.

The church was acquired from the predominantly Euro-centric mainline Protestant denomination when its congregation had declined to the point where they could no longer support the cost of the building. Rev. Shipley was a teacher who spent his Sundays preaching to the 40-50 people who would gather in a local hall. His small congregation was "on its way up" and the grand structure represented their dreams for the future.

The liberal denomination, perhaps embarassed that the congregation had succumbed to the trend of white flight, offered the new African American Baptist congregation affiliation status. This would be mutually beneficial: the congregation could buy the church at a greatly reduced price and the denomination could maintain a presence in the neighborhood which reflected the changing demographics of the area. And so the move into the stately church also brought about dual affiliation for Sanctuary -- with the United Church of Christ (Congregationalists) as well as the National Baptist Convention, Inc.

The marriage worked for a while, according to the pastor. Congregation members eagerly took advantage of the educational resources available through their new denomination. There were also some requirements with which they had to comply. For example, the pastor was now required to go to seminary. Rev. Shipley earned his M.Div. through a denominational school, an experience which he found quite alienating.

After several years the denomination began to pressure the church to change its worship style to comform to the style of the Congregationalists. "They wanted us to become European in our worship. I asked (the staff person), 'Why should we do what didn't work for you here?'" At that point the pastor and people reaffirmed their identity as African American Baptists and distanced themselves from what they saw as a Euro-centric denomination. "We're still affiliated, but its very, very loose," said Shipley.

The members of Sanctuary expressed belief patterns much more similar to their Baptist counterparts than to those of the Episcopalian congregants. Just as the Advocate was the most theologically liberal congregation in the study, so Sanctuary was among the most conservative. For example, while only about 1/4 at Advocate believed the Bible should be taken literally, 3/4 of the Baptist congregation did. The pattern persisted on beliefs about salvation. Over half of the Sanctuary members thought that only those who were born again would be saved by God; at the Advocate, only a few did (Chart 6.1).

Despite the bifurcated social strata at the Advocate, its membership came from poorer neighborhoods[5], with higher poverty rates[6] and higher concentrations of African Americans[7] than did members of Sanctuary (Charts 3.1, 3.2, 3.4). Members from the Advocate were almost three times more likely to walk to church from the immediate neighborhood (Chart 6.2).

In addition to the members of Sanctuary having more conservative theological views and more widespread middle class status, they also differed from the Advocate in their political perspectives. The Baptist congregation favored the government in its interpretation of what causes poverty, but the Episcopalians primarily blamed the structural problems of racism and lack of jobs (Chart 6.3).

When it comes to resolving the problem of poverty, both looked first to the government, although at Sanctuary support for this position was not as strong. There was not as much belief that the government, which they saw as causing poverty, could reverse itself and become the solution to the problem. These Baptists looked more toward the church and community organizing to help end poverty (Chart 6.4), although they agreed more strongly than the folks at the Advocate that signficant economic change was needed (Chart 6.5).

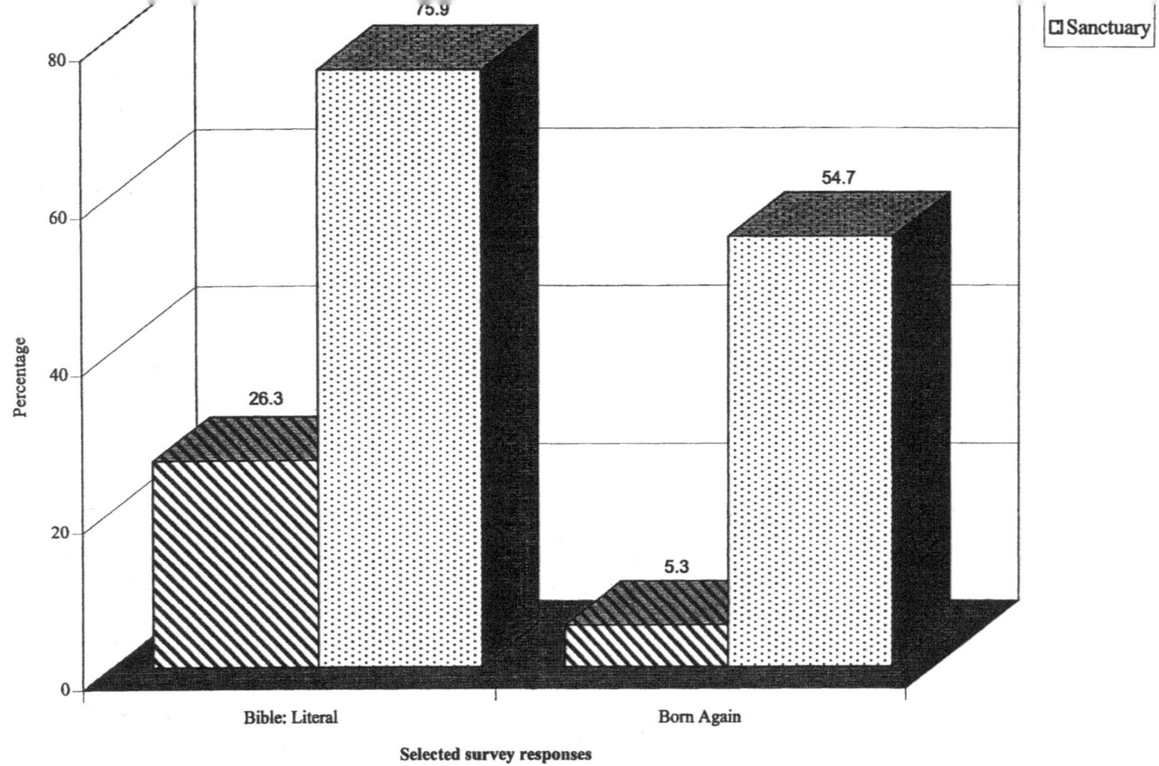

Chart 6.1 Religious Views: Advocate and Sanctuary

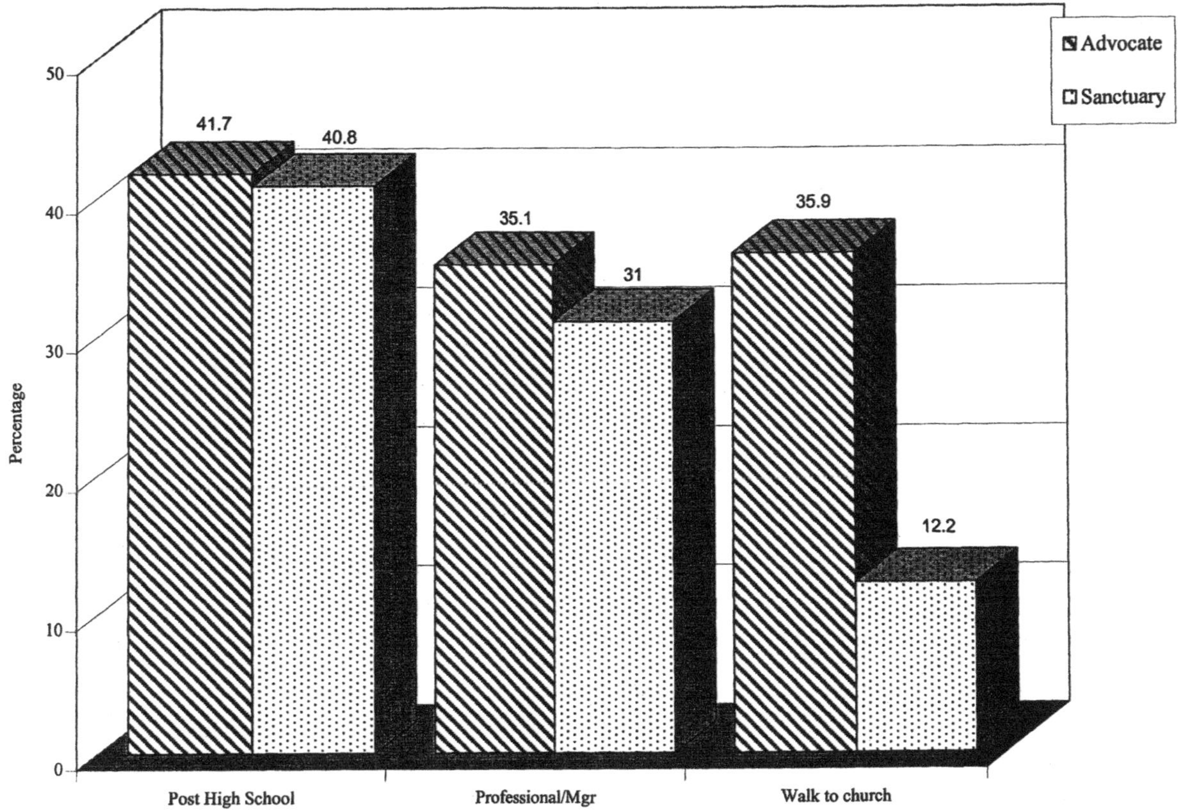

Advocate
Sanctuary
50
40
30
20
10
0
Percentage
41.7
40.8
35.1
31
35.9
12.2
Post High School
Professional/Mgr
Walk to church

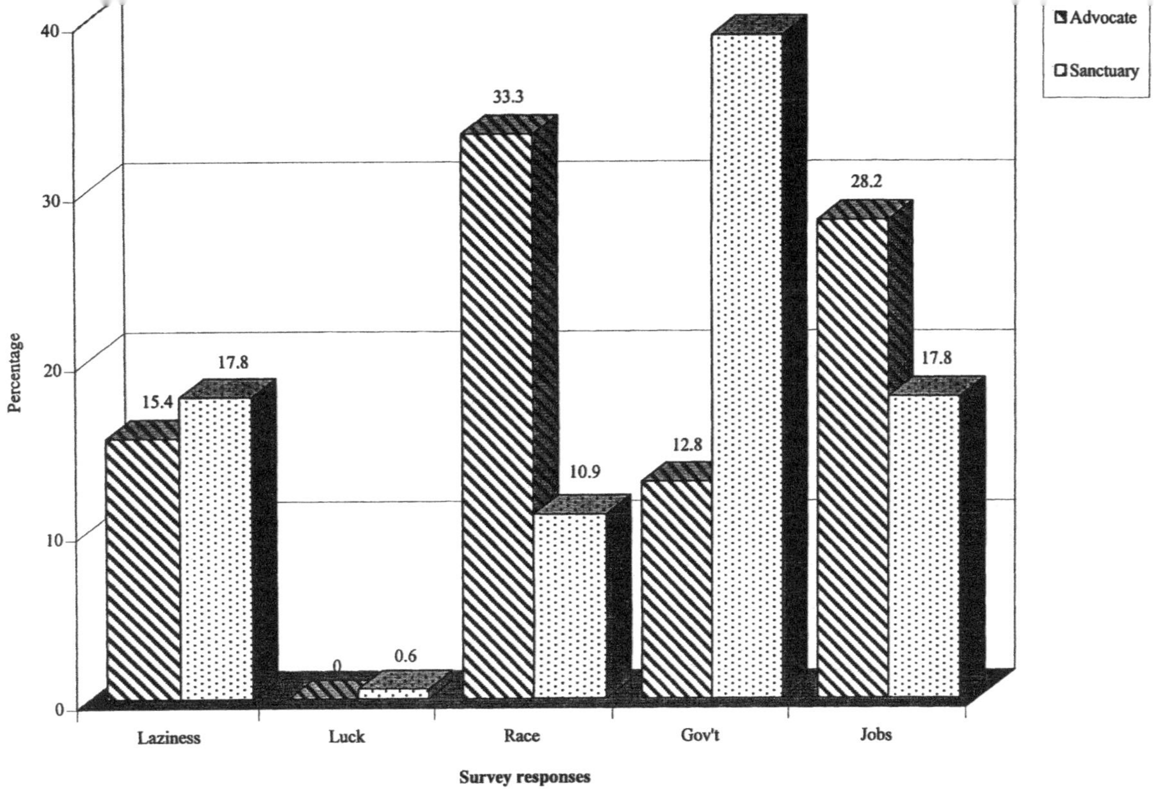

Chart 6.3 Views on Cause of Poverty: Advocate and Sanctuary

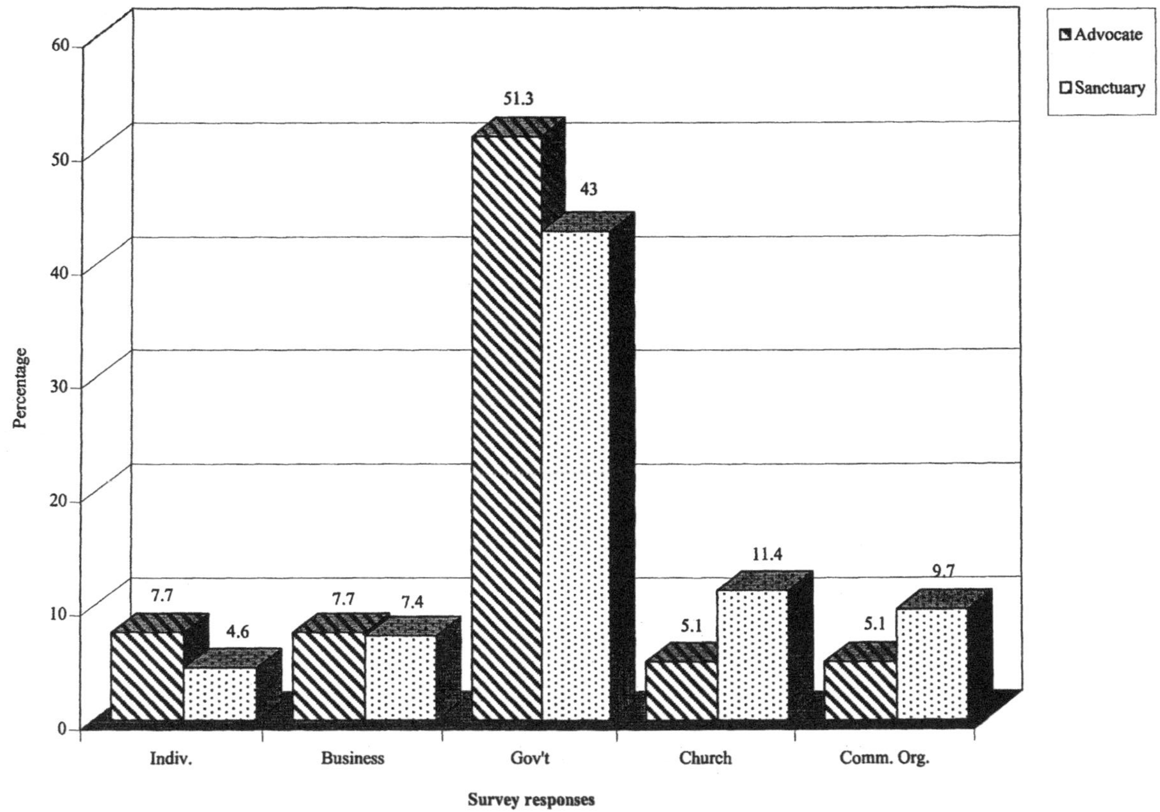
Advocate
Sanctuary
Percentage
60
50
40
30
20
10
0
51.3
43
7.7
4.6
7.7
7.4
5.1
11.4
5.1
9.7
Indiv.
Business
Gov't
Church
Comm. Org.
Survey responses

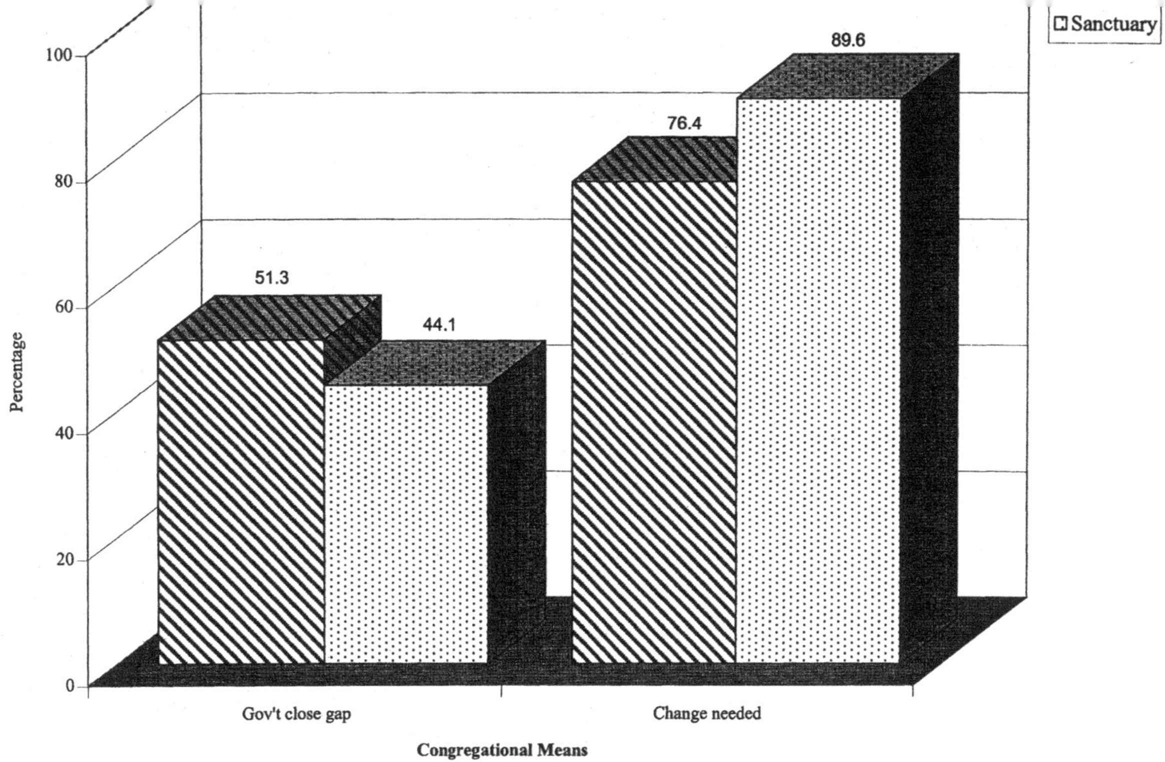

Chart 6.5 Perspectives on Change: Advocate and Sanctuary

When it came to strategies for social change, those at Sanctuary favored spriritual conversion, although not as strongly as did the other churches from the traditional African American denominations. At the Advocate, electoral politics was actually the strategy of choice, although there was also an appreciation for protests, as could be predicted from their past involvements (Chart 6.6).

The Role of the Preacher as Instigator

Sanctuary Baptist does not have a radical past on which to draw; in fact, they do not even have a history which reflects much attention to politics at all. They are a very typical African American Baptist church in many ways in their commitments and perspectives. They have spent the last twenty years developing their congregation and its ministry, all under the leadership of 42-year-old Shipley. He has never served anywhere else and seems to view his position at Sanctuary as a commitment for life. His leadership is strong, yet he resists mythologizing his role.

Rev. Shipley has sought to develop his ministry out of "a theology that's relevant." Consequently the relatively young congregation has an impressive resume of programs, organized around the dual foci chosen by Shipley -- programs for youth and social ministry. There are recreational, educational and religious programs for young people, particularly young men. Like Grace Memorial, they have also "adopted" a junior high school and provide tutoring for students.

The church owns and manages a "guest house" for twenty-one previously homeless residents. They have developed their own drug-rehabilitation program called FANS (Former Addicts Now Saved). These two programs have brought recovering addicts and unemployed people into the church -- two groups largely underrepresented in most religious congregations.

Prior to joining P.I.A. in 1991, Shipley had been trying to break into housing development. He had been meeting with community residents and exploring alternative solutions to Logan's housing crisis. He had been talking about organizing a CDC (Community Development Corporation) based at Sanctuary, a first step in church-based

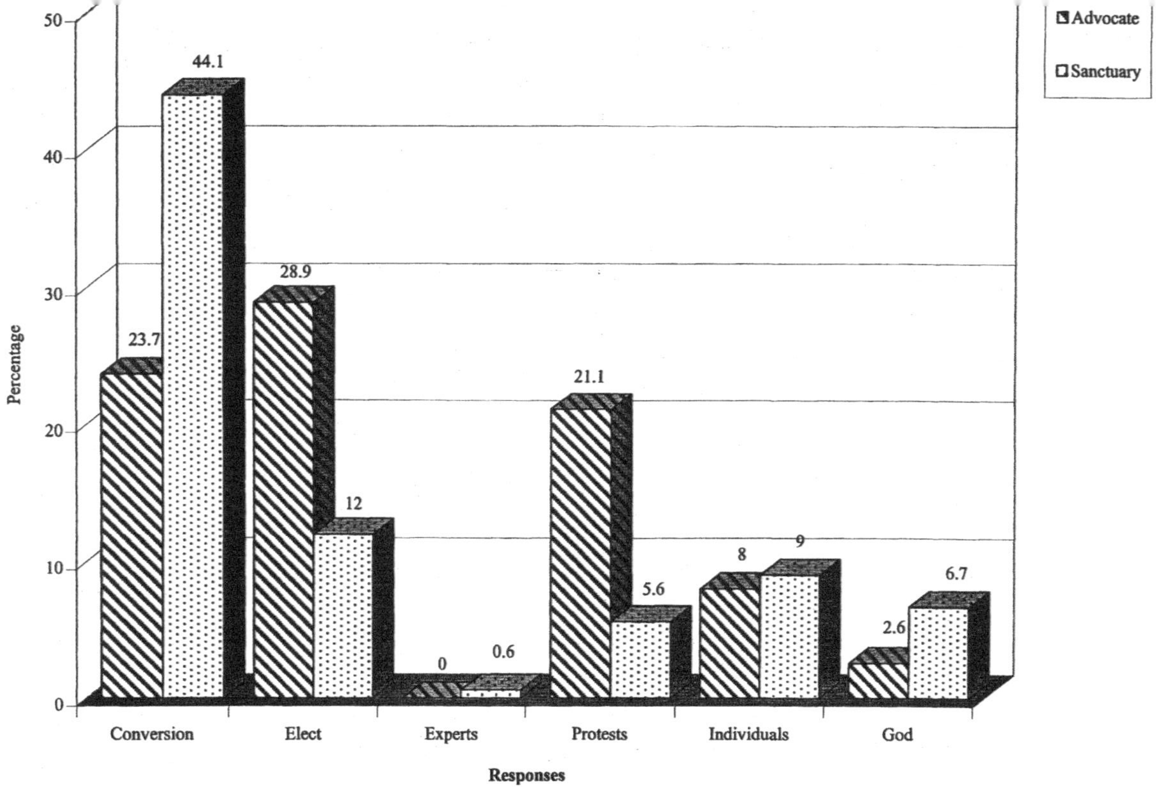

Chart 6.6 Strategies for Social Change: Advocate and Sanctuary

community economic development. During this period he had also joined with six other clergy to develop a parcel of land owned by one of the churches in another part of North Philadelphia. Each church put in $2000 so that additional public monies could be leveraged. Having secured the land, the funding, and the contractor, the small group was now looking for a management agency within the community for the new units for low-income renters. Rev. Shipley admitted that he had joined this effort outside of his own neighborhood so that he could learn from one of the pastors who was more experienced in housing development. In the organizing effort, he clearly deferred to the elder mentor -- a protocol he did not seem to mind in his quest to make the necessary contacts and learn the ropes of CED. Once housing could be built, he felt, economic development will result --stabilized communities become more viable for commercial development, thereby creating jobs and the conditions for improved services. Housing, for him, was the lynchpin.

It was out of his commitment to community development in Logan and his own pragmatism which first led Rev. Shipley into P.I.A. He would not have resonated with the whole philsophy of the Industrial Areas Foundation. For example, he readily admits his tendencies toward clerical, rather than shared, leadership in his pre-P.I.A. days and an assumption that change could result only as clergy could access power. Indeed these marked the approach taken by the seven clergy in developing housing, even though this effort also represented for Shipley a move beyond a strict parochial focus and into a limited coalition.

But underlying the pragmatism and commitment to housing development, there was a pre-existing understanding for Shipley, regularly shared in his preaching, that religion must be relevant. Beliefs must result in action; faith should create a sense of responsibility. 'What is your ministry?," he challenges the congregation consistently in worship. Action born of faith is rewarded: those who are faithful in their responsibilities are publically recognized. For example, those who tithe (give 10% of their income to the church) come forward in the service to deposit their envelopes with great musical fanfare; students making good grades have their report cards read by the pastor in front of the 400-500 people at the 11 a.m.

service. Those who help with the homeless shelter, visit the prison, teach in the church's school and help with the youth programs are recognized in worship and in other ways, including being given prominent leadership positions. Religious faith at Sanctuary Baptist Church is not a private affair: the so-called "comfortable pew" where one can engage their personal faith in worship and then leave, does not exist here. Members are constantly challenged to demonstrate their piety in action. Throughout the discourse at Sanctuary this identification of belief and action is articulated -- to have faith is to take responsibility.

> When I first came here I went through a spiritual transition. I became more convicted about what I was doing. I wasn't interested in just social involvement..but I got involved out of a deeper feeling of responsibility.
> - Young professional woman, church leader

> We can't sit on this corner without getting involved in the neighborhood. Our outreach has to be to body and soul. We need to show we care, that we love. - Male church leader

In this heightened sense of responsibility there coexists a pessimistic view of the world but a highly optimistic perspective on the role the larger church can play in bringing about social change. This perspective was shared by both pastor and members.

> Too many organizations are splintered. But the church brings a social organization with a moral dimension. Its all in the Word (Bible). We have common goals, we can get beyond our differences. - Male church leader

> I'd like to see a lot of change: workfare, raising the minimum wage, available day care for working parents, good housing for everybody, good schools, plenty of jobs, better health care..but that's not the direction the country is going. Things are getting worse. The rich are getting richer. We're moving to the apocolypse...The church is what is holding back anarchy..Everyone needs to have a minimal standard (of living). Those who have should share..They (the rich) hear the word of economic distribution, but do they like it? No! But we're talking about Black survival here. And if the Black church doesn't do it, who will? - Rev. Shipley

The very pragmatic concern for developing the residential community around the church, coupled with their faith/action paradigm and strong view of the church in social change, contributed to a sense of urgency which Rev. Shipley felt in the summer of 1991. Soon after hearing about P.I.A., he attended a meeting for clergy. It was not long after that that Sanctuary Church joined the coalition through Shipley's decision. There was no resistance to the move; the church appropriated its dues of $2000, "no problem."

Sanctuary Church is typical of all of the P.I.A.-related churches in the study on this point. Despite P.I.A.'s commitment to shared leadership and the attraction of some pastors to that, the decision to join the coalition has been made largely, if not solely, by the pastor.

> The pastor's role is important. If he likes something, he gets the congregation involved..How he feels about things is how the congregation feels and acts. - Young woman, church leader

As different as the congregations of Sanctuary and the Advocate are, they felt more strongly than did the other eight churches that "The pastor of a congregation should be involved in politics and issues of public concern" (Chart 6.7). These two pastors and some of their church members continue to be in the leadership core of P.I.A.

Shipley's attraction to P.I.A. was driven by pragmatism. He had learned through his own efforts that working with six others increased his effectiveness. But for the scale of change which was needed (the first step of which was extensive housing redevelopment), more political power was needed. He saw in the new broad-based coalition the possibility for such power. This perception was shared by many in the congregation. One church leader, a retired police officer, said: "I know Philadelphia politics. And P.I.A. is the only way we can be heard. We couldn't do Nehemiah on our own." Another church member with experience in economic development had been in conversation with Rev. Shipley about the possibility of a CDC:

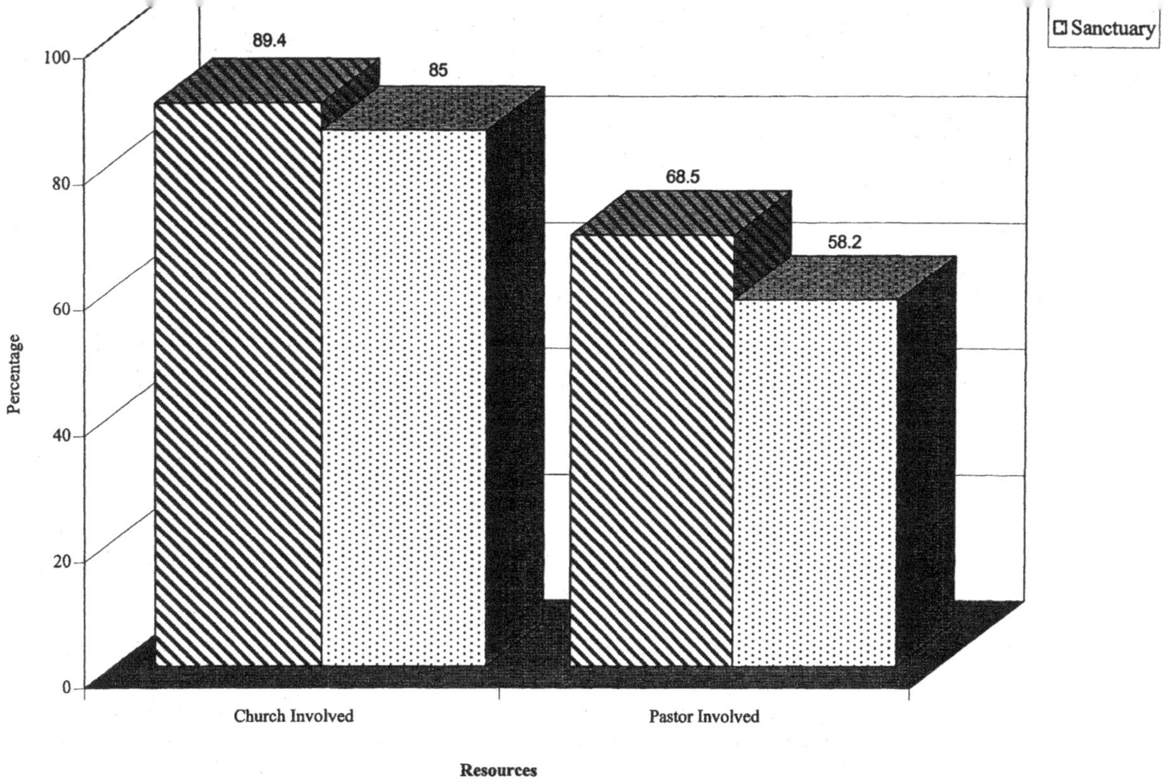

Chart 6.7 Church Involvement in Social Change: Advocate and Sanctuary

He was talking about big projects, but I just wasn't comfortable..Then came P.I.A., which is a much better strategy for us. They were already organized, they already had a plan. The ball still falls in our court. P.I.A. is a resource for us to train our leaders to do local work. We have to take care of those at home (in Logan) first. - Young professional, church leader

Correspondence between Congregation and P.I.A.

Rev. Shipley had a unique strategy for getting his fairly traditional Baptist congregation involved in P.I.A. Rather than trying to sell some of the older more conservative members in the congregation on the idea, he instead developed a new leadership group within the organizational structure. Since identifying and appointing leaders in the congregation was already part of his management style, he tapped nine members in the congregation for P.I.A. involvement and sent them to 10 day training. Most of those chosen were baby-boomers, professionals, and relatively new to the congregation (having joined in the last 2-5 years). They had initially been attracted to the congregation because of its programs and had each become involved in various activities. All spoke of being flattered, if not surprised, that the pastor had chosen them for special leadership in the church so early in their tenure there.

> I can now relate to people of all ages because of Pastor Shipley who kept putting me in different situations...He can see potential in you and delegates responsibility to you. - Young woman in Core Group

> First the Pastor asked me to be a Deacon. 'Why me?', I asked. There are other men who are so much more worthy. But I had grown spiritually. Then he approached me about P.I.A. He thought it was a viable organization and I liked the idea of empowering people. - Male church leader

The Core Group began meeting regularly (Saturdays at 7:30 a.m.) and expanded to include a few who are involved with P.I.A. but have not yet been through the training. They worked not only on projects for the coalition but using their community organizing techniques to bring change within the congregation.

Those in the group found a resonance in the approach taken by the coalition. Like their counterparts at the Advocate, most did not find the training to be as transforming as it was intensifying of their own perspectives:

> It wasn't new material for me. It reminded me of my training in acting at college. But the style was new -- this was much more relational. It felt like the stuff we were already doing (at the church) but we just didn't know what it was. It taught us how to channel our energies; how to focus.
> - Female member, Core Group

> It was the same as my training at IBM. It was very good on leadership development. - Female member, Core Group

There was an attraction among Core Group members to P.I.A.'s commitment to **shared**, rather than clerical leadership. As professionals, the members of the Core Group clearly regard their pastor as a peer. He attends their meetings, but the responsibility for convening rotates among all. At one point, there was a conflict between him and other members of the group on the issue of whether or not to include those who had not been to training. The rest of the group prevailed against what they perceived as elitism on his part. "He doesn't always change his mind so easily. We have to work on him," one reported.

Others described their experience of sharing power with the pastor:

> Pastor Shipley doesn't want to hoard power. Actually, the more he delegates, the more power he has. - Female member, Core Group

> The pastor moves us from awareness to action. He is pivotal, yet he has faith in the Core Group. He has given up much of his power -- he doesn't have the ego thing. - Male member, Core Group

Again, there is the juxtaposition of strong female leadership within a congregation which maintains a patriarchal organizational structure. The irony is more striking here than it is at Grace Baptist because this church, and particularly the Core Group, have so publically and privately embraced the shared leadership approach of community organizing. Still, the women here offer the same explanation as did the women at Grace --their leadership is recognized, affirmed and utilized, if not in the pulpit or the governing board.

Female members take heart from Rev. Shipley's movement to a more democratic style. This was observed not only by members of the Core Group, but it was also how he understood his evolution as a leader. Moving beyond a traditional authoritarian perspective on the pastorate, the members of Sanctuary and particularly the Core Group gravitated to a more functional understanding of his role in the congregation. They saw their pastor less as an authority figure and more as an **interpreter**. He is needed to interpret what is happening in the city and with P.I.A., as well as interpreting the faith in terms which will mobilize for action. Shipley stresses the importance of his interpretive role, and feels that if people really hear what is going on, they will be motivated to work for change.

Members of the Core Group also found an ideological home in the strategic approach of **empowerment** -- even though some are so positioned within the power structure as to facilitate access or at least to discourage grassroots confrontation tactics. One example of this was the member working in city government whose immediate supervisor was the target of a lot of pressure by P.I.A. At work, she sits on a committee which is actively resisting the group's efforts. Not only did she not try to further the organizational goals through her contacts within the system, but she felt that the empowerment approach would be more appropriate and effective.

> I'm not sure if there's a conflict of interest here, but there's not a moral conflict for me. We had to get the mayor's attention..I trust this process. The Arch St. action[8] took boldness, but we were responsible. There's got to be accountability (of the mayor). I'll confront him, but I won't lose my integrity. - Female member, Core Group

The pastor and members of the P.I.A. Core Group were true believers in the effectiveness of working in **coalition**, through **shared leadership** and **empowerment** of the grassroots. Although research in the congregation took place after they become involved in P.I.A., they did not indicate that affiliation had necessitated a great change in consciousness. While there were individual stories of transformation, the congregations of Sanctuary and Church of the Advocate both indicated that, for the most part, P.I.A. resonated with their pre-existing perspectives. It represented a vehicle through which their prior commitments could be more fully articulated, and moved them more clearly in directions in which they were already going.

Tensions between Congregation and P.I.A.

This is not to say that participation in P.I.A. had come about without tension at Sanctuary Church. Certainly the rise of this new leadership group within the congregation has created some resistance on the part of the "old guard." In response, the Core Group implemented a microcosm of P.I.A.'s citywide strategy by organizing a series of individual conversations ("one-on-one's") throughout the congregation. The purpose of these meetings was to give people an opportunity to voice their dissatisfactions and then to find common cause with them on issues. Eventually, they hoped that the few detractors within the congregation would become supportive. There were also indications that the highly visible actions and organizing victories had eroded much of the resistance within the congregation. Within months of affiliating with P.I.A., Sanctuary hosted its second Delegates' Assembly, a rousing ralley with 400 representatives from the 14 member churches. While Sanctuary was not yet visible in the leadership of the organization, the event served to heighten its profile within the coalition and to broaden the support of the congregation.

A second point of tension with P.I.A. was not around their organizing strategies, but the eventual goal of such efforts. Rev. Shipley maintained a utopic vision of an egalitarian society, a scenario which would necessitate fundamental social change which he believed could come about through both divine and political power. While some of his social views were quite conservative ("There is no such thing as 'alternative lifestyles.'"), politically he could be described as a democratic socialist. Rev. Shipley did not conceal his critique of the economic, political and institutional systems, nor did his views elicit a disagreeable response. It is important to note that Sanctuary had the highest proportion of respondents (89.6%) who agreed to some degree with the statement, "In order to bring poverty to an end there will have to be changes in our economic system."[9]

The congregation brought this widespread critique of the economic system to their involvement with P.I.A. There were some who saw in P.I.A. affiliation the hope for systemic change:

> P.I.A. is in the toddler stage, but its going to have a huge effect..We're demanding change in City Hall. Its not going to be 'business as usual.' We need a whole new political system that doesn't depend on corruption and patronage, but provides housing and employment, especially for our youth. - Male Core Group member

But for most in the congregation, and for some Core Group members, there was a reluctance to seek systemic change. A retired police officer, for example, was uncomfortable with P.I.A.'s struggle with the Police Commissioner to implement a program of community policing because he was not convinced the system needed changing.

> I'm working with the Education Group (in P.I.A.) now. I was soured in the community policing effort. After being on the beat for 23 years, I saw a lot that was right. - Male Core Group member

His was a more positive view of the system, or at least part of the system. For others, a certain reticence to work for systemic change was fueled by an ingrained pessimism about the system. If things have become so bad in our government, economy and culture, it was reasoned, is it realistic to expect change? Just getting housing built was change enough. Even one who considered himself radical limited his expectations of what was, finally, possible.

> I felt this rage at the way things were getting so much worse (for African Americans)..I had my one-on-one with the Pastor. I told him about my anger and he told me how to cool off with Jesus Christ. He showed me how to focus my energy in constructive ways..At 10-day-training I got more insight into how to build bridges instead of building walls...We need to be realistic about what can be done. - Male Core Group member

He communicated that his anger around racism had been channeled into the pragmatic goals of community development, but it had not been eradicated.

There were boundaries to the idealism of this congregation. Unlike rhetoric at the Advocate, at Sanctuary they spoke more of "responsibility" than they did of "justice," more pragmatically of what could be done rather than what should be done. And so, ambiguity around the issue of broad social change was left unresolved.

For Pastor Shipley, the Core Group and many members at Sanctuary Church, involvement with P.I.A. became an extension of how they could, as individuals and a corporate body, be faithful. P.I.A. became for Sanctuary Baptist Church not only a vehicle for action, but an extension of their religious commitment. It corresponded with their perspectives and world view, but not without tensions.

Because of this identification of piety and action they were not always comfortable with the compromises that working with a coalition meant. Because the I.A.F. is not a religious organization but is made up largely by congregations at the local level, there was a suspicion among some that "it is using the church." One member of the Core Group questioned some of the tactics he saw during his training being used in another city:

> Sometimes their values are different from ours...I thought they were lying to the mayor, conning him to do what they wanted. If they (I.A.F.) want to use devious means, we'll have to draw the line and do things right. - Male Core Group member

While their religious dedication led them to critique some organizing tactics, it also justified others -- including confrontation. Even though most people at Sanctuary did not have histories of political activism, their fusion of faith and action fueled a "righteous rage" which could result in symbolic action and civil disobedience. The same man who was critical of what he saw as manipulative tactics had "no problem" with the recent P.I.A. action in publically confronting the mayor: "He lied to us!" he said.

For Sanctuary Baptist Church, P.I.A. came along at the right time with the right approach. It has enabled the church to extend its effectiveness outside the church, and deepen its commitment to action within. One member summed up the relationship this way: "P.I.A. strengthens our agenda." It is perceived as "a vehicle which can take the congregation where it wants to go" -- but only because Rev. Samuel Shipley had set the direction and chosen the vehicle.

---

[1] This recurring metaphor for Father Washington is a reference to W.E.B. DuBois' concept of the "double consciousness" developed by African Americans existing within an oppressive dominant culture, articulated in his book, The Souls of Black Folk.

[2] This is a reference to Jesus' words as recorded in the Bible meaning that he had a responsibility to those outside of his "fold," the Jewish community.

[3] 41.7%; the sample mean was 48.6%

[4] 25%; the sample mean was 7.1%

[5] Sanctuary, $26,294; Advocate, $18, 052

[6] Sanctuary, 18.2%; Advocate, 32.7%

[7] Sanctuary, 61.7% Black in members' tracts; Advocate, 75.5%

[8] In July, 1993, three hundred P.I.A. members crowded into a meeting room at Arch St. Methodist Church, across from City Hall, demanding to talk to Mayor Ed Rendell who had promised that he would give them an answer that day about the land acquisition for Nehemiah Housing. A delegation kept going to his office while the larger group sang and made speeches next door. He finally met with the group and stated that the status of the land was not yet clear.

[9] The mean for the sample was 83.2%

Chapter 7

Conclusions

The question being pursued in this study has been quite focused: Why have some African American churches in North Philadelphia affiliated with the coalition P.I.A. and others have not? This research also engages larger issues of the dynamics of religion and social change. What are the conditions in which African American churches will utilize the strategy of community organizing to improve the quality of life in their city and neighborhoods -- a strategy which not only works the system, but seeks to change it, when that is deemed to be necessary?

As stated in Chapter 2, one cannot generalize beyond the particular context of this sample. Still, the data represented from the ten churches have theoretical implications for interpretations of the relationship which exists between communities of faith and social change. Predictions about religious involvement in change movements cannot be easily reduced to one or two variables. This study shows that the relationship is a complex and dynamic one.

The short answer to my research question is simply, "Whether or not a congregation participates in community organizing is up to the pastor." Yet the data resist any reductionist explanation. How and why these pastors have come to their choice of direction requires that we bring the culture back into the analysis, a conclusion consistent with current scholarship among scholars of social movements:

> ..it makes little sense to deny the importance of culture, ideology, symbols, media framing, collective identities, and meaning construction in the origins and outcomes of collective action. Indeed, the evolving consensus is that theoretical and empirical work on the cultural-social psychological aspect of collective action must lie at the center of the intellectual agenda if a comprehensive explanation of collective action is to be realized. (Morris and Mueller, 1987, p.369)

The decision about strategy clearly is not driven by characteristics of the congregation, although the congregation cannot be left out of the equation. There were distinctions which emerged between the two groups of clergy, but their decisions were not entirely individual. These pastors functioned not in isolation but in relationship to their congregations as their interpretation of what would be the best course of action developed. The interest of the congregation is socially constructed in the context of the pastor-people relationship. Neither the self-interest of the pastor nor the interests of the congregation can be extricated like threads from what is, in reality, a social knot.

The Congregational Factors

From the survey results reported in Chapter 3, it is clear that important differences exist among the congregations in their beliefs and demographics and that there were patterns to the diversity. For example, those in traditional African American denominations were consistently more conservative theologically and had lower levels of education than those in the predominantly Euro-centric "mainline" Protestant groups. However, patterns of class and belief could not, finally, be associated with the strategies the churches employed in the public aspects of their ministries, specifically, whether they joined P.I.A.

Throughout the quantitative data relationships are demonstrated between religious beliefs, social class (education, occupation, income), and denominational affiliation.

It had been hypothesized in Chapter 3 that theological beliefs and social class would impact not only denominational affiliation but the formation of political opinion which would express the class interests represented. This, in turn, would determine whether a congregation would embrace a strategy which could collectively mobilize their individual class interests (Figure 3.1). More specifically, I had fully expected to find that the more middle class congregations would be attracted to the traditional approach to CED which does not challenge the status quo. Those congregations with greater proportions of members with lower socio-economic status were expected to have more liberal political views which they would perceive as being better represented by P.I.A.

However no clear trends emerged which would support such a Weberian interpretation. There were no discernible relationships leading from socio-economic status to conservative (or liberal) theology to conservative (or progressive) politics to affiliation with P.I.A. Class cohorts were conservative on some questions and more liberal on others when it came to faith and politics, as were members of P.I.A. churches.

P.I.A. affiliation was slightly related to the variables of individual characteristics and perspectives. When there was a significant relationship it was often counter-intuitive. For example, members of P.I.A. churches believed less in organized protests and more in spiritual conversion as strategies for social change. Obviously community organizing is not a natural inclination for them. Another finding was equally curious. In terms of education and occupation, members of P.I.A. churches were indistinguishable from the general sample. Yet a significantly higher proportion came from residential tracts with income levels above the mean for the city[1]. If this indicates that personal incomes are high, why would they want to participate in an organization which might be antagonistic to the system which rewards them? Again, Weberian assumptions are challenged.

In analyzing the data by congregations, no significant differences existed on any of the questions or in the demographic data. There was a lot of variation among the P.I.A. and the non-P.I.A. churches. Yet when the sample means of the two groups were compared, even the few significant differences in the individual data disappeared.

In reviewing the data further, other interpretive schemes may be eliminated. For example, earlier explanatory frameworks of mass movements would have looked at the level of grievance articulated by the congregations. That is, when the proverbial "boiling point" is reached, a group decides to take action. However, it is clear that in this study there was a level of dissatisfaction shared throughout the sample regardless of the CED strategy being utilized. The question on the survey which demonstrated the highest level of agreement (83.2%) related to the need for major change in the economic system in order to end poverty. As with so many of the questions, denomination and socio-economic class made a significant difference in the responses, but not P.I.A. affiliation. Non-affiliates were just as likely to think that change was needed.

This was interesting in light of the observations made in the ethnographic research, in which dissatisfaction with the system was more often verbalized by those within the P.I.A. churches. The verbalization might have been encouraged by a heightened sense of viability for change (to be discussed later). Nonetheless, it is important to keep in mind that an almost equal level of longing for change existed even among non-P.I.A. church folk, and more strongly among those in traditional African American denominations and representing a lower socio-economic stratum.

Just as the data indicated that P.I.A. did not represent an opportunity to mobilize individual class interests, it can also be said that the coalition does not attract more politically disenfranchised African American church members. The coalition is diverse in its membership, bringing together college graduates and high school drop-outs, fundamentalists and liberals, political conservatives and progressives. This parallels the socio-economic and ideological diversity of the whole sample and makes it resistant to demographic or ideological distinctiveness.

While differences can be seen by denomination and congregation, in general the African American church is far less stratified than Anglo churches and can accommodate much more diversity (Lincoln and Mamiya, 1991). The shared legacy of slavery and racism provides a "glue" which can transcend differences of class and belief. Similarly, P.I.A. cultivates an awareness of shared experience not based on race but as citizens of a common city.

It is interesting that P.I.A. affiliates were not distinct from individuals in non-P.I.A. churches in their views about the Bible, but they were more likely to believe to a significant degree that "only those who are born again will be saved by God." A possible explanation is that both this theological perspective and P.I.A. affiliation are based on a clear delineation between "who's in and who's out." This is not to suggest a causal relationship between a point of faith and coalition affiliation, but a social-psychological resonance. However, when comparing the congregational means, the two groups did not show significant difference on the question of salvation.

In summary, the analysis of the responses to the questionnaires does not demonstrate any of the expected relationships between the variables. Whether looking at the data individually or as congregations, it is clear that socio-economic class (and the presumed interests thereof), political beliefs and religious ideology are not the determinative factors for these churches as they construct their CED strategies. This challenges the conclusions of other studies which have found that conservative theological beliefs, as well as higher social class status, have a conservative influence on political perspectives and behaviors (Baer and Singer, 1992; Roof and McKinney, 1987; Marx, 1967; Pope, 1942; Himmelstein, 1986; Tamney, 1991; Beatty and Walter, 1988; Buell and Sigelman, 1985; Guth and Green, 1988; Kellstedt, 1988; Shupe and Stacey, 1983; Smidt, 1988). However, much of the research which has contributed to dominant theories within the sociology of religion has been conducted among non-African American populations. In this study, the theoretical approaches which focus on the characteristics of class and belief as their basis clearly do not have explanatory power: protest exists where accommodationism might be predicted and moderation exists where more radical action might be expected. Conservative Christians and those of higher socio-economic status are just as likely to be mobilized through CBCO in this research.

The Pastors Revisited

If the religious beliefs, political perspectives, and class interests of the congregations did not drive the strategies for CED, what did? Attention is easily drawn to the pastors, all of whom frankly disclosed the fact that it had been their decision whether the congregation should join with P.I.A. or not. What led clergy who were facing the same realities of life in North Philadelphia at the same moment in time into very different strategic approaches?

The clergy in both groups represented a wide theological range, from those who could be described as fundamentalist to liberal. Further, those who had chosen to join the coalition as well as those who had declined represented a spectrum of activism in their personal histories and current activities. While these two aspects of experience -- religious beliefs and political involvement -- undoubtedly were part of their decision about strategy, there was no clear pattern from which behavioral predictions could be drawn. For example, it cannot be said that activist pastors are more drawn to broad-based community organizing, or that Pentecostals are not. Some with no political background were attracted as a way of getting involved; inversely some with activist backgrounds eschewed the coalition. Further, those with conservative theologies interpreted both their attraction to or rejection of P.I.A. in terms of faith.

The recognizable patterns of difference which did emerge were in two areas: consciousness (through the "action frames") and social location.

Clearly, as demonstrated in Chapters 4, 5 and 6, the two groups represented contrasting action frames: P.I.A. clergy described their perspectives on effective organizing in terms of shared leadership, coalitional organizing, grass roots empowerment, and systemic change. The non-P.I.A. clergy were, by and large, the reverse image. They articulated their approach to CED predominantly in the opposite terms -- of clerical leadership, parochial organizing, accessing power structures and not challenging the institutions and systems which distribute resources.

The P.I.A. clergy indicated that the training they had received through the coalition had not reformed their consciousness as much as it had confirmed their own perspectives and given them the context in which to develop. The sources of their own consciousness, as represented by the action frames, were as diverse as their individual biographies. Yet in this small sample some trends did emerge in their personal narratives of how and why they found either resonance or dissonance in CBCO.

The most striking differences existed in their own social location. The non-P.I.A. clergy had, for the most part, lived, learned and moved almost exclusively in the African American community. On the other hand, the clergy who had affiliated with P.I.A. had been educated in, and now resided in, more racially integrated contexts. (Certainly this pattern should be tested in other contexts.) Whether at a conscious level or not, such exposure might be related to the P.I.A. pastors' openness to joining a multi-racial coalition.

For some theorists, a comfort level with racially integrated religious organizations would signify accommodationism, an expression of racial compromise and political co-optation. (Marx, 1967) But the philosophy of the parent group, I.A.F., is decidedly anti-accommodationist, seeing its very reason for being as training and empowering people to challenge the system. At the local level, P.I.A. does not focus on overtly racial issues, yet it does, through an integrated coalition, provide an opportunity for more radical forms of activism on issues of common concern to all racial groups in the city.

The non-P.I.A. clergy maintained a stronger identification with the African American community. As well as residing in census tracts with significantly higher proportions of African Americans, there were also signifiers of higher status attainment within that community. When compared to their P.I.A.-affiliated colleagues, the non-P.I.A. clergy were older, and had longer tenures in churches with larger memberships. Further, they also had higher levels of education, including both earned and honorary doctorates. All of the non-P.I.A. clergy had earned their undergraduate degrees from Black colleges.

It was because of their cultural status within the African American community that they could cultivate contacts and access the power structure as representatives of the community. While no one described himself as being co-opted by dominant institutions within the public and private sectors, interviews with the non-P.I.A. clergy included stories of rewards received (material and social) from power structures. Further, they described the value and good behavior of the institutions which held power over their communities. They were unwilling to challenge these systems, and indeed felt that their relationships with those in power would be a more effective means of keeping them in line.

In summary, the political capital held by these pastors was a result of their primary identification with, and status within, the African American community of North Philadelphia. Indeed it had paid off in terms of getting resources for their CED projects -- they had a power base from which they could realistically negotiate.

On the other hand, the P.I.A. clergy were willing to take greater risks in confronting the power structure -- they had far less political capital to lose. And, coming from a somewhat lower cultural status, they had more to gain. Younger and leaner in the accouterments of status, they were the "up and coming" clergy in a city where there is a social hierarchy among African American clergy.

As all of the pastors discussed their decision whether or not to join the coalition, it was always in pragmatic terms: Is P.I.A. going to indeed help us do what we need to do? Is it going to finally further our interest? The non-P.I.A. clergy expressed a concern that affiliation with the broad-based coalition might dilute the primary focus of the church on its immediate neighborhood. Given the experience and cultural identification of these clergy with the African American community, would affiliation also mean a betrayal of racial politics and, at the same time, a loss of status for the pastor? Apart from analyzing the data through an intensely psychological lens, these meanings cannot be known. However, it is apparent that the decisions are complex. Such intangibles as experience, cultural status, world view, the location of threat, and one's web of loyalties are all brought into the process of deciding on a strategy for community development.

Based on the data from the interviews and later ethnographies, it did not seem that personal self-interest on the part of the pastors was driving the decision. Certainly these pastors had healthy egos, and there were ego rewards (social recognition) through both strategies of CED. But pursuit of either course did not guarantee that this self-interest would be realized; in fact, P.I.A. affiliation meant that power and glory would be shared. Further, personal involvement in CED through a coalition or more localized efforts represents a significant risk to self-interest.

The pastors in the study were attracted to the goals of CED and identified with the values which the two strategies represented. Pastors in both groups expressed the same refrain: "If the Black church won't do it, who will?" Through different means they all sought self-determination and improvement in the quality of life for disenfranchised people in Philadelphia.

Rather than self-aggrandizement, the decision about strategy represented collective interests. The good being sought is a collective good -- housing, jobs, education/training, and other resources for those who need them. The collective interest of the congregation was also considered. What course of action made sense for this congregation and its future? Moving into a capital and neighborhood development campaign, Rev. Johnson did not want to take his congregation's focused commitment off their immediate neighborhood. Rev. Miller, on the other hand, felt that the future survival of his congregation depended on their activism in the coalition.

The pastors made the decision whether or not to affiliate with P.I.A., to be sure. The decision was pragmatic, based on how they understood their congregation, the community, and themselves. It was a decision to which they brought their experience, values, loyalties, personalities and relationships. It was a decision wrapped in their understanding of collective interests and how they could best be served. It was a decision which made sense in the context of the sub-culture of the congregation.

The Pastor in Community

It was not in isolation, but in the pastors' embeddedness in their congregations that the construction of the collective interest took place which led to the decision about strategies. The relationship is a dynamic one, as both the congregation and its leader bring their own history, values, and identity to the mix. To greater or lesser degrees, they shape and are shaped by one another.

Leadership

The first area this is most apparent in is the construction of the pastor's leadership itself, and how his power and authority are understood and exercised. All the clergy in the four ethnographic studies were clearly strong leaders. The two Baptist and the Presbyterian pastors fall within Weber's description of the charismatic leader.

> ..he is set apart from ordinary men and treated as endowed with specifically exceptional powers or qualities..[which] are not accessible to the ordinary person (Weber, 1947, pp. 358, 359).

The two non-P.I.A. clergy, Revs. Johnson and Smith, acted as Hero, Representative, and Patriarch of the their congregations. These expressions of charismatic leadership continued to be reinforced rather than challenged or changed within the congregational dynamic. The P.I.A. clergy and congregations described the pastoral role in more relational, process-oriented terms. They were seen as Interpreter, Instigator, Facilitator. Rev. Shipley was in transition between a more classic charismatic leadership role to one in which power was shared. As the parameters of his interest expanded beyond the immediate neighborhood, so too did he come to believe that a broader base of leadership was needed. He was looking for his "70 elders," as had Moses; however, he still clearly identified himself with the great patriarch.

The construction of the different leadership modes preceded the decision about P.I.A. However, the coalition was more compatible with those clergy and congregations that were not completely invested in maintaining charismatic leadership. Its commitment to shared leadership does not accommodate charismatic leadership within the organization. The organization also strives to de-mythologize such individual leadership as a critical step in bringing more people into collective leadership. In so doing, it was correctly perceived to be a threat to charismatic leadership by some African American clergy who had opted out of the coalition.

Worldview

A second area in which the correspondence between the congregations and their clergy impacted on their strategic approaches to CED was in what might be called world view. This had a stronger influence than did ideology. While the religious beliefs were deeply held convictions, they did not emerge as the source of actions as much as they served to interpret and justify social action. The world view, on the other hand, operated on an even more basic level, bringing coherence to the congregations in the process of understanding their place in the world which prompted how they would engage their context in action.

The four congregations described in Chapters 5 and 6 displayed strikingly different world views. In sermons, prayers, and interviews Grace Baptist and Knox Presbyterian communicated what defined their sense of threat -- those forces which need to be resisted and defeated. These were most often interpreted in personalistic, spiritual terms. Temptations, doubts, immoral and unproductive behaviors all threatened to undermine their attempt to live lives of faith. There was also a sense of threat to the survival of their churches, particularly as related to the future of their neighborhoods: as goes the neighborhood, so goes the church. These dual threats, to their person and to their church, contributed to a social cohesion which was not antagonistic to the dominant culture and its systems. Their battles were against the Devil, at a personal level, and the deterioration of their neighborhoods.

As can be expected, there was a salient individualistic orientation in these two churches, which came out in the interviews, as even collective action was interpreted and justified through personal experience. (For example, recall the woman at Grace Memorial Baptist who had finally been persuaded to support the elder housing development when she realized that she might need to use it when she became old.) Individualism was also evident in the survey results. Grace Memorial Baptist ranked first among all ten churches in the sample in its proportion of members who blamed individual laziness for poverty[2] and looked to the individual to take the initiative in reversing poverty[3]. Knox was also above the mean on this latter question.[4]

Consistent with these dynamics, and notwithstanding programs which served the neighborhood, the primary orientation of the two non-P.I.A. churches -- in their perspectives and their programs -- was toward their membership. Knox's emphasis on Afro-centrism served to develop a sense of racial identity which cultivated pride and power among individuals and the congregation as a whole, but little attempt was made to connect it with political issues, much less action. The thrust of the ministry of Grace was to strengthen individuals in their lives, and to stabilize the economic and social well-being of their parochial area, and in so doing, to improve the future prospects of the church.

On the other hand, the two P.I.A.-affiliated churches exhibited more of an external orientation. This was not without tension in either congregation. At the Advocate, there had even been a power struggle between those who represented the membership and external orientations, a process which resulted in a recommitment to an other-oriented ministry. The tension continues at Sanctuary Baptist Church where the older more traditional Baptists desire a member-oriented ministry despite the external orientation which has become more dominant.

At these two P.I.A. churches members and clergy were more likely to discuss their sense of threat in political, systemic and cultural terms. Often using crusade language, they described themselves as warrior churches, engaged in battles with City Hall, their own denominations, and the broader cultural forces which threaten not only individuals but neighborhoods, cities, and groups of disenfranchised people.

Seeking Change

These elements of subcultural mileau -- leadership, threat, worldview and internal/external orientation -- all contributed to what kinds of change were sought, how, and why.

The congregations reflected the difference in the scope of change expressed by the clergy. The P.I.A. churches, sensing threat as originating in the larger systems, expanded their analysis into visions of what needed to be changed. If the problem in finding available, affordable housing was lodged in the city's unwillingness to invest in the neighborhood, then the solution was not in helping individuals to find housing, or even to provide it, but to force change within the government itself. In contrast, the non-P.I.A. churches were led out of their own consciousness, to direct their energies to changing the individual (through social ministries) and the resources available to them (by providing housing or jobs). The difference in the two strategies is not as subtle as it may appear on the surface; the non-P.I.A. churches did not direct efforts toward changing the system. Either they did not see it as ultimately problematic or they did not see that changing it was a viable option. I would suggest that both explanations could be true, and to varying degrees, depending on the church.

The individualistic, parochial, and membership orientation of the non-P.I.A. churches created a different understanding of the power that was needed for change. In these churches, power would come from within (individual faith) and from the congregation itself. Hence, the sources of power for change were from the prayers answered, and the dollars raised from the congregations, as well as the connections the pastor had developed. However, for P.I.A. churches with a more external orientation and systemic analysis of threat, power was needed from outside themselves. In order to change the city, a broader base of players was needed, and so linkages with other congregations were sought through P.I.A. as a way of garnering power and increasing the possibility for change.

As with the clergy, a history of activism was no predictor of affiliation with P.I.A. Recall that two churches with strong activist pasts -- Knox and the Advocate -- had gone in different directions in their participation in the coalition. The same could be said of churches with no history of political activism.

The congregations also paralleled the clergy in their understanding of what could be gained through P.I.A. affiliation. Secure in their size and public identity, neither Grace nor Knox expressed a widespread need to join with P.I.A. or to collaborate in a substantial way with other churches[5]. They had the resources within themselves to bring about the changes which they sought. They also had critical connections to those in the power structure on whom they could call.

However, the congregations as well as the clergy at the Advocate and Sanctuary Baptist Church were opportunistic in their interpretation of working in coalition. They saw how much they had to gain as congregations, beyond the possibility of systemic change. They saw themselves as outside of the power structure, not having "strings to pull." Leadership training, increased energy and relevance, a heightened public profile --these were considered to be attractive outcomes for an older church sensing its institutional vulnerability (the Advocate) as well as a young, growing, up-and-coming church (Sanctuary).

As a way to further clarify this conclusion -- that the construction of a strategy for CED is forged by the pastor in the cultural context of the congregation -- it is instructive to return to the two anomalous congregations, one of which is uncomfortably in and the other uncomfortably out of P.I.A.

The best explanation for why Corinthian Baptist Church joined the coalition is that they have had and continue to have a strong external orientation. They have been aggressive in developing programs which serve the neighborhood, particularly in the area of CED. They interpret threat at both an individual/spiritual level as well as being systemically-based. However, the pastor (as was described in Chapter 4) is uncomfortable with shared leadership and the confrontational tactics of P.I.A. -- he wants to protect the connections which have enabled him to successfully access the power structure. While he is highly articulate in his analysis of the systemic roots of problems experienced at a local level, he is just not sure that social change is possible, or even desirable. Finally, there is not a strong compulsion to link with others. The pastor and people of this large, active and well-established church are not convinced that there is much they can gain from P.I.A. The pastor maintains a strong belief in their ability to generate whatever resources might be needed to accomplish their goals from the congregation itself. They pay their dues and participate minimally in the organization.

St. John's Baptist Church was not in P.I.A. at the time the research was done. They had a long history of strong pastoral leadership and successful CED projects. The pastors had been very active politically and had been able to access the power structure and direct resources to their neighborhood. However, things were changing within the congregation. The pastor's health problems had necessitated that leadership be shared within the congregation. In addition, the church sat across from an empty lot for which they had dreams of housing development. However, in a new political climate in which African American clergy did not have the clout that they once had, St. John's Baptist Church had not gotten very far in this development process. Finding the power structure unresponsive (city and federal agencies, specifically), the pastor and congregation were becoming disillusioned with the access-to-power strategy and were talking about the need to accumulate more political power. They had chosen not to affiliate with P.I.A. at first, but were beginning to reconsider it as circumstances forced a shift in their consciousness.

P.I.A. and the Churches

Since the issue of what is to be gained is so critical in the decision about affiliating with a broad-based community organization, it is important to consider just what P.I.A. membership does for its member congregations.

It was clear in the ethnographic research with the P.I.A.-related congregations that there were few testimonies of radical transformations of either individual or corporate consciousness. Even the intensive 10-day training process did not, according to participants, bring new insights and perspectives as much as it reinforced those which pre-existed. As P.I.A. has developed its own collective identity, it has served to attract congregations with compatible consciousness, as has been argued, and moreover has served to "enlarge the identities" of the participants (at both an individual and congregational level).[6]

Those coming into the coalition from African American churches find that their congregational culture can certainly be challenged, as around the issue of inclusion of a synagogue. But more often congregations found that their cultural identity enhanced through participation. The coalition addressed the same issues which they cared about --the quality of life for people in their communities. In meetings and large assemblies the symbols which were part of their tradition were incorporated -- prayers, songs, enthusiastic preaching. The religious overtones of P.I.A. activities were church-friendly for these African American congregations; they did not have to cease being themselves in order to participate.

While P.I.A. is not cause-oriented, and therefore does not focus its efforts on issues which are exclusively defined in racial terms, the content as well as the format of their organizing efforts resonate strongly with the concerns of African Americans living in the city. The agenda of P.I.A. -- the safety of neighborhoods, the availability of affordable housing, the allocation of public moneys and the quality of education -- represent the complex relationship of class and race interests. No one interviewed communicated a sense of betrayal of Black interests by working on these city-wide issues. (That is not to say, of course, that the feeling did not exist; just that it was not evident in this study.) Certainly identification with the coalition was aided by the fact that the "lead organizer," a paid staff person from the I.A.F., was an African American man.

Politically, as well as culturally, the interests and identity of the P.I.A. churches were enlarged by participation in the larger coalition. The public profile of the churches and their clergy was heightened, as those who were known only to a limited population gained visibility to those outside their denominations and neighborhoods. Their sphere of interest also expanded enabling those from North Philadelphia to incorporate the concerns of those from other parts of the city in their analysis.

The dimension of enlarged identity which was most dramatic was in the area of power. Participation in the coalition had been a heady experience for many of the churches. "Regular folks" had confronted public officials. Publicly touted "successes" had increased their sense of viability, of what was politically possible. The sheer numbers of people at P.I.A. events, and their enthusiasm, was empowering for participants.

As the culture of the coalition itself is developing, it is corresponding to that of many African American congregations, and is indeed a vehicle for enhancing their cultures. By expanding their sphere of interest, heightening their visibility, and magnifying their sense of viability and political power, their own collective identity is enlarged, rather than diminished, through participation in the larger whole.

Conclusion

This research, it should be kept in mind, was conducted early in the organizational life of P.I.A., and in the relationship of five of its African American congregations. More longitudinal study is needed to determine if the trends described would continue. Would member African American churches continue to find that, indeed, participation enhanced their culture, enlarged their identity and furthered their agenda? Would P.I.A. membership pay off for the Advocate, which is concerned about its survival? Would Sanctuary Baptist Church find that indeed the coalition did facilitate housing development in their neighborhood?

The findings from this study should also be tested in other contexts. The quantitative research in congregations suggests that there are no discernible patterns of class, religious or political beliefs which would make the adoption of broad-based community organizing for working on CED predictable by congregation. This runs contrary to research in predominantly Euro-centric churches which has historically found that social class and denomination, more than beliefs, is critical in determining whether a congregation will be change-promoting or change-inhibiting (Pope, 1942; Roof and McKinney, 1987).

The data on the pastors suggests they make the decision about strategies for change based on pre-existing consciousness about leadership and social change which finds affinity in the social movement organization and gets reinforced by it. Their consciousness is reflected in congregation, the context in which their leadership is constructed. Although the social location of the church members is unrelated to the choice of strategy, the patterns of education, residential segregation and status (including their relationship to the power structure) do emerge as distinctive among the clergy. All of this points to a decision-making process which is complex -- at once the product of the individual pastor, but only as he is embedded in the context of his congregation. Would the same pastor in a different context make a different decision? This, of course, is difficult to know. More research should explore the complexities of the social construction of consciousness among clergy and their congregations.

This research begs a final question of its implications. It is premature to construct a universal profile of what types of congregations are most likely to join a broad-based community organizing coalition, although characteristics were identified among African American churches in this study. But is this approach to CED preferable? Is it more effective?

In terms of housing units built, jobs created, capital mobilized, the two approaches seem comparable. While at the present time, the more traditional approach has produced more fruit, P.I.A. has a lot to show for its short history. (In less than four years they have built 170 units of Nehemiah houses in West Philadelphia, and are projecting a total of 1000 units in the next few years in two other sites. One of them is the lot across from St. John's Baptist Church, now a member). The more traditional approach, as modeled so prominently by Rev. Leon Sullivan of Zion Baptist Church, has served North Philadelphia well. It would be a far less viable section of the city had it not been for the efforts of Sullivan and other entrepreneurial clergy who follow in his footsteps -- like the Rev. Joe Johnson and the Rev. Dr. Curtis Smith.

However, it is difficult to compare the traditional and the community organizing approaches solely on the basis of community economic development projects. The community organizing approach has other, less quantifiable goals: leadership development, increased democratic public process, and change in the ways policies are developed through "holding officials accountable" by an empowered populace. These, too, must be considered when comparing effectiveness.

In theory, two approaches should be complementary as congregations pursue their common goals of CED through the strategy which makes sense for them. In reality, tensions are inevitable between the two paradigms, as was the case in Philadelphia. Having secured the funding and political support of the city administration for Nehemiah Housing, ground-breaking was blocked by a single pastor of a large African American Baptist church and a city official who was a member of his congregation. The fact that he was able to stop the process for six months without apparent cause was testimony to the political capital he in fact had garnered over a lifetime. However, P.I.A. finally prevailed by getting support from a larger, more diverse set of power-brokers.

Was this a turning point in Philadelphia? Will church-based community organizing become the dominant paradigm for religious involvement in community economic development? As urban centers move into leaner times and the competition for funding intensifies, this chapter, at least, is still to be written.

---

[1] 80.7% of P.I.A. members came from high income tracts, compared to 57.8% of non-P.I.A. members.

[2] Grace: 22.5% Sample Mean: 16.1%

[3] Grace: 10.5% Sample Mean: 6.2%

[4] Knox: 7.9%

[5] The exception was the member at Grace who discussed the need for working with other churches, but didn't know how to go about it. He confessed that his was a unique perspective in his congregation.

[6] Gamson develops this idea of social movement identity serving to enlarge individual identity in his article, "The Social Psychology of Collective Action" in Morris and Mueller (1992)

Appendix

Survey

<u>Check the response that best represents what you believe:</u>

<u>Group A</u>:
____ The Bible is an ancient book of fables recorded by humans.
____ The Bible is the inspired word of God, but not everything in it should be taken literally.
____ The Bible is the actual word of God and is to be taken literally.

<u>Group B</u>:
____ Everyone is saved by God.
____ Only those who have been born again are saved by God.
____ All those who have been baptized are saved by God.
____ All true believers, of any religion, are saved.
____ I don't know about this.

<u>Group C</u>:
Theologically, I would call myself:
____ fundamentalist
____ conservative
____ moderate
____ liberal
____ other:

<u>Group D</u>:
I believe that poverty is cause <u>primarily</u> by:
____ laziness, lack of motivation
____ bad luck

____ racism, discrimination in hiring
____ inadequate government support and services
____ unavailability of good jobs

Group E:
Those most responsible for ending poverty are:
____ individuals who are poor
____ businesses and banks
____ the government
____ the Church
____ community organizations
____ others:

Group F:
"It is the responsibility of government to reduce the difference in income between people with high incomes and those with low incomes." In response to this statement, I:

____	strongly agree	____	agree
____	both agree and disagree	____	disagree
____	strongly disagree	____	don't know

Group G:
"In order to bring poverty to an end, there will have to be major changes in our economic system." In response to this statement, I:

____	strongly agree	____	agree
____	both agree and disagree	____	disagree
____	strongly disagree	____	don't know

Group H:
The best way to change society is:
____ through spiritual conversion
____ through electing better officials
____ to leave it to the experts
____ to join with others and organize protests
____ for individuals to speak up
____ to wait for God to act
____ don't know
____ other:

Group I:
"Working for change in society is an important part of the mission of the church."

In response to this statement, I:

____	strongly agree	____	agree
____	both agree and disagree	____	disagree
____	strongly disagree	____	don't know

Group J:

"The pastor of a congregation should be involved in politics and issues of public concern." In response to this statement, I:

____	strongly agree	____	agree
____	both agree and disagree	____	disagree
____	strongly disagree	____	don't know

K. How much formal education have you completed?

____ elementary school/middle school
____ high school (or G.E.D.)
____ some college
____ completed college degree
____ some graduate school
____ completed graduate degree
____ vocational training

L. Check the category which best describes your work situation:

____	professional	____	clerical/office worker
____	salesperson	____	manager
____	merchant/proprietor	____	tradesperson
____	factory worker	____	student
____	unemployed		

____ service worker (such as restaurant worker, health care aide, etc.)
____ volunteer or non-paid worker (such as housewife)
____ other:

M. Do you work

____ full time
____ part time

N. How do you come to church?

____ walk
____ public transportation
____ drive from within the neighborhood
____ drive from another part of the city
____ drive from outside the city

<u>O.</u> What is your zip code? ____________________

<u>P.</u> What is the closest intersection to your home?____________________

Please indicate which of the above questions were confusing or difficult for you to answer:

Thank you so much for your help!

References

Articles:

Alexander, Bobby C. "Correcting Misinterpretations of Turner's Theory: An African-American Pentecostal Illustration." JSSR 30 (1991): 26-44.

Alston, John P., Charles W. Peck, and C. Ray Wingrove. "Religiosity and Black Militancy: A Reappraisal." JSSR 11 (1972): 252-261.

Baer, Hans A. "Black Mainstream Churches: Emancipatory or Accomodative Responses to Racism and Social Stratification in American Society?" RRR 30 (1988): 162-176.

Beck, Carolyn S. "Our Own vine and Fig Tree: The Authority of History and Kinship in Mother Bethel." RRR 29 (1988): 369-384.

Broom, Jack. "The Negro Church and the Movement for Equality." MA Thesis, University of California at Berkeley, 1966.

Chaves, Mark and Lynn M. Higgins. "Comparing the Community Involvement of Black and White Congregations." JSSR 31 (1992): 425-440.

Demerath, N. III, and Rhys H. Williams. "Religion and Power in the American Experience" Society 26 (1989):29-38.

Dixon, Richard D., Roger C. Lowery and Lloyd P. Jones. "The Fact and Form of Born Again Religious Conversions and Sociopolitical Conservativism." RRR 34 (1992): 117-131.

Ellison, William and Darren E. Sherkat. "Patterns of Religious Mobility among Black Americans." The Sociological Quarterly 31 (1990): 551-568.

Goode, Erich. "Social Class and Church Participation." AJS 72 (1966):102-112.

Gorenstein, Nathan. "Faith and Capitalism." Philadelphia Inquirer July 21, 1995.

Greeley, Andrew M. "Ethnic Variations in Religious Commitment." in Robert Wuthnow (ed.) The Religious Dimension: New Directions in Quantitative Research New York: Academic Press, 1979.

Jacobson, Cardell K. "Religiosity in a Black Community: An Examination of Secularization and Political Variables." RRR 33 (1992):215-228.

Jacobson, Cardell K., Tim B. Heaton and Rutledge M. Dennis. "Black-White Difference in Religiosity: Item Analyses and a Formal Structural Test" Sociological Analysis 51 (1990):257-270.

Johnson, Stephen D., Joseph B. Tamney, and Sandy Halebsky. "Christianity, Social Traditionalism, and Economic Conservatism." Sociological Focus 19(1986): 299-314.

Johnson, G. David, Marc Matre, and Gigi Armbrecht. "Race and Religiosity: An Empirical Evaluation of A Causal Model." RRR 32(1991):252-266.

Johnston, Ronald. "Negro Preachers Take Sides." in The Black Church in America, Hart M. Nelsen, et.al., editors. New York: Basic Books, 1971.

Kosmin, Barry A., Ariela Keysar and Nava Lerer. "Secular Education and the Religious Profile of Contemporary Black Americans." Presented at the Annual Meeting, Society for the Scientific Study of Religion, Pittsburgh, PA, (Nov. 1991).

Marx, Gary T. "Religion: Opiate or Inspiration of Civil Rights Militancy among Negroes?" ASR 32(1967): 67-68.

Nelsen, Hart M. "Unchurched Black Americans: Patterns of Religiosity and Affiliation." RRR 29(1988):398-412.

Peck, Gary R. "Black Radical Consciousness and the Black Christian Experience: Toward a Critical Sociology of Afro-American religion." Sociological Analysis 43(1982):155-169.

Petersen, Larry R. and K. Peter Takayama. "Religious Commitment and Conservatism: Toward Understanding an Elusive Relationship." Sociological Analysis 45(1984): 355-371.

Pyle, Ralph E. "Faith and Commitment to the Poor: The Link Between Religious Orientation and Economic Conservatism." Presented at the Annual Meeting of the Society for the Scientific Study of Religion, Pittsburgh, PA, (Nov. 1991).

Rokeach, Milton. "Religious Values and Social Compassion." RRR 11(1969):24-39.

Sasaki, M.S. "Status Inconsistency and Religious Commitment." in Robert Wuthnow (ed.) The Religious Dimension: New Directions in Quantitative Research. New York: Academic Press, 1979.

Sawyer, Mary R. "Black Ecumenical Movements: Proponents of Social Change." RRR 30(1988): 151-161.

Shaw, Talbert O. "A Tentative Profile of the Black Clergy in Chicago." Journal of Religious Thought 30 (1973), 39-51.

-----. "Responsibility and Black Middle Class Religion." Ph.D. Dissertation, University of Chicago, 1973.

Stellway, Richard. "The Correspondence between Religious Orientation and Socio-political Liberalism and Conservatism." The Sociological Quarterly 14(1973):430-439.

Tamney, Joseph B. "Social Class Composition of Congregations and Pastoral Support for Liberal Activism" RRR 33(1991):18-31.

Tamney, Joseph B., Ronald Burton, and Stephen D. Johnson. "Christianity, Social Class, and the Catholic Bishops' Economic Policy." Sociological Analysis 49(1988):78-96.

-----. "Religious Diversity and Ecumenical Social Action." RRR 32(1990): 16-26.

Taylor, Robert J. "Correlates of Religious Non-Involvement among Black Americans." RRR 30(1988): 126-139.

-----. "Structural Determinants of Religious Participation among Black Americans." RRR 30(1988): 114-125.

Trulear, Harold Dean. "A Critique of Functionalism: Toward a More Holistic Sociology of Afro-American Religion." Journal of Religious Thought 42(1985): 38-50.

Turner, Ronny E. "The Black Minister: Uncle Tom or Abolitionist?" Phylon 34 (1974): 86-95.

Wilcox, Clyde. "Blacks and the New Christian Right: Support for the Moral Majority and Pat Robertson among Washington D.C. Blacks." RRR 32(1990): 43-55.

Wuthnow, Robert. "Religious Commitment and Conservatism: In Search of an Elusive Relationship" in Charles Y. Glock (ed.) Religion in a Sociological Perspective: Essays in the Empirical Study of Religion. Belmont, CA: Wadsworth Publishing,(1973) pp. 117-132.

Books:

Ahmann, Mathew and Margaret Roach (eds.). The Church and the Urban Racial Crisis. Techny, Ill: Divine Word Publications, 1967.
Baer, Hans and Merrill Singer. African American Religion in the Twentieth Century: Varieties of Protest and Accommodation. Knoxville, TN: University of Tennessee Press, 1992.
Childs, John Brown. The Political Black Minister: A Study in Afro-American Politics and Religion. Boston: G.K. Hall, 1980.
Cone, James. The Black Church and Marxism: What do they have to say to each other? Democratic Socialists of America, 1980.
Davidson, James D., C. Lincoln Johnson, and Alan K. Mock (eds.). Faith and Social Ministry: Ten Christian Perspectives Chicago: Loyola University Press, 1990.
DuBois, W.E.B. (ed.). The Negro Church. Atlanta: Atlanta University Press, 1903.
-----. The Philadelphia Negro: A Social Study. New York: Schocken Books, 1970 edition.
Freedman, Samuel G. Upon This Rock: The Miracles of a Black Church. New York: Harper Collins, 1993.
Goffman, Erving. Frame Analysis: An Essay on the Organization of Experience. New York: Harper, 1974.
Greider, William. Who Will Tell the People: The Betrayal of American Democracy. New York: Simon and Schuster, 1992.
Hamilton, Charles. The Black Preacher in America. New York: William Morrow, 1972.
Harris, James H. Black Ministers and Laity in the Urban Church: An Analysis of Political and Social Expectations. Lanham, MD: University Press of America, 1987.
Kling, Joseph M. and Prudence S. Posner (eds.) Dilemmas of Activism: Class, Community and the Politics of Local Mobilization. Philadelphia: Temple University Press, 1990.
Kluegel, James R. and Eliot R. Smith. Beliefs About Inequality: Americans' Views of What Is and What Ought to Be. New York: Aldine De Gruyter, 1986.
Lincoln, C. Eric. Race, Religion and the Continuing American Dilemma. New York: Hill and Wang, 1984.
-----.The Black Church Since Frazier. New York: Schocken Books, 1974.

Lincoln, C. Eric., and Lawrence H. Mamiya. The Black Church in the African American Experience. Durham and London: Duke University Press, 1990.

Marable, Manning. How Capitalism Underdeveloped Black America. Boston: South End Press, 1983.

Marx, Gary. Protest and Predjudice. New York: Harper and Row, 1969.

McAdam, Doug. Political Process and the Development of Black Insurgency 1930-1970. Chicago: University of Chicago Press, 1982.

McDougall, Harold A. Black Baltimore: A New Theory of Community. Philadelphia: Temple University Press, 1993.

Morris, Aldon. The Origins of the Civil Rights Movement. New York: Free Press, 1984.

-----, and Carol McClung Mueller (eds.) Frontiers in Social Movement Theory. New Haven: Yale University Press, 1992.

Mukenge, Ida Rousseau. The Black Church in Urban America: A Case Study in Political Economy. New York: University Press, 1983.

Nelsen, Hart M. and Nelsen, Anne K. The Black Church in the Sixties. Louisville: University of Kentucky Press, 1975.

Nelsen, Hart M., Raytha L. Yokley, and Anne K. Nelsen, eds. The Black Church in America. New York: Basic Books, 1971.

Paris, Peter. The Social Teaching of the Black Churches. Philadelphia: Fortress Press, 1985.

Pinkney, Alfonso. The Myth of Black Progress. Cambridge: Cambridge University Press, 1984.

Roof, Wade Clark, and McKinney, William. American Mainline Religion. New Brunswick, N.J.: Rutgers University Press, 1987.

Pope, Liston. Millhands and Preachers. New Haven, CN: Yale University Press, 1942.

Roozen, David, William McKinney and Jackson Carroll. Varieties of Religious Presence: Mission in Public Life. New York: Pilgrim Press, 1984.

Stack, Carol B. All Our Kin: Strategies for Survival in a Black Community. New York: Harper and Row: 1974.

Stark, Rodney and Charles Glock. American Piety: The Nature of Religious Commitment. Berkeley: University of California Press, 1968.

Tucker, David M. Black Pastors and Leaders: Memphis, 1819-1972. Memphis, TN: Memphis State University Press, 1975.

Wald, Kenneth D. Religion and Politics in the United States. New York: St. Martin's Press, 1987.

Washington, Joseph R. Black Religion. Boston: Beacon Press, 1964.

-----. Black Religion and Public Policy. New York: Joseph Washington, 1978.

Washington, Paul M. and David McI. Gracie. Other Sheep I Have: The Autobiography of Father Paul M. Washington. Philadelphia: Temple University Press, 1994.

Weber, Max. The Sociology of Religion. Boston: Beacon Press, 1964.

Williams, Melvin D. Community in a Black Pentecostal Church: An Anthropological Study. Prospect Heights, Ill: Waveland Press, 1974.

Wilmore, Gayraud. Black Religion and Black Radicalism: An Interpretation of the Religious History of Afro-American People. (2nd Edition) Maryknoll, N.Y.: Orbis Books, 1983.

Wuthnow, Robert. The Restructuring of American Religion: Society and Faith since World War II. Princeton: Princeton University Press, 1988.

Indexer's note: Author citations in italics indicates multi-authored works

A

Action frames, 8, 12, 17, 18, 21, 119
Advocate Community Development Corporation (ACDC), 149–50, 157, 162–63
African American churches and study, 19, 36, 188–89, 190
  activism of clergy in, 23
  community economic development (CED) and, 1, 5, 7, 12, 24, 203–04
  complexity of traditions, institutions in, 22–23
  P.I.A. affiliation and, 187, 202
  paradoxical terms in, 23
  social change strategy and, 187
  traditional paradigm in, 5
African American Protestants, 57
African Methodist Episcopal Church, 15
Alinksy, Saul, 1, 2, 6, 18
Alinksy groups, 6–7
All Our Kin, Stack, Carol B., 39

B

Baer, Hans A., 14, 191, 211, *214*
Baltimoreans United In Leadership Development (BUILD), 3, 6
Baptism, rite of, 55
Baptist groups, 15
Baptist *vs.* Presbyterian religious views, 136, 140
Beatty, Kathleen Murphy, 191
Bible, views on, 51, 55, 58, 168
Billy Graham Crusade, 127
Black Baltimore, McDougall, 3
Black bank (Unity Bank), 126
Black Clergy, Inc., 129
Black Clergy Association (B.C.A.), 13, 92, 101
Black Clergy of Philadelphia and Vicinity, 5, 126
Black colleges, 193
Black Consciousness Scale, 92, 94
"Black Friday", 150
Black Panther Convention, 152
Black pastors, inspiration of, 91
Black People's Unity Movement, 150, 152
Black Power Conference, 152
Black Unity Rally, 152, 154
"Born again" religious view, 49, 51, 54, 55, 136, 168, 190
Bright Hope Baptist Church, 13
Broad-based community organizing predictability, 203
Broom, Jack, 14, 211
Buell, Emmett, 191
Burton, Ronald, 16, 29, *213*

C

Carmichael, Stokely, 152
CBCO (*see* church-based community organizing)
CED (*see* community economic development)
Chambers, Edward T., 2
Childs, John Brown, 23, 214
Christian fundamentalism, 55
Church-based community organizing (CBCO), 1, 2, 3, 19
  and the clergy, 14, 22
  and conservative Christians, 191
  in Philadelphia, 5–6, 21, 204
  and viability of, 22
Churchill, John, 154
Church of the Advocate and study, 149, 150, 152, 163–64, 168
  Advocate Community Development Corporation (ACDC) and, 149–50, 157, 162–63
  bifurcated social strata and, 168
  Black power and denominational funding in, 153, 154

Black Unity Rally and, 152, 154
Churchill, John and, 154–55
classes and races of, 159
coalitional organizing of, 162–63, 166
community economic development (CED) and, 150–51, 159, 162, 163
commuting patterns of, 159
cultural enhancement of, 166
education and, 159
electoral politics and, 174
empowerment in the subculture of, 164–65
Grace Memorial Baptist Church and, 159
Harris, Barbara (bishop of Boston) and, 162
identity conflict in, 158
ideological consensus in, 159
income levels in, 159
liberal theology in, 168
Miller, Rev. Isaac of, 160–62, 163, 164–65
ordination of woman and, 154, 162
pastor as prophet in, 154–57
pastor's involvement with politics question and, 178
Philadelphia Interfaith Action (P.I.A.) and, 160, 161, 163, 165–66
physical structure of, 158–59, 163
poverty, view of, 168
poverty rates of, 159, 168, 186*nn5–6*
and salvation, view of, 168
Sanctuary Baptist Church and, 168, 174
shared leadership in, 161–62, 165
Smith, Rev. Ann Robb of, 159
social change and, 165–66, 174
social dislocation and, 159, 160
vestry of, 156, 158
Washington, Christine and, 149–50, 156, 157, 162
Washington, Rev. Paul and, 151–57, 162, 163, 165
Civil Rights Movement, 100, 105, 108
Class stratification in religion, 15–16, 59, 81, 190
Clergy activism, 14–15
Clergy in study, 100, 107, 187, 195–96, 203
accommodationism and, 193
action frames and, 192
activism of, 23, 94, 104, 192
approaches to power of, 102–06
charismatic leadership of, 195–96
coalition and, 101, 192
and the collective good of the community, 195
community economic development (CED) and, 92, 95, 96, 101, 110
community organizing of, 187
community solidarity of, 110
confrontation with power structure of, 194
cultural status of, 193, 194
demographic factors of, 92–93
dominant institutions and, 193
education of non-P.I.A. clergy and, 193
electoral politics and, 94
empowerment approach to power of, 102, 104–06
entrepreneurial pastors and, 5
and the goals of community economic development (CED), 194–95
Johnson, Rev. Joseph and, 116, 117–22, 126–28, 135, 144, 145, 146, 147*n*1, 196, 204
metaphorical language of, 111, 112
Miller, Rev. Isaac and, 11, 160–63, 164, 166
non-P.I.A. affiliated churches and, 98–99, 101
P.I.A. affiliation decisions of, 195
P.I.A. *vs.* non-P.I.A. pastor comparisons in, 92, 93, 94, 95–96, 99–100, 111–12, 191–94, 196
paradigms of, 106–09, 110, 112
parochial strategies of non-P.I.A. pastors and, 101–02
parochial *vs.* coalitional organizing of, 100–102
pastor-people relationships and, 188, 194–95
political capital of, 193–94
political consciousness of, 91, 94–95
political involvement and religious

beliefs of, 192
political votes and, 105
power and personal compromise of, 102
pragmatism of, 102, 109–10, 194, 195
racial consciousness of, 94–95
self-interest of, 194–95
Shipley, Rev. Samuel and, 166, 167, 174, 176, 177, 178, 180, 183, 196
Smith, Rev. Ann Robb and, 159, 162
Smith, Rev. Curtis and, 20, 140, 143, 144, 145–46, 196, 204
social change and personality of, 112–13, 119
social change perspectives of, 109–10, 192
social location of, 192–93, 203
strategic approaches to power of, 102, 104
strategies for change of, 106–09, 110–12, 191, 203
Sullvian, Rev. Leon and, 4, 5, 26, 94, 203, 204
Washington, Rev. Paul and, 150, 151–57, 158, 160, 162, 163, 165
Clinton, William Jefferson, former president of the U.S., 146
Community development corporations (CDC'S), 95, 174
Community economic development (CED) and study, 1, 25, 115, 119, 202–04
accommodation *vs.* change in, 10–11
action frames in, 8–11
African American clergy consciousness and, 92, 192
Black power structure and, 13, 92
class status and, 17
clerical *vs.* shared leadership in, 8, 96–100, 192
comparative effectiveness of, 203–04
congregational questionnaire results and, 50, 87–88, 189, 190, 192
Corinthian Baptist Church and, 200
dominant model for, 5
federal funding and trend toward, 3–4
Grace Memorial Baptist Church and, 117–19, 134
leadership in, 8, 100
parochial *vs.* coalitional collaboration in, 8–9
Philadelphia Interfaith Action (P.I.A.) and, 8–9, 10
political capital of pastors and, 192–93
political consciousness and attitudes for, 29, 30
power access *vs.* empowerment in, 9–10
predictability of, 203
self-interest of pastors and, 194
strategies for (compared), 203–04
theory and reality of approaches to, 204
traditional model of, 10–11
traditional strategy in, 5, 26
Congregational consciousness, 30, 203
Congregational questionnaire results, 41, 49–50, 81, 93, 191
activism and P.I.A. affiliation in, 199
beliefs and demographic diversity patterns in, 87, 188
Black Consciousness Scale and, 92, 94
"born again" religious view in, 49, 51, 54, 55, 84, 168
census data and, 42, 43
charismatic leadership findings in, 195–96
the church and social change in, 77–80
churches clustered by denomination in, 84
class indices among P.I.A. members in, 59
class indices trends in, 72
class status and, 83
class stratification along denominational lines in, 59, 81
class trends and opinion patterns in, 84, 188–89
commonalties among congregations joining P.I.A. finding, 87–88, 189
community economic development (CED) and, 49, 50, 87–88, 189, 202–04
community economic development (CED) and collective interest finding, 195
and community economic

development (CED) strategy conclusion, 199–200
commuting patterns and, 43, 49, 58, 59, 77, 83–84, 88*n*7
congregational factors in, 188–91
conservative theology and, 49, 51, 54, 57, 58, 59, 65, 69, 72, 79, 83, 84, 86, 88*n*3, 191
consolidated categories in, 50
contrasting action frames of pastors in, 192
Corinthian Baptist Church and, 200
demographic profile in, 57–59, 88
denominational affiliation and, 51, 54, 83, 88*n*8
dissatisfaction indicator in, 73
distinctiveness of individual churches in, 87
dominant theories within sociology of religion and, 191
economic and political change opinions in, 69–73, 83, 105
education levels and, 42, 58, 79, 83, 88*n*4
fundamentalist theological orientations and, 49, 55
and Grace Memorial Baptist Church, 197, 199, 204*nn2 and 3*
hypothesized relationship of variables in, 50
income levels and, 42–43, 49, 51, 59, 88*n*6
individualism in, 197
and Knox Presbyterian Church, 197, 199
leadership findings in, 195–96
mainline Protestant denominations in, 50, 54, 57, 58, 61, 67, 77, 83, 84, 88*n*8
null hypothesis in, 51, 77, 87
occupational levels and, 41–42, 51, 58, 59, 79, 83, 88*n*4
P.I.A. affiliation decision findings, 191–95
P.I.A. and the churches, conclusions from, 201–02
paradigms in, 106–07
pastors and community economic development (CED) goals finding, 194–95
pastors' behavior patterns in community economic development (CED) strategies decision findings, 192–93
pastors' religious beliefs and political involvement findings, 192
patterns of religious belief (summary of), 57
perceptions of wealth and poverty in, 61–64
Philadelphia Interfaith Action (P.I.A.) and, 41, 49, 51, 54, 55, 58, 79, 84, 86, 88*n*9
political perspectives and, 191
poverty, opinions in, 59, 61, 65, 67, 69, 197
pragmatism of pastors in, 194, 195
religious beliefs in, 51–57, 188–89, 196
residential patterns in, 43
response rate in, 41–42
rite of baptism and, 55
Sanctuary Baptist Church and, 198, 199
self-identification in, 55, 57
self-interest findings in, 83, 194–95
Shipley, Rev. Samuel and, 196
Smith, Rev. Curtis and, 196
social change and church mission consensus in, 77, 79
social location differences of pastors in, 192–93
socio-economic profile in, 43, 84
socio-economic status (s.e.s) in, 49, 50, 51, 54, 57–59, 83
St. John's Baptist Church and, 200
strategies for social change and, 73–77
subcultural milieu and seeking change findings, 198–200
theological non-conservatives in, 57, 58, 67
theological perspectives in, 79, 81, 83, 191
theological self-identification in, 55–57
theological spectrum in, 49, 81

theoretical approaches of class and beliefs in, 191
theoretical implications of, 187
unemployment and, 49
validity in, 55, 87
variations in intensity of opinions in, 81, 83
views on salvation and, 51, 55, 191
views on the Bible and, 51, 55, 190
world view findings in, 196–98
zip code data in, 49

Congregations in study
action frames and, 12, 17, 18
beliefs and demographic diversity patterns of, 188
church-based community organizing (CBCO) of, 20, 24
class interest and, 16, 18
class stratification in, 15–16
clerical *vs* shared leadership in, 12
community economic development (CED) and, 12, 17, 23, 29
competing paradigms in, 23
conservative theology in, 16, 29
cultural identity and, 21–22
determinant of political and economic views in, 16
education and income levels in, 39
frame extension and, 20
incorporating movements in, 20
Industrial Areas Foundation (I.A.F.) and, 18, 20
personal theology and, 29
Philadelphia Interfaith Action (P.I.A.) and, 17
political views and beliefs in, 16–17
racism and, 18
shared meanings in, 20
social class functions and, 30
social movement and, 20
socio-economic status (s.e.s) in, 17, 23, 30
the urban poor and, 17, 18, 30
Weberian framework in, 16, 17, 59, 189

Congress on Racial Equality (CORE), 152
Connections, publication, 26
Conservative Christian theology, 72–73
Corinthian Baptist Church, 200
Cose, Ellis, 18

D

Demerath, N. III, 16, 29, *211*
DeWitt, Rt. Rev. Robert, 153
Dixon, Allen, Rev., 123
Dixon, Rev. Allen, 123
DuBois, W. E. B., 4, *214*

E

Edelman, Marian Wright, 104
Edmonds, Walter, 158
Eliot, R. Smith, 61, 64, *214*
Episcopal Church of America, 153–54
Ethnographic research, 36–38, 115, 190, 195, 201
Ethnographies, 25, 194
Evening Bulletin, The, 153

F

Ford Foundation, 150

G

Gamson, William A., 20
Girard College (1965), 151
Glock, Charles, 16, 29, *216*
Goffman, Erving, 7, *214*
Goode, W. Wilson, mayor of Philadelphia, 13, 126, 143, 149, 154
Grace Memorial Baptist Church and study, 7–8, 115–17, 120–21, 124, 174
accessing power and, 127–30
action frames in, 119, 147*n2*
Church of the Advocate and, 159
Commission on Leadership and, 124–25
community economic development (CED) in, 117–19, 134
commuting patterns of, 120, 131
cultural context of, 121, 135–36
Department of Housing and Urban Development (HUD) and, 117, 118, 120
Dixon, Rev. Allen, of, 123
empowerment and, 128, 129–30
Grace Memorial Non-Profit

Development Corporation, 118
history of, 125–26
individualism and, 133, 197
Industrial Areas Foundation (I.A.F.) and, 129–30, 147*n*3
Jenkins, Oscar and, 128–29
Johnson, Rev. Joseph, pastor of, 116, 117–18, 119–20, 121, 122–25, 126–28, 133–34, 135, 147*n*1, 196
"Johnson Era" in, 123
Joseph Johnson Manor housing project and, 117–19, 126
narrative and identity of, 123
pastor as benevolent patriarch of, 122–25, 130, 135
pastor as hero in, 119–22, 130, 135
pastor as representative of the people in, 125–28, 135, 147*n4*
Philadelphia Interfaith Action (P.I.A.) and, 119, 129, 133, 134
public policy and, 135
relationship to other churches, 131–32
Sanctuary Baptist Church and, 182
Southern African American Baptist traditions and, 121, 123–24
status quo and, 134–36
strategic approach to social change of, 127–30
systemic change and, 134
women and leadership of, 123–25
world view of, 197
written history of, 123
Grace Memorial Non-Profit Development Corporation, 118
Gracie McI., David, 151, 152, 153, 155, 156, 162, *216*
Gray, Rev. William (congressman), 13, 118
Green, John C., 191
Greider, William, 2, 3, *214*
Guth, James, 191

H

Habitat for Humanity, 3
Halebsky, Sandy, 16, 29, *212*
Harris, Barbara (bishop of Boston), 162
Harris, James H., 23, 214
Heritage Foundation, 1
Himmelstein, Jerome L., 191
Hirschman, A.O., 110

I

Industrial Areas Foundation (I.A.F.), 1, 9, 19, 100, 193
approach to power of, 104–05
Church of the Advocate and, 166
frame extension in, 21
leadership training in, 2, 22
lead organizer of, 6, 202
reform goals and, 11
strategy of, 2
suspicion and criticism of, 6
systemic change and, 11–12
viability of, 22

J

Jennings, James, 6
Johnson, Rev. Joseph, pastor of Grace Memorial Baptist Church, 116, 126–28, 135, 147*n*1, 196
as benevolent patriarch, 122–25, 196
as entrepreneurial clergy, 204
as hero, 119–22, 196
and Joseph Johnson Manor housing project, 117–19
parallels with Smith, Rev. Curtis, 144, 145, 146
and the Philadelphia Interfaith Action (P.I.A.), 133–34
Johnson, Stephen D., 16, 29, *212*, *213*
Joseph Johnson Manor housing project, 117–19, 126

K

Kellstedt, Lyman A., 191
Keysar, Areila, 16, 30, *212*
King, Martin Luther, Jr., 108, 152
Kling, Joseph M, 7, 9, *214*
Kluegel, James R., 61, 64, *214*
Knox Presbyterian Church and study
African American identity in, 145
Afro-centrism of, 197
charette (covenanted dialogue) of, 140, 143
community economic development (CED) and, 143
and Grace Memorial Baptist Church

comparison, 115
parochialism of, 143
pastor as hero in, 145–46
patriarchal status of pastor, 144
People's Community Developers Corporation (PCDC) and, 143, 145–46, 149
"People's Village" and, 140, 143
Philadelphia Interfaith Action (P.I.A.) and, 140
political issues and, 197
Presbyterian affiliation of, 136, 144, 145
Smith, Curtis Rev., pastor of, 140–43, 144, 145–46, 196
social change and, 140
strategies for community development of, 140
Temple University and, 140, 143, 145
world view of, 136, 140, 197
worship service of, 144–45
Kosmin, Barry A., 16, 30, *212*

L

Lerer, Nava, 16, 30, *212*
Liacouras, Peter, 140
Lincoln, C. Eric, 4, 14, 15, 23, 29, 30, 33, 91, 92, *215*
Lincoln and Mamiya study of African American churches, 91, 92, 93

M

Mainline Protestant denominations and study, 160
and "born again" belief, 54
and education, 57, 188
and Knox Presbyterian Church, 136
and non-conservatives in, 58
and opinions on poverty, 61, 67, 83
and social change, 77
Mamiya, Lawrence H., 4, 14, 15, 23, 29, 30, 33, 91, 92, *215*
Marable, Manning, 14, 23, 214
Marty, Martin, 16, 29
Marx, Gary T., 14, 191, 193, 212, 215
McAdam, Doug, 19, 20, 22, 33, 215
McCoy, Hilda, 145
McDougall, Harold A., 3, 4, *213*
McKinney, William, 191, 203, *215*
Methodology of research, 25, 34, 36–37, 38, 187
age question in, 33
analysis of data in, 33, 35
anonymity in, 34
assumptions and biases in, 40
attitudes toward poverty questions in, 31, 33–34, 190
class status considerations in, 30–31
community economic development (CED) and, 25–26, 28, 30
congregations sampling, 25–26, 34
continua in, 26
dissatisfaction, level of in sample, 190
diversity of congregations in, 26
educational attainment question in, 32
ethnographic problems (inherent) in, 39
ethnographic research in, 27, 34, 36–38, 115
gender question in, 33
Hawthorne effect in, 39
hypotheses in, 33, 36
income distributions question in, 69, 72
institutional factors in, 28–29
interpretive schemes and, 189–90
limitations of, 38–40
marital status question in, 33
and McAdam's contention on social change, 33
North Philadelphia and, 26–28, 38
occupational category question in, 32
pastors and, 27, 35–36, 91
personal belief questions in, 31
perspectives on social change questions, 32
Philadelphia Interfaith Action (P.I.A.) and, 28, 33, 35, 39
political opinion questions in, 31–32
politics, pastor involvement with question in, 178
poverty and economic change question in, 72–73
poverty and government responsibility question, 69–72
poverty and theological orientation in,

64–65
pre-existing instruments and, 38
procedures for administration of, 34–35
proximity to church question in, 32
rationale of questionnaire, 28–31
sample congregations attendance and membership in, 27, 40*n2*
social distance between interviewer and subject in, 35
social location of respondents in, 32–33
socio-economic status (s.e.s) in, 32
structured interviews in, 35–36
structure of questionnaire in, 31–34, 38
suspicion and, 39
Weberian framework and, 33
zip code data in, 43
Miller, Rev. Isaac, pastor of Church of the Advocate, 11, 160, 164, 166
activism of, 161–62
and Philadelphia Interfaith Action (P.I.A.), 161
and shared leadership, 160–61
and Washington, Rev. Paul, 162
Model Cities program, 149, 150
Moore, Rev. William B., 13
Morris, Aldon, 7, 188, 205*n6*, *215*
MOVE community, 154, 157
Mueller, Carol McClung, 7, 188, 205*n6*, *215*
Muhammad Kenyatta, 153
Mumia Abu Jamal, 154

N

National Baptist Convention, Inc., 167
National Congress on Community Economic Development, 1
National Opinion Research Center (NORC), 31
Nehemiah Housing developments, 6, 22, 106, 203, 204
Nelson, Anne K., 29, *215*
Nelson, Hart M., 29, *215*
Northern Student Movement, 152
North Philadelphia and study, 2, 4, 15, 149, 176
Broad Street corridor of, 43, 146
commercial developments by clergy in, 95
commercial ventures by individual churches in, 5
corporate investment in housing and, 107
Diamond Street corridor of, 150, 157
Grace Memorial Baptist Church and, 129, 131, 134, 146
Knox Presbyterian Church and, 146
mainline Protestant groups in, 15
Master Street corridor of, 121
Opportunities Industrial Centers (OIC) in, 4–5, 94
pastor identification with, status within, 193–94
Philadelphia Interfaith Action (P.I.A.) and, 15, 26
Progress Plaza in, 4
strategies for change in, 12
Washington, Rev. Paul and, 151

O

Opportunities Industrial Centers (OIC), 4–5
Other Sheep I Have, Washington, Rev. Paul, 156, 186*n2*

P

Paris, Peter, 29
Pentecostal groups, 15
Petersen, Larry, R, 16, 29, *212*
Philadelphia and study, 4, 30, 126, 151, 178
African American clergy in, 13, 19, 22, 194
and Black Clergy Association of Philadelphia and Vicinity, 5
Board of Education (1967) of, 149
census data of, 42
church-based community organizing (CBCO) and, 5–6, 204
Community economic development (CED) strategies in, 4, 9–10
congregational identity and culture in, 21
and credit unions in local African American congregations, 5
educational levels in, 42

Episcopalians in, 153
Goode, W. Wilson, mayor of, 13, 126, 143, 149, 154
history of P.I.A. in, 100
Industrial Areas Foundation (I.A.F.) and, 4–5, 6–7
lead organizer in, 6, 202
Logan area of, 167, 176, 180
MOVE community in, 154
Philadelphia Interfaith Action (P.I.A.) and, 5–6
Rendell, Ed, mayor of, 161
Philadelphia Divinity School, 155
Philadelphia Inquirer, 11, 121
Philadelphia Interfaith Action (P.I.A.) and study, 5–6, 10, 13, 19, 26, 58, 176
accomplishments of, 203
affiliation and theological perspective in, 190–92
appropriateness or necessity of, 146
Arch St. action of, 182, 186*n8*
belief patterns and, 87
benefits to member congregations of, 201
"born again" religious view and, 55, 190
Church of the Advocate and, 161, 166
class interest and, 84
clergy in, 92–93, 191–93
clergy leadership *vs* shared leadership and, 100
commonality among congregations joining, 87–88
conclusions of research in, 202–03
congregational identities and, 41, 201–02, 205*n6*
congregational questionnaire and, 49, 84, 86
conservative theology and, 84, 86
cultural identity and, 21–22
demands of, 96
dissatisfaction (with the system) and, 190
diversity in, 8–9, 190
dues in, 178
economic change and, 86–87
educational levels and, 58
empowerment and, 106
fundraising of, 9
government income distribution and, 72, 86
Grace Memorial Baptist Church and, 119, 129, 133, 134
Hansen, Judith and, 161
individual class interest within, 190
individual leadership and, 198
informational booklet quoted, 11
intensity of belief and, 86
laypeople training of, 105
leadership in, 8
local neighborhood concerns and, 86
opinion patterns in, 84, 87
pastors and, 88, 191–95
political perspectives of, 67, 84, 88
poverty, opinions on, 67, 86
power and political strategy of, 10, 106
and question of affiliation with, 187
race and, 190
racial issues and, 193
shared leadership commitment of, 178
Shipley, Rev. Samuel and, 174, 176, 178
social change and, 77, 84, 86
socio-economic profile of, 84
socio-economic status (s.e.s) and, 57
St. John's Baptist Church and, 200
strategy team of, 8
theological conservatives and, 84, 86
views on salvation and, 54, 191
Philadelphia Tribune, the, 26
Pope, Liston, 14, 29, 191, 203, 215
Posner, Prudence S., 7, 9, *214*
Poverty, opinions on (in study)
commuting patterns and, 64
education, occupational levels and, 72
education and, 61, 64, 65
fatalism and, 61
government responsibility and, 67, 69
income and, 61
individualism and, 61, 64, 65
individualistic interpretation and, 65
mainline Protestants and, 61
motivation and, 61
occupational status and, 61
perceptions of wealth and poverty in, 61, 64

Philadelphia Interfaith Action (P.I.A.) members and, 65, 72, 84, 86
primary cause belief and, 59
racism and, 61, 65, 168
socio-economic status (s.e.s) and, 64
summary of opinions, 65
theological orientation and, 64–65
Poverty, solutions to opinions (in study), 65–73, 168
class effects and, 72
community organization and, 67
conservative theology and, 72
denominational affiliation and, 67
denominational groups and, 69
economic change and, 72–73
education, occupational levels and, 67
government responsibility and, 65
individual data *vs* congregational mean data and, 65
intensity of perspective in, 65
Philadelphia Interfaith Action (P.I.A.) affiliation and, 67, 72, 73
theological orientation and, 69, 72
Presbyterian *vs.* Baptist religious views, 136, 140
Protest and Prejudice, Marx, Gary, 29

Q

Quantitative research in congregations, 202–03

R

Racial consciousness, 18
Reagan-Bush administrations, 13
Reagan era, 5
Religious beliefs and study
and the Bible, 51
"born again" belief, 49, 51, 54, 55, 168
Philadelphia Interfaith Action (P.I.A.) and, 51, 190
Presbyterian *vs.* Baptist, 136
summary of (in congregation questionnaire), 57
theological self-identification in, 55–57
and views on salvation, 51, 54, 55, 168, 191
Rendell, Ed, mayor of Philadelphia, 161
Research, conclusions of, 202–03
Research, implications of, 203–04
Rokeach, Milton, 16, 29, 212
Roof, Wade Clark, 191, 203, *215*

S

Salvation, views on, 51, 54, 55, 168, 191
Sanctuary Baptist Church in study
belief patterns in, 168
and the Bible taken literally, 168
and Church of the Advocate, 168, 174, 182–83
coalition activism in, 180–81
commitments and perspectives of, 174, 176–77, 185
commuting patterns of, 168
congregation size of, 167
Core Group of, 180–81, 182, 183, 184, 185
criticism of economic system in, 184
denominational affiliation and, 167–68
economic and political change opinions in, 183
education and, 174
empowerment and, 182, 186*n8*
female leadership in, 181–82
Former Addicts Now Saved (FANS) program of, 174
and Grace Memorial Baptist Church, 182
National Baptist Convention, Inc. and, 167
Philadelphia Interfaith Action (P.I.A.) and, 166, 178, 180, 183–86
physical structure of, 166–67
political activism and, 185
political perspectives of, 168
politics and pastor involvement with question in, 178
poverty and economic, political change opinions in, 186*n8*
and salvation, view of, 168
shared leadership in, 181
Shipley, Rev. Samuel of, 166, 167, 174, 176, 178, 186, 196
social change and, 174, 177
spiritual conversion and, 174
United Church of Christ

(Congregationalists) and, 167
and view of poverty in, 168
Shipley, Rev. Samuel, pastor of Sanctuary Baptist Church, 166, 167, 178, 183
Community Development Corporation (CDC) and, 174
community economic development (CED) and, 176
criticism of economic system of, 183
as democratic socialist, 183
and Philadelphia Interfaith Action (P.I.A.), 174, 178, 180
and shared power, 196
and social change (quoted), 177
Shupe, Anson, 191
Sigelman, Lee, 191
Singer, Merrill, 191, *214*
Smidth, Corwin E., 191
Smith, Rev. Ann Robb of Church of the Adocate, 159, 162
Smith, Rev. Curtis, pastor of Knox Presbyterian Church, 140–43
as entrepreneurial clergy, 204
as hero, representative and patriarch, 196
parallels with Johnson, Rev. Joseph, 144, 145–46
Social change beliefs, 73–81
and consensus of church mission, 77
and empowered posture, 73
and mainline Protestantism, 73, 77
and P.I.A. affiliation, 79
and passive orientation, 73
and pastoral involvement in, 79
and role of the church in, 79
and spiritual conversion, 73, 77, 84
and strategies for, 73–77
and theological orientation, 79
Social movement theory and study, 18–19
action frames in, 7
and African American congregations, 20, 23
boundaries of self-identification and, 21–22
critical component of social movements and, 22
culture and, 187–88
explanatory power of, 23
frame extension in, 20–21
ideational materials argument in, 20–21
intolerance and imperative in, 22
political culture and, 19
political opportunities and, 19, 20
theological conservatism and, 29
transformation of consciousness and, 20, 22
Socio-economic status (s.e.s.) in study
and African American congregations, 17, 23, 30
in congregational questionnaire, 49, 50, 51, 54
denominational categories and, 57–58
education and, 58
indices of, 29, 57
occupations and, 58
theological orientation and, 58–59
South African Blacks, 5
St. John's Baptist Church, 200
Stacey, William, 191
Stack, Carol B., 39, 215
Stark, Rodney, 16, 29, *215*
Student Non-Violent Coordinating Committee (SNCC), 152
Sullivan, Rev. Leon, 4, 5, 26, 94, 203, 204
Sullivan Principles, 5

T

Takayama, K. Peter, 16, 29, *212*
Tamney, Joseph B., 16, 29, 191, *212*, *213*, 213
Tarrow, Sidney, 19
Temple University, 103, 140, 143, 145
Texas, 6
Theology and congregational questionnaire results, 188, 190–91
the Bible and salvation views in, 49
and the Bible and salvation views in, 51, 55
"born again" belief in, 54, 55
class stratification along denominational lines (summary of), 59
conservative theology and, 57, 58, 83, 88*n3*

denominational affiliation and, 51, 54–55, 57, 58, 65, 81
non-conservatives and, 67
P.I.A. affiliation and, 84, 86
self-identification and, 55–57
socio-economic status (s.e.s) and, 57–59
spectrum of theological perspectives in, 49, 81
and theological orientation, 59, 72, 79
Theology and study
conservative, 16, 29, 30, 58–59, 72–73, 188, 191
liberal, 168
liberation, 33
P.I.A. affiliation and, 191
personal, 29
and poverty, 64–65
and social change beliefs, 79
and social movement theory, 29

U

United Church of Christ, 167

W

Walter, Oliver B., 191
Washington, Christine, 149–51, 156, 157, 162
Washington, Joseph R., 151, 152, 153, 155, 156, 162, *216*
Washington, Rev. Paul of Church of the Advocate, 150, 151–57, 160, 163, 165
and Advocate Community Development Corporation, 157
and the Black Manifesto, 153
and the Black Unity Rally, 154–55
as lone prophet, 155–56
and the MOVE community, 154, 157
and Muhammad Kenyatta, 153–54
and Mumia Abu Jamal, 154
and separatist Black Power movement, 152
and social change, 165
and "Theology of Black Power", 152–53
and vestry of the Church of the Advocate, 156, 158
and women in church leadership, 162
Watson, Richard, 158
Weber, Max, 16, 195, *216*
Weberian framework and, 16, 17, 31, 33, 59
Williams, Rhys H., 16, 29, *211*
Wilmore, Gayraud, 14, 216
Wuthnow, Robert, 16, 29, 216

Z

Zion Baptist Church, 4, 26, 27, 203

www.ingramcontent.com/pod-product-compliance
Ingram Content Group UK Ltd.
Pitfield, Milton Keynes, MK11 3LW, UK
UKHW012034150926
475560UK00001B/6

9 780761 821540